"In *Tantric Intimacy*, Katrina Bos provides an exciting and easy to follow guide that is inclusive of all genders and orientations. She delivers her expertise through colourful stories and heartfelt sharing that connects the reader and holds them in kindness, trust and passion so they may find this in themselves. When I finished reading I felt truly changed. This book intersected with me at the perfect moment of my life, propelling me forward to the next level of exploration."

KRISTIN SULIS, USA

"Katrina invites us into her personal journey, which is a pleasure to read and relatable. When I tell people I am a student of tantra, they often have preconceived ideas about it. This book tells it how it is with no mumbo jumbo and no imaginary theory. You could give this book to anyone who has an initial inquiry into tantra or someone who has been practicing for years."

RICHARD COOPER, AUSTRALIA

"The world of tantra can seem like a daunting prospect when deciding which lineage to follow or technique to use. Yet the real terrain of tantra is so simple. Brave, timely and on point, Katrina shares profound insights that most modern-day tantra teachings avoid; that being tantric is our truest nature. Tantric Intimacy is for anyone looking to dive deeper into their inner and outer worlds. This is the book I would have wanted when beginning my exploration of tantra; one that offers a clear path for connecting to oneself, another and the world at large. Pure genius."

COCO OYA CIENNAREY, UNITED KINGDOM

"A perfect primer for anyone wanting to discover tantra. This book is an enlightening and refreshing take on a subject that is often bogged down in mysticism. Ms. Bos presents the foundations of tantric thought in a beautifully simple and personal way. Packed tight with gems of insight, this book helped reveal the preciousness of EVERY moment and continues to challenge my ways of thinking and being in the world. This book is well worth a read...and a re-read with a highlighter!"

ANITA NI NUALLAIN, NORWAY

"In this book I found answers to all my questions about tantra. Until now, tantra seemed to me like something strange and difficult. Katrina writes about it like it's the way of life – nothing strange, nothing unreachable. It is our birthright; it is true connection with ourselves and others. Now I feel that tantra is not only for sex. It's how I look at my life, my deep connection with my body, nature around me, how I see beauty around me. It's really a way of life."

LEA VEIDER, SLOVENIA

"This book is powerful. Every word speaks quietly and insistently to your soul, and as you read you will find yourself whispering softly and then shouting 'yes' as the words resonate with the part of you that knows the truth. At the end of the journey, you will know the feeling of true connection and that tantra ultimately is about you."

AIMEE MOORE, AUSTRALIA

"Brilliant! I love, love, love this book! In *Tantric Intimacy*, Katrina takes us on a sacred journey into our own personal mysteries. In implementing Katrina's teachings, I discovered the part of myself that was forced into submersion; the creative, wise, life-giving, feminine held prisoner after generations of oppression. The warrior masculine aspect of myself stepped forward to protect her deep within my internal ocean. Now is the time for resurrection – bringing the feminine forth into divine union with the masculine for integration and wholeness. Katrina gently guides us on this life-changing and healing process. A must read for anyone who dares to free themselves and who longs for a connection with the divine, allowing us the opportunity to (re)discover the ultimate bliss that lies in wait."

JULIE TALBOT, CANADA

"This book is for anyone who is curious about Tantra and feels there is nothing out there that explains its true essence. Her book could have many titles: How to connect to people in this world. How to connect in a relationship. Kindness. A different approach to sexuality. Loving yourself. The essence of tantra. Just breathe. There is so much useful information in this book, I will continually reference its wealth of information."

LOU PORRAZZO, USA

TANTRIC INTIMACY

Discover the Magic of
True Connection

BY KATRINA BOS

Editor: Sara Stibitz
Artist: Lynn Borth

Tellwell Talent
www.tellwell.ca

ISBN
978-1-77302-913-9 (Paperback)
978-1-77302-914-6 (eBook)

TABLE OF CONTENTS

TANTRA

It's not what you think.

It's so simple,
we don't believe it's true.
It's so subtle,
we will miss the ecstasy
if we aren't present.

It's how we are made, our design.

When we feel completely unafraid.
When every cell is completely present.
When we allow love to permeate
our whole being.

When we become hollow like a bamboo flute
And allow the Divine to flow through us...
filling us with magic and light
and infinite joy.

This is tantra.

PROLOGUE

Anthropologists say that we are social creatures. Up until this point in history, we have recognized this as our need to "live together." We needed the safety of the clan to have food, protection and to procreate the next generation.

However, our social need is greater than that. We desire to deeply connect with each other. We are capable of incredible closeness and love. Somewhere inside, we know we are meant to feel completely satisfied, loved, and held in the world. So, the disparity between what we know deep down is possible and our current reality nearly makes us crazy. Just think of our wide-spread use of alcohol and drugs (prescription and recreational), where we try to experience the peace, relaxation, and ecstasy we know is possible.

This distance between our deepest desires and our reality causes us incredible pain and struggle.

Up until this point, we have been thoroughly trained in a set of rules and "shoulds" that protect and serve the clan. All of these rules serve whoever is in charge, and all of our guidance comes from those around us. We must do whatever it takes to be strong, contribute, and do what's "best" for the society we live in.

But these rules were never designed for us to find happiness, personal power, or nurture deep connections with each other. Most of our religions have told us we are sinful, shameful and lowly, so we delete our connection to the divine and believe that we are not lovable or worthy.

We have advertisers who use our own psychological makeup to plant fear and a sense of lack within us so we feel we must buy their goods. I first learned about this while studying psychology in university. To learn that marketers and advertisers are using our own human psychology against us to convince us of things that aren't true was the beginning of the end of my studies in psychology. Just imagine how many of the ideas that are driving our behaviour and self-worth have actually been planted there by others.

Obviously, there are also political and a myriad of other influences, and none of these are meant to bring us to a place of happiness, joy, and loving intimacy with each other. This simply has never been a priority.

This is why tantra is now rising. One of the basic tantric principles is to recognize the constructs society has taught us.

The consequences of failing to nurture our closest relationships for centuries are now showing themselves right on the surface. There is no question we are off path. We experience distance even in our closest relationships. We feel alone.

Sexually, we are less than satisfied, so we constantly try new tricks, new partners, or we give up completely. Some people don't believe they will ever find a truly loving relationship. Others are addicted to porn. We are exploring every possible permutation to find the excitement, thrill and connection we know is possible - kink, edging, multiple partners, toys, movies - anything to make us feel truly alive.

Truthfully, all of this is understandable because we have barely gotten out of the gate when it comes to what's possible in true sexual intimacy. It is only in the last fifty years that it has been widely accepted (even by doctors) that women could experience orgasm. Imagine the ripple effects of that belief – one half of every heterosexual partnership not only didn't have to find pleasure, there was simply no pleasure to be found. Her experience of the sex act was irrelevant, except perhaps to please her partner or to bear a child. This has created a difficult and dysfunctional foundation in the heterosexual world that will take some time and work to undo.

The greater challenge here is that we are taught nothing about sex, relationships and pleasure. As young people, we are either told not to do it or at least to use protection. So, we naturally default to our body's primal wiring to procreate: get in, get off, and get out. (This applies to all orientations.) We can dress it up and increase our pleasure along the way, but because we are taught nothing, we believe this is all there is. And then we wonder why we aren't satisfied.

It's like we are stuck on the first floor of a huge tower. We know there are upper floors. We know there is so much more. We just don't know how to get there.

So what would happen if love and connection became our priorities, perhaps for the first time in history? What if they became the foundation on which we built a whole new reality?

What if love, kindness, trust, and openness were always present in our relationships? What if deep connection and passion were cultivated every day with our intimate partners?

What if we felt fully connected to everything and everyone around us? What if we were happy, passionate and hopeful in every moment?

This is the world tantra describes for us. It is the world where we are all as big and expansive as we know we can be. We are effortlessly open and deeply connect with each other because we know there is nothing to fear.

We develop deep bonds with our children, family, friends, and lovers.

Our days are filled with possibilities, infinite solutions and true peace and happiness.

This world is right at our fingertips. All we need to do is wake from our slumber. We need to see what is real in the world. We need to connect with our deepest truths. We need a new perspective and a whole new set of priorities.

It is a beautiful world that we are all meant to be a part of, and if you're reading this book, deep down, you already know that.

My First Teacher

When I was 29, I went through a healing crisis that completely changed my life. The man, Jim, who helped me through it, was the person who introduced me to this beautiful world I was seeking.

He would wonder why people didn't walk around fully orgasmic all day long. He couldn't imagine making love for less than three hours at a time. He would talk about how crazy it was that men ejaculated. He couldn't understand our obsession with orgasms since, if we wanted one, all we had to do was think about it.

My husband and I would listen to him intently, but we really had no idea what he was talking about. What would we do for *three hours*? What did he mean about no ejaculation? How could you walk around completely orgasmic? What did that even mean? And how could you have an orgasm just by thinking about it?

However, the greater lesson for me at that time was a very spiritual journey. He taught me how to connect with God/the divine/spirit and truly trust and follow the guidance I heard. This was a great challenge for me because I had a lot of issues with organized religion. Even more importantly, I trusted my brain completely to guide me through life. I had a degree in mathematics. I was a "good" girl. Logic and rules told me what was acceptable and expected in life.

Gurus and teachers appear when we are in crisis. Everything I had believed was right in the world had led me right to this point. I was 29 years old, had lumps growing in my breast, two small children, a husband, and my whole life ahead of me. My mom had died of breast cancer four years before. Her mom and sister had died of cancer as well. I was at a turning point. I didn't want to continue that legacy and I didn't want to pass it on to my daughter. And so, I was totally open to trying something new because I didn't want to die.

Through my healing journey, I got to spend many hours with Jim. He was my first true teacher. I trusted him completely. I stayed completely open to everything he said, even though I had no idea how to get to this magical place he was talking about.

I now understand that Jim created the foundation for my lifelong tantric journey. I learned to trust the perfection of the universe. I learned how to release my mind and listen to higher guidance. I learned how to let go of everything I had ever been taught and trust something much greater than myself.

I'm not saying it was easy. I had many, many dark nights of the soul as I released all the constructs that defined every aspect of my life. And afterwards, I was completely different.

I include Jim in some of the stories and teachings in this book. His teachings are now part of me and as you read this book, he, and all of my teachers, are sprinkled through all of the pages. (The complete story of my healing journey can be found in my first book, "*What If You Could Skip the Cancer?*")

THE UNFOLDING OF TANTRA

When I was 35, I found myself lying awake in bed as my husband slept. Something wasn't sitting with me. Everything in our life was apparently perfect, but something was gnawing at my insides.

We were happily married. We loved each other. We had passion, love, touch, and lots of pleasure. We did everything "right." And yet, I knew something was missing. I couldn't describe it. I didn't know where to look for it, and I didn't know anyone else who had found it.

I remembered that once, in our early 20s, my husband and I were making love in my dorm-room at university and "something" happened. It began as normal sex, but then energy started coursing through us in a totally different way. It was like we were being carried on a river. It was the most incredible and indescribable pleasure I had ever felt. Of course, we tried to recreate it many times over the years. But no matter what position, angle or technique we tried, nothing worked. We just couldn't make it happen again.

As I lay there thinking about this, the word "tantra" started bubbling up inside of me. I didn't even know what it was, and no matter how I tried to put it out of my mind, this word, *tantra*, kept repeating itself. I knew I had to find out what it meant.

To begin my study, I went to our local library (this was pre-internet) and asked the librarians to order in all of the books they could find on tantra. When I went to pick them up, the elderly librarian would stare at me from behind the stack of various tantra books. She would look at each book, then at me over her glasses. Then she would slowly stamp the book with this look of curiosity, judgement... and something else. I don't know what she was really thinking, but I got quite a giggle out of it.

Most of what I found in those books was definitely not what I was looking for – rituals under the full moon, sexual practices and exercises, communes, etc. But I did find many books pointing to the spiritual essence of tantra, the role of an open heart in relationships, and how true intimacy works between a couple. I studied for a couple of years and then my husband and I took off for a week in Jamaica – a lovely bubble where we could try everything out.

Well, we definitely found it. Three hours of lovemaking was nothing! We made love for six to seven hours every day (not all at once). And in between, we had all the magical intimacy I had been seeking – an effortless, loving connection that felt like we were always making love, whether we were walking on the beach, having lunch, or relaxing by the pool.

The love-making was like nothing I'd ever experienced. The feeling of orgasms flowing through our bodies in unending waves... the playfulness and deepened connection. It was truly amazing.

MY TANTRIC AWAKENING

The week was filled with a lot of healing tears and amazing pleasure, but on the fifth day, I was changed in a profound way.

During one of our lovemaking sessions, he was deep inside of me. On the outside, we were quite still, but on the inside energy was flowing through us like crazy. My yoni (vagina) was doing crazy things to him – completely independent of me. Whatever she was doing was sending the most exhilarating waves of orgasm all the way through me.

I don't know how long this went on, when suddenly energy shot up through me like the warmest golden light right out the top of my head. It was absolute ecstasy. It flowed and flowed and flowed.

As it happened, something unfolded inside of me. A knowing. Memories. It was like a tiny cube unfolding into a huge tree. It was an experience that, to this day, I really can't articulate.

After this experience, I now understood tantra. I understood everything my first teacher had taught me. I knew what we were all capable of. A huge treasure chest had been opened.

And I knew that I was meant to share it.

THE BIRTH OF FUSION TANTRA & THIS BOOK

I began travelling to attend tantra retreats and trainings, not only to learn and see what was out there, but also to find community and see if others were having the same experiences I was.

I met wonderful people and experienced healing and personal revelations in my travels. But, similarly to when I first researched tantra through books, I kept thinking, "But this isn't what I know to be tantra." And when I shared my sexual experiences with the others in my classes, they would look at me wide-eyed and tell me they'd never heard of that before.

It was also strange to me that so many workshops and teachings included nudity, sexual exercises, multiple partners, kink, and rituals. None of this rang true as being tantric for me. I knew tantra was a natural part of every person. It was our birthright. You could be old, young, naked or dressed in a parka. It was the most natural thing we could do. Yet, tantra had become something only for outliers, people on the fringe of society, and this was so far from the truth.

Then I met a man on one of these retreats who was a self-professed "tantra junkie." He had been studying tantra for over 30 years. He had attended lots of different schools, gone to all the festivals. We spent hours chatting about tantra, spirituality, and connection. I showed him how to feel total bliss simply through breathing together. How through non-sexual touch, you could have a full-body orgasm. None of this was intentional. It just flowed from our open-hearted connection.

Afterwards he said, "Do you know that I have never experienced anything like this before? Never. I've never even heard teachers talk about it. I don't know why. Being with you is so simple. It's like we aren't doing anything, and yet it's so completely different. I don't get it. All I know is that you have to teach it. People need to know this is possible."

Whatever had unlocked within me on that beautiful day in Jamaica was simply beyond my understanding. I didn't have to study further. I already knew it.

As I figured out how to share this with others, I realized that every experience in my life had created a foundation for me to share this ancient teaching in ways that our modern world could understand and put into practice.

I had been a scientific, analytical mathematician *and* a flowy, yoga teacher. I'd been the computer programming city-slicker *and* the earthy, organic dairy farmer. I'd been the housewife *and* the feminist, the mystic *and* a skeptic. I'd had highs that continue to blow my mind *and* lows that I never want to repeat. I had been a mother, foster mother, and unofficial mother to so many (and still am).

This all created a very grounded foundation to share a very spiritual teaching.

So, I launched my school, Fusion Tantra. Our "tantra-junkie" friend from the story actually came up with the name because I showed him what it felt like for two people to fully merge - to actually "fuse" together (even without being sexual). I soon began teaching online courses that are now studied by students all around the world.

My greatest break was an article that I wrote called "Tantra is the Opposite of Porn," which you can read in the appendix. It was based on a discussion with a friend of mine before I began openly teaching tantra. At the time it was published, I was living in a very small, conservative town and was convinced I might be "tarred and feathered" or driven out of town if it became known that I taught tantra (people often link tantra with orgies and wild sex lives). I told my friend this fear and he said, "Don't you understand what you're offering? The world is addicted to porn. And you are teaching the opposite. This is an incredible gift." The next day, I wrote the article. I shared it on the internet. It went viral and continues to be shared and translated into languages all over the world.

I have also taught around the world. What intrigues me the most is watching the people in my classes look at me, spellbound, while I talk. When I ask them how they are doing, their response is always something like: "It's so strange to hear you speak. It's like I already know what you're saying. I have just never been able to put it into words before. Even though I have never had the experiences you've had, some part of me knows that they are completely possible. It's like you are describing something I already know deep inside... Please keep talking. It's all good."

This is when I knew I was right on track.

As more and more people found me, they would ask me to recommend a book for them to get started. The best I could do was recommend books that had helped me on my journey. But none of them really covered what I knew and taught.

That was when this book, *Tantric Intimacy: Discover The Magic of True Connection* was born.

THE STORIES IN THIS BOOK

Stories are our favourite way to learn. When my kids were teenagers, we hosted many evenings with their friends gathered in our living room sharing stories about tantra, love, sex and relationships. No matter what I'm teaching, it always seems to turn into "story-time with Katrina." And so, it made sense for this to be the format of this book.

The stories in this book are all true. All of the people in the stories are happily living their lives, so I have obscured most of their identities so we don't get hung up on who they are and miss the point of the story.

CHAPTER 1
ENTERING THE WORLD OF TANTRA

I had been driving for about 12 hours and was so happy to find this little motel in Montana. I was even more excited when I saw the lovely man with a buzz-cut, muscles and tattoos standing by his truck, drinking a beer.

And he just happened to be staying in the room right beside me. Hmmm. I had definitely picked the right motel.

As I got out of my car, he turned, looked at me with a twinkle in his eye and said, "Well you're a long way from home" as he glanced at my Canadian licence plate.

He was an ex-soldier. He had been overseas in the war for eight years and had been home for four. He was tough, angry, and disillusioned, but he was a sight for my sore eyes.

We spent the evening chatting on the white plastic chairs in front of our rooms. When he learned that I taught tantra, this sparked his curiosity and a very interesting conversation (definitely increasing the already strong sexual chemistry between us). I told him about deeply connecting, making love for hours at a time, and how it was completely mind-blowing and out of this world. (Yes, I know... the conversation was a ridiculous tease.)

Eventually, he asked me, "Soooo, do you think **we** could try out any of this crazy sexy stuff you're talking about?"

"I don't know. It depends if we can have *that* kind of connection," I said.

"How do we know?"

"Well, let's see."

We turned our chairs to face each other, held hands and then looked into each other's eyes. He was pretty uncomfortable with this – most people are. Over the evening, he had shared with me that women were all crazy, life was hard, and it pretty much sucked. To openly stare into someone's eyes would be pretty uncomfortable for him.

"Why are we doing this?" he asked.

"I want to connect in a deeper way than just physically. Obviously, we could just have sex. But so what? That's not very interesting. Our physical bodies are the tiniest part of who we are. Just having physical sex is like having an entire box of crayons and only using one colour. We are also spiritual. We have infinite, divine energy flowing through these bodies. What if we could connect that part of us too?"

He had this look on his face somewhere between "Damn, I really picked a crazy one here..." and "I have no idea what you're talking about and I don't want to admit it, but I'm in."

So I said, "What do you believe in? Do you believe in God or spirit or anything like that?"

He looked down. "I don't know."

"Do you believe that we are just physical bodies - just muscle and bones? Or is there something more?"

"I think there's something more."

"OK. That's all that matters. Just close your eyes and tune into to *that.* Tune in to what's inside of you that is beyond these muscles and bones."

He closed his eyes for a bit, took a few deep breaths, and then opened them. His eyes were totally different. Something had relaxed inside of him. There was a glimmer of life.

We gazed into each other's eyes for a bit longer, and then I brought him closer and let our noses rest together side-by-side.

"Can I breathe with you?" I whispered.

"Yes."

I began inhaling his exhale and allowing him to inhale my exhale. We breathed this way for a few minutes. We were so relaxed, everything was so calm. Then suddenly, he pushed me away.

"What the f*@# are you doing? What is this?"

"It's just closeness, intimacy, compassion."

"Oh."

He came closer again and this time, we breathed with our mouths together. It was so euphoric. It's impossible to explain what happens, but it's like letting go of the world and completely joining with another in total bliss.

After a few minutes, he pushed me away again. I could tell that he was losing his bearings. He kept looking around at his truck, at traffic going by, anything familiar. I let him find himself again. We have strong programs inside that help us feel safe in a crazy world. These are hard to let go of.

He then came close one more time. We weren't kissing or doing anything sexual – just holding hands and breathing together. It was really beautiful. This time when he pulled away, he was gentle and he only moved a couple of inches from me. And there were tears flowing down his cheeks.

As he gazed into my eyes, he whispered, "I can't be this innocent again. You wouldn't believe what they [the Army] made us do over there. You wouldn't believe what I've done. You wouldn't believe what I've seen."

He quietly shared for a few more minutes. And then he kind of "snapped out of it."

"What the f#@&?! I never talk about this! I never tell anyone this stuff. What the f#%@?!!"

He took a deep breath and stared into my eyes. We sat together in beautiful silence. Hearts open. Completely present.

(And yes, this lovely heart-connection turned into hours and hours of "all that sexy stuff we'd been talking about.")

WHAT IS TANTRA?

Tantra is an incredible body of teachings that we can't begin to grasp in one book. Some people study tantra to learn sacred sexual practices from exotic lands. Others seek the deep spirituality, mystery and happiness tantra can bring us. Tantra is all of these things and so much more.

The earliest stories are of ancient tantrikas going into towns and rebelling against the rules of that society. If the town's religion said that they shouldn't eat meat, then the tantrikas would eat meat. If sexuality was taboo, then they would have sex. They would do whatever was needed to "wake the townspeople from their sleep." These stories ring an important note of truth inside of us because we too know that we are asleep and need to wake up.

Because tantra, at its core, is about integrating the divine experience with the physical world, its principles were picked up by many faiths. There are Buddhist, Hindu, Taoist tantric lineages, and many more. The mystics of all faiths are also tantrists because their only desire is to be in constant connection with the divine.

Tantra is a Sanskrit word that means many things. When we look at its syllables - *tan-tra*, the Indo-European root of "*tan*" means "to stretch" and the "*tra*" means "technique." So, the most valuable definition of tantra for our journey is "techniques that stretch us" or "tools of expansion."

TANTRA TODAY

Many things are called tantra today. As with all teachings that come out of a different culture, the adopting culture will take what it can understand and what it needs most right now.

This is why a lot of the tantra we hear about is so focused on sex and relating to each other. This is considered "Red Tantra" and it focuses on our physical experience. Many of these teachings and workshops help participants to release shame, guilt, and unhealthy programming around sexuality. There is normally nudity (because we have so much shame tied up in our bodies) and there are often sexual exercises designed to help us face sexual taboos and break out of our limited boxes.

The word *tantra* is also used by many industries to make their services sound exotic and mysterious. This is where we must be very discerning on our tantric journey. A "tantric massage" might simply be a sexual massage with exotic music and a masseuse dressed in a sari. Or it might truly be a wonderful healing experience where you can heal shame, guilt, re-sensitize your body, and retrace the pathways where your natural orgasm wants to flow.

"Tantric dance" is usually learning how to pole dance and move like a stripper. However, it might also be a fascinating inner exploration of the divine feminine where you integrate spirit, breath, movement and sound, resulting in a beautiful tantric awakening.

This book is based on the teachings of "White Tantra" because we focus on the growth of our spiritual side and integrate it into our lives. Historically, White Tantra is purely a spiritual study with no mention of sexuality. And although there is an entire section dedicated to applying it to sexual intimacy, this book isn't really about sex, either. It is part of this book because it is a beautiful aspect of our lives that is meant to be both a spiritual and physical experience. But it is only a part of our lives; we can't start there.

When we apply the philosophy and techniques of tantra, we actually *become* tantric. We change from the inside out. We become happier, stronger, more open, and more trusting. We have a different perspective in romantic relationships, how we connect with our children, finding joy in our careers, how we enjoy a cup of coffee, and of course, our intimate lives are changed forever.

TANTRA IS FOR EVERYONE

We are energetic beings. Regardless of our gender and whom we choose to be intimate with, we all desire happiness, love and connection.

This book applies to everyone because the goal is to *become tantric*. This has nothing to do with sex, gender, or even relationships. Once you become tantric, I won't actually need to tell you anything about relationships and sex. Your sexual experiences will flow naturally and magically from who you are.

Within tantric philosophy, we talk about magnetism – the polarity of positive and negative energy. This translates into the joining of masculine and feminine energy and how they interact to create oneness. When we interact with a partner, we will often have a preference as to which magnetic pole we feel most comfortable in.

However, this isn't necessarily about the interaction of men and women. What matters most is which polarity you personally identify with. We all need to be internally balanced in our masculine and feminine (which is often the most challenging feat to accomplish).

I am sensitive there might be parts in this book where anyone who isn't strictly cisgender* might find the gender-specific words used are exclusive. My goal has been to write as inclusively as possible and still be readable. Most of the time, I will use the words "masculine" and "feminine" because it is our magnetic polarity that matters. And when I actually say "man" or "woman," I am specifically addressing the issues and situation of cisgender men and women.

Today, we are living in an exciting time where we can openly discuss and explore all possibilities. And as more people who identify as LGBTQ study and practise tantra, our teachings will truly evolve with the times.

---

* Cisgender means that you are currently the same gender you were assigned at birth. It is the opposite of being transgender, where you are actually a different gender than you were assigned at birth. They both have Latin roots: "cis" meaning "on this side of" and "trans" meaning "on the other side of."

THE TRANSFORMATIVE POWER OF TANTRA

You cannot travel the path
until you have become the path itself.
BUDDHA

We are taught that information and knowledge are important. We study, learn, and talk about ideas, concepts and theories - our best guesses as to what the world is really all about. It is the best our brains can do to explain the world around us.

But knowledge doesn't transform us. In fact, it is easy to separate what we have learned and should believe from our true feelings and experiences in our lives. When our brains are filled with ideas it is easy to ignore what is really happening around us. Until we bring these worlds together and we have a deep and personal experience of anything, we are simply filled with information. What we are looking for is wisdom. This is what will change our lives. And it only comes from experience.

When I was young, I was a real philosopher. I'm still a philosopher now, but when I was younger, I actually thought I knew what I was talking about.

I was well-educated. I had it all figured out. I was pretty clear about how things worked in the world.

Then one day, I was sitting by my mom's hospital bed, close to the end of her life. She was terrified of dying because she was afraid of going to hell, since she hadn't continued going to church like she was supposed to have done. (Which is ironic because she was such an angel in all of our lives.)

As I sat with her, she looked at me and said, "I'm so afraid."

I had studied every major world religion. I'd read about reincarnation. I'd read countless accounts of people's near-death-experiences. I knew a lot about what happened after you died. So, in all of my 24 years of knowledge, I looked at her and genuinely said "Mom, don't you worry. It will all be just fine."

She looked at me with an anger and clarity that I'd never seen before and said "How do you know?"

And in that moment, every theory in my mind disappeared. I stared into her eyes, started crying and said "I don't know. I'm sorry."

That was the last time I believed I knew what happened after we died. I am still aware of different theories and ideas, but something important passed between my mom, me, and God in that moment. A knowing. A reality that I now know deep in my bones.

I no longer knew anything on this topic.

But I was a whole lot wiser.

Tantric wisdom comes from our life experiences. It comes from all the jobs we've ever had, the relationships that have come and gone. It comes from our upbringing, whether happy or sad. It comes from raising children and experiencing sacrifice.

Wisdom is deeper than knowledge. It lies in an unknowable and indescribable place. It exists in the "oneness." There is no inner battle. No illusions, ideals or "ought to's."

Wisdom just is. It is simply a truth. No arguments. No debates.

It comes from helping others. It comes from times of depression and despair. It comes from times of great sacrifice and hardship and suffering.

It also comes from times of extreme happiness and joy and the feeling of wonderful love and togetherness.

This is a wisdom that comes from living your life.

It is good to learn and expand our minds through reading books and studying under gurus and teachers, but this learning is only valuable when we apply it to living.

It is our experiences that transform our knowledge into wisdom. It is only in our lives that tantric transformation happens.

We must allow tantra to transform us and shift us to a whole new paradigm, from a limited existence to an infinite one. This is not something we can do academically. We must live it. As we study tantra, we can learn a bit from those who have gone before, but then we must release what we've learned and start with a beginner's mind. We must allow *ourselves* to unfold according to what actually happens, loving the exciting journey.

This new paradigm is completely different. This is why it can't be studied with our minds. It isn't a theory we can learn. Without applying it to our lives and truly transforming, we will still have all of our old issues, hang-ups, opinions, histories and expectations. Without transforming all of these aspects of ourselves, we might understand the words we are reading, but we won't experience the real magic.

This is why when we read books written by people who have academically studied tantra, they will often state that the ecstasy a tantrika experiences is simply a metaphor for life, something for us to strive for. Or they will say that only serious yogis are capable of such "miracles."

This is not true.

Tantra is for everyone. This is how we are made. It reveals our potential as humans – nothing added. We simply have to return to our true nature.

We must shift how we see the world, ourselves and each other. Many people come to tantra to be great lovers, but the greatest hurdle for most people is changing "why" they are making love, not "how." Once we change the "why," tantric intimacy is the most natural, fulfilling and ecstatic experience we can have. There are no tricks. We actually already know everything.

We must do the work. It is in our everyday lives that the real transformation happens. It is when we take these concepts, ways of being, and the guidance we receive into both the hard days and the easy days that we truly transform ourselves and every aspect of our lives. This is the true arena. Our current lives have been formed around us. As we shift, everything shifts.

This is how we become truly tantric.

BECOMING TANTRIC

Do not be satisfied with stories,
How things have gone with others.
Unfold your own myth,
Without complicated explanations,
So everyone will understand the passage,
We have opened you.
RUMI

Tantra isn't something we *do*. It's something that unfolds from inside.

The key is to *unlearn* everything that blocks us from this wisdom. We need to experience the world around us for what it actually is. We need to connect with the inner wisdom that energizes our transformation.

Our first step is to wake up and look around.

AWAKENING FROM THE
SPELLS WE ARE UNDER

The ancient tantrikas were famous for being the rebels who woke people from their "day-to-day slumber." Their call was to awaken! Start to live again! Think and feel in this moment! Forget all of the rules you've ever been taught!

Life can easily become like living under a spell. When we are young, what we naturally learn easily becomes second nature. It's like learning to tie your shoes. We really have to focus in the beginning, but once we've mastered it, the knowledge slips into our subconscious and we can do it without thinking.

This happens in every aspect of our growth – physically, mentally & emotionally. We learn many things from our parents, friends and society so we can effortlessly move through our days, grow, and be a part of the world.

A lot of what we learn is simply the "story" of our culture. We adopt the mythology of our society because we are immersed in it. We don't even realize it.

Years ago, people believed that women's ankles were too sexy to be shown. This wasn't even questioned. It was just a "fact." It couldn't be discussed because no one actually knew *why* they believed it. It was simply a cultural belief.

These cultural beliefs create the story that we are woven into creating the fabric of who we are. Because we are immersed in it, it can be challenging to know the difference between what *we* really think from the "spell that we are under."

Being aware of this story is fundamental to becoming tantric because when we act according to external rules, we are not actually present to what is happening. The rules tell us what is right and wrong, so there is no need for us to be present and truly respond (or even exist) in the moment.

Of course, breaking free of society's rules can seem a little anti-social. The people close to us might not understand our choices. They may not be comfortable with us discarding their "rules" and "expectations," but this is only *their* discomfort. It may be difficult in the beginning, but after a while, life will actually be a much nicer experience than before.

This is because the path of tantra is very loving and creates much deeper connections than are possible when we simply exist on the surface. We connect on a deeper level with everyone around us. We become kinder. We listen to intuition in all situations. So many situations that might have been very difficult or even unsolvable previously now smooth out with beautiful ease.

Also, because we become whole ourselves, we are loving and accepting of all of our own quirks, gifts, and challenges, and we naturally extend that privilege to everyone around us. They get to be themselves, too.

When this happens, magic occurs and our entire lives transform.

TRUSTING OUR SOUL

However, there are fears that rise when we think of letting go of all the constructs we were raised with, all of the patterns we have set up over the years, and even our definition of self.

What would happen if we had no rules to follow? Would "all hell break loose"? Would everyone just "run wild"? Would you stop feeding your children? Would you start lying to everyone? Would you become a mean person? Would you never do anything nice for anyone again?

We must ask ourselves what we believe about our basic human nature. Do you believe humans are "intrinsically good" or "intrinsically evil"? This is an important question because many religions teach us that we are "sinful by nature" and require a "shepherd" to guide us.

The fear is that without rules, how would we know if what we were doing was "right"?

That is the big question! We are obsessed with knowing what we are doing is right. We need to know we are making the right decisions, making love properly, raising our children properly. That we are being a good partner/parent/friend/member of society...

But what if the point isn't whether what we're doing is right or wrong? What if the point is our experience? What if our soul is meant to experience everything here? What if the idea of right or wrong is actually just a concept that confuses us on our path?

Right and wrong is a filter of judgement. In the Christian faith, this idea is traced back to Adam and Eve living in paradise until they eat fruit from the tree of knowledge of good and evil. Afterwards, they begin to judge the world around them and they are banished from paradise forever.

This right/wrong filter is our greatest twist in our experience of life. As long as we carry this judgement with us, we will not listen to our deepest self. We will not allow our soul to experience the world and be wild.

Even as I'm saying this, you might be thinking, "Yes but there are still limits. You can't go around murdering people just because you want to." We are taught that without rules, we will want to do crazy things and cause havoc in the world. This is the trick of the mind that keeps us enslaved. **We are taught that we can't trust our soul.**

Luckily, we have another option.

What if we trusted our deepest, truest self? What if we could completely relax the armour and the rules and let our soul free? What if we said to ourselves, "Go. Experience. Play. Have fun. Don't worry. You can't get in trouble. Everything you do is simply an experience. That's why you're here."

The idea that humans are "intrinsically good" is an important foundation in tantra because it allows us to release the external rules and listen for divine guidance within instead.

Of course, there is no such thing as "good" or "bad" in spirit. There is only oneness. When we listen to our soul, we are tapping into our deepest truth. We are listening to what simply *is* in that moment.

The rules, expectations and social ideals are built to protect and control "the tribe." Many of these rules create a structure and stability that truly helps us all live together in harmony. But there are also many ideas, principles and dogma that actually separate us from our hearts and our truth. We become like robots simply living according to the beliefs of previous generations.

Instead, we want to have faith in ourselves. We need to believe that we can follow our soul's truth. That it is connected to a deeper reality.

This gives us the freedom to choose in every moment. We can choose to follow certain rules in the world and discard others. We can stay awake, observe the world around us, listen within and then follow our unique and exciting path.

This freedom and faith is what allows us to be fully alive.

PERSONAL EXPLORATION: WHAT ARE THE CONSTRUCTS THAT YOU GREW UP WITH?

Our early years form us in ways that are sometimes hard to see. We learn ideas as children casually sitting on the laps of our parents, around the dinner table and at family gatherings. Many values and beliefs naturally become part of our beings. We never question them. We don't even know they are there.

Our first exercise is to become aware of what these constructs might be. Some may serve you well in life. Others may create great barriers to intimacy.

Step One:

Ask yourself the following questions and write them in your journal:

1. What did I learn from my family? What were their values? What phrases did I hear a lot growing up?
2. What did I learn from my church or spiritual community?
3. What did I learn from the society that I grew up in?

It's best to be complete and include the "negative" and the "positive." All of these beliefs are intertwined and we don't want to edit as we write. Plus, it's good to see it all in its proper context. Perhaps there was love *and* judgement. This isn't an exercise in hating our childhood. It's about shining light on what has been written in our consciousness.

Step Two: Add more that apply

The list below contains constructs that my past students learned from their families, religious communities and their society in general. Although they are from all over the world, there were definite similarities.

There were also those who felt their upbringing was very open and inviting to new ideas. They were taught to be loving, kind, to think outside of the box, and that they could truly do anything. I have included the more "negative" constructs so that we can understand what is limiting us and keeping us from living in a tantric way.

After you've made your own list, please look through these and add any additional constructs that are also true for you. It's often amazing to realize how many of these are present in our consciousness, but we aren't even aware of them.

Step Three: Look at the Effects

For each construct, rule or belief, write down how this belief has shaped your life. How has it made decisions for you in the past? Has it served you? Has it caused trouble? Do you want to continue forward with this belief? If not, what will you replace it with? How will this shift your personal life and relationships?

Possible Constructs:

- A girl/woman's opinion is irrelevant
- A woman's work is never done.
- Adults are always right.
- All that's important is having kids and making money.
- Always appear as if everything is fine. Put on a happy face.
- Always be brave.
- Always be honest.
- Always have good manners and be presentable.
- Always put others ahead of you.
- Anger is not acceptable. Ignore sadness.
- Avoid confrontation. Don't make a fuss.
- Be a good girl/boy and others will like you.
- Be a good member of society.
- Be a good wife. Man is head of the household.
- Be aware of what others might think. Act normal.
- Be careful with money. Nothing comes for free.

- Be fearful. Don't think for yourself.
- Be guilty for "everything."
- Be kind to those who need help.
- Be logical about your emotions.
- Behave or you will go to hell.
- Being sensitive is self-centred.
- Being sexually adventurous is not OK.
- Believing in a God is stupid.
- Business before pleasure.
- Busy people are better people.
- Children should be seen and not heard.
- Conformity means inclusion and safety.
- Crying is manipulative.
- Divorce is failure.
- Do a good job or don't do it at all.
- Doing something wrong makes you a bad person.
- Don't be so sensitive.
- Don't be too big for your britches. Don't bite off more than you can chew.
- Don't cause trouble.
- Don't expect anything and you won't be disappointed.
- Don't feel that way. Don't wear your heart on your sleeve.
- Don't let your feelings show. Don't let anyone see you cry.
- Don't make others uncomfortable by showing that you're upset.
- Don't show your true self.
- Don't talk about negative events. They will just go away.
- Don't talk about sex.
- Don't talk back.
- Don't trust anyone.

- Fat girls aren't happy and no one will love them.
- God is separate from me.
- God will punish you.
- Good children fit into the family.
- Good girls are quiet and well-behaved. Women must sacrifice.
- Good people finish last.
- Hold your cards close.
- Homosexuality is wrong.
- How you look is more important than your health. Clothes make the man.
- I am a sinner needing forgiveness.
- If you want it done, do it yourself. Be self sufficient. You only have yourself to rely on.
- If you're not the best, you've failed.
- It's not safe to feel secure. Watch your back.
- Keep family secrets.
- Keep the peace at all costs. Never say no. Follow the rules.
- Keep your husband happy so he won't stray.
- Life is tough.
- Look outside yourself for validation.
- Love means losing and sacrificing myself.
- Marry for life. Have children.
- Masturbation can cause madness.
- Men are the breadwinners and must support his wife and children.
- Men are unfaithful, violent and abusive. Men just want sex.
- Men make the decisions.
- Men must be strong and macho.
- Men should hide their feelings and not show weakness.
- Money is evil.

- Monogamy is all that is acceptable.
- Must be thin and fit.
- Never admit to being tired.
- Never let them see you sweat.
- Never marry beneath you.
- Nice people don't do that.
- No one likes a show-off.
- No physical displays of affection.
- Nudity is shameful.
- One partner for life.
- Put a positive spin on everything.
- Put other people's needs above your own.
- Reject others before they reject you.
- Rich people are greedy and bad.
- Sex before marriage is a sin.
- Sex for enjoyment is sinful and wrong.
- Sex is a duty. Sex is shameful.
- Stay small so others aren't envious.
- Stay small. Stay humble.
- Success is marriage, owning a home, a good job, kids.
- Talking about your feelings is a sign of weakness.
- Temptation comes from the devil.
- The world is a scary place.
- The world is against you.
- There's something wrong with a woman who wants sex. Sex is all men want.
- There's something wrong with you if you're single.
- Who you are in your career is who you are.
- Women are inferior to men. Man is the leader of the household.

- Women are inferior. They are here to please men.
- Women focus on family. Men are intelligent and spiritual.
- Women have to be seductive. Women have to be pretty.
- Women must control men to get what they want.
- Women need to be pure, reserved and lady-like.
- Women should only have one sexual partner.
- Women stay home and take care of the house and children.
- Work hard. Business before pleasure. Laziness is a sin. Work through the pain.
- Work requires us to sacrifice our relationships.
- Work to your potential. Enough is never enough.
- You are alone in the world.
- You are as much as your achievements.
- You are not good enough.
- You have to be an important person.
- You have to be in a relationship to be happy.
- You must always be perfect.
- You must fit into society. Be normal. Don't be different. What will the neighbours think?
- You've made your bed. Now sleep in it.
- Your desires and needs are selfish.

SECTION I:

REDEFINING LOVE AND CONNECTION

Your task is not to seek for love,
but merely to seek and find all the barriers within yourself
that you have built against it.

RUMI

LOVE: THE MAGICAL RIVER OF ENERGY

I recently polled university students to learn why they wanted to study tantra. Many responded they would love to learn about sex and have new experiences. But the most common answer was they wanted *real* connection and *true* intimacy.

We long to connect with each other. We know that we are made for it. When we lack genuine connection in our lives, we truly suffer. Because many of our relationships have been based on things that have nothing to do with love, we end up feeling very alone, frustrated, and filled with longing for something more.

So let's begin with understanding what love really is.

Love is what connects all of us. It is that invisible "something" we feel when we stand in front of a lover, when we hug a child, or when we think of a good friend. It is what we feel for the stranger who smiles at us as we walk down the street; it's a sense that we are all in this together.

When we say love is foundational for studying tantra, we are talking about this ethereal, indescribable "river of energy" that connects us to everything – to God, ourselves and each other.

We must agree with the poets that this connection, this love, is impossible to describe. However, in the same way the average person can drive a car without understanding the inner workings of an internal combustion engine, we too can accept that love exists and experience its power in our lives.

We will explore the different depths of this river in the next three chapters. We will look at three kinds of love – kindness (agape), trust (philia), and passion (eros) – and understand how they all work together to create the closeness, connection, and magic we all know is possible.

CHAPTER 2

AGAPE: A NEW FOUNDATION OF KINDNESS

"It wouldn't matter to me if you were an axe-murderer. I would still love you."

This was Jim, my first teacher. In the beginning, it was a little shocking to sit with him. He didn't look like your typical guru. There were no flowing robes, sandals, or incense anywhere. He looked like a big guy with curly hair and the friendliest face you'd ever seen.

But it was his eyes that got you.

When he looked at you, his eyes shone with love. He looked right into your soul, saw everything you liked and didn't like about yourself, and loved every part of you. There was no judgement in him. There was absolutely nothing you could say that would make him love you less.

To be in the presence of that kind of compassion and non-judgement was overwhelming. Slowly, all my guards dropped. Without even meaning to, all the "bad stuff" inside that I worked hard to suppress rose to the surface and became part of the conversation.

I would apologize for something about myself or explain what I was working on and trying to improve in myself.

He would listen politely and say, *"It all sounds great Katrina. But you really are perfect just the way you are."*

And then I'd get the biggest smile.

Simply being around him changed me. Every time I was with him, more of me was allowed to rise and I became a little more whole. I understood how being in the presence of a "holy" person could instantly heal you.

THE FOUNDATION OF TANTRA

This is my simple religion.
There is no need for temples;
no need for complicated philosophy.
Our own brain, our own heart is our temple;
the philosophy is kindness.

DALAI LAMA

Creating a life of kindness, non-judgement, and compassion is the foundation for all love and connection, and our study of tantra.

The ancient Greeks called this *agape.* This is the love we need to feel for everyone. There is no judgement; there is only total compassion and complete respect for each other. This is where we understand we all are fragile, vulnerable, and truly trying our best with the life we've been given. We know that inside we are the same and we are all connected.

Agape is often described as the highest form of love. This is because it is the foundation of all other love. It is an absolute necessity. Without it, we simply cannot have any deeper connections.

It is often considered "God's love for man" and "man's love for God." Later, we will discuss more about our perceptions of the divine. For now, let's imagine agape means that we step into the divine part of ourselves and look at each other through a lens of pure kindness and love.

ON THE LACK OF AGAPE

The lack of agape is the root of all our problems in relationships. ALL OF THEM.

The truth is that many of us have never experienced actual love. We are told that we are loved by our parents and partners, but it is often something else that is called by the name of love. (It's no one's fault. They didn't know any better either). Anything that makes you feel separate from someone isn't love. Love always connects us. More than likely we've never experienced full, unconditional kindness and respect, ever.

By definition, our relationship is how we are connected. Love connects us. But when our connections are based out of obligation, expectation, or contract (like having children or marriage), we have been told we are loved. There is a kind of connection. It might be familiarity, and there might be moments of love. But it isn't love.

If the love comes with judgement, punishment, correction, possession, control or anything else that often comes with the territory, we lose our faith in love. We develop beliefs that love is painful, difficult, "love hurts," you can't trust love, there are ups and downs, etc. These aren't signs of love. These are the results of our own dysfunction, pain, and fears projected onto those closest to us. This isn't love.

Without this foundation, we will struggle to experience philia – the ability to fully disclose our deepest self with a true confidante – even with a close friend or family member. We will always keep a certain distance from others. We may not even know we are doing it, or that it is possible to be closer.

If we try to have love or sex in our relationships, which we will, we will never be able to take it past the physical level. Without kindness, respect, and trust, how can we share our deepest, most intimate selves with another person? If we become vulnerable in this situation, we will always risk having our hearts ripped open. We aren't going to take that risk.

How do we come to a place where we can experience love as we describe it in this book when we have never experienced it in our lives? We must begin with finding agape in our lives. We must look around us and figure out how to find genuine kindness and respect for everyone who comes into our lives. We must find this for ourselves. We truly must find this personally for anything else to work.

We can't skip this step. If we skip agape, there will always be distance between us and everyone around us – our friends, children, partners, colleagues, everyone. We will struggle to live in reality. Our judgement of our lives and everything we've ever done will not allow us to look in the mirror and be okay with who we see. We won't have the basic kindness we need for ourselves, much less for other people.

The foundation of this book is kindness. Everything I talk about is built on this foundation.

There is a whole other reality that assumes complete love. This is the world I want us to play in. And it is important to know that there is no bridge waiting for you between the worlds, and no direct path. You have to build your own bridge.

This is why tantra is about personal transformation. Your tantric experience is the journey that will take you from your current reality based on the past to a different reality (still yours) based on what we are truly made for.

It's right here for all of us. We know it inside. We have to trust and take the first step.

Why We Struggle with Kindness

One of the first questions I ask my students is whether they believe they could be 100% kind to their loved ones all day long. Some say it would be nice. About half think it's possible. Some say it would be boring and that it's not even a worthy goal if they want to feel alive in the relationship.

I realized I had to define kindness better. Kindness doesn't mean we are always happy, agreeing with, or going along with other people. Being kind doesn't change how you feel in a situation or whether you agree with someone. Being kind is an action. It is how you treat other people (and yourself).

Let's say you are absolutely furious about something. This is how you feel. What you do with that fury is the point. If anger is your tendency, then you might choose to yell at the closest person, whether they are the reason you are angry or not. But this will cause them to step away from you in some way. This is not kindness because it creates separation.

Instead, if we don't want to create separation, then we can own our feelings. Maybe we recognize we are angry about something at work, so we ask our partner if it's OK if we vent for a bit, and assure they know it isn't about them. Or maybe it *is* about them. Still, we don't unleash the anger *at* them. We are angry about the current situation, *and* we want to be connected to them. So, in order to maintain connection, we have an honest, but kind, conversation instead.

This requires a level of emotional maturity we might not have ever seen. If it's new for you, then it will take a concerted effort in the beginning to avoid falling into old patterns. And it starts with practicing kindness toward ourselves.

RELEASING JUDGEMENT

When we have kindness in our relationships, we love people for who they are. We don't believe we are better than them or that we can see their situation clearer than they can. We honour their journey. We recognize that our judgement comes from the fact that *we* would be very uncomfortable if we were in their situation.

We come by this judgement honestly. Nearly all societies and families teach us that there are certain ways we are supposed to be. We are told there are "right" ways to live; there are "good" choices and "bad" ones.

But do any of these judgements matter? The reality is we have absolutely no idea about each other's life paths. We don't know why some of us make certain choices and others make other choices. Maybe it's their upbringing or culture. Maybe it's fear. Maybe they are making conscious choices that are very personal. Or maybe it's some kind of karma – a big picture far beyond our understanding.

The important thing to realize is that every one of these judgements creates distance between us. It harms our connection. We feel separate. If we are the one judging, then we know "better" than the other. This is not love. This is separation.

WHEN TRUTH AND FIXING ANOTHER ISN'T KIND

"I'm only saying this because I love you."

When someone says this, it is not love or kindness because it does not create connection.

Kindness is always considering how our actions towards someone will affect them. Will our words push them away? Will our actions cause them to shut down? To feel shame? To feel guilty?

For example, sometimes we want to fix others – children, friends and especially partners. We tell ourselves it's for their highest good. In reality, we are making them feel that there is something wrong with them, that they aren't capable of making good choices in their lives and they are somehow less than you. Is this really in their highest good? Is it really kind?

Or maybe we tell ourselves we are being kind because someone needs to know a brutal truth. But truth without kindness is simply cruel. This is not truth. This is your judgment of their situation. What are your motives? Do you believe you have a better or superior view of their life? Do you believe you are smarter or more intuitive than they are? Is this why you feel called to share your "truth" with them?

Whether we are clear about our intentions or not, the receiver will get exactly the message you are sending – that you believe you are smarter than them, more intuitive, more evolved, and superior. If the other person is in a vulnerable state, they may take it to heart and it will reinforce their own self-doubts and lack of self-worth. This is not very kind.

This also applies to our children. It's important to not fix them. They are here to have their own experience. We are simply their caregivers. We can create an environment for them to grow, but we cannot do it for them. In fact, the more we do try to do it for them, the more they will believe they can't do it themselves because this is what *you* showed them.

PERSONAL PRACTICE:
SADHANA OF KINDNESS

A *sadhana* is a daily spiritual practice. It is a discipline we choose to do because in order to accomplish it, we must grow and expand spiritually. Each day, we stretch a little more towards our goal, transforming our life in small ways, with profound, long-term effects.

On the Mat

Many of us struggle with meditation. In fact, many of us give up on meditating because we say we aren't any good at it.

Instead, let's look at meditating as a time to practise a new skill. In this exercise, we are going to practice kindness for ourselves. It can be surprisingly more difficult than we think in the beginning. Soon, it becomes effortless and second-nature.

Sit comfortably on the floor, on a chair, or even lying in bed. Your form isn't important here. What is going on inside is what matters.

Breathe deeply and think about your life. Are there areas in your life where you are struggling? Work, relationships, health, hope? Allow your thoughts to flow naturally. Are the thoughts about yourself kind? Compassionate? Non-judgemental?

If not, start to think the opposite of your thoughts. Find your kindest inner voice. Ask for inner guidance to find kinder words. Feel compassion for your inner child who is truly vulnerable. Look at yourself through the eyes of someone who loves you and honours everything you've been through.

Do this whenever you have the chance, until one day, your inner voice is always kind. It learned its old ways somewhere. It can learn new habits this way. Soon, you will default to kindness and non-judgement.

In Our Lives

We also want to practice this kindness with others. This will make all the difference with your loved ones. Simply look at them and understand they are like you inside. They are trying.

Maybe they don't have all the tools you have. Perhaps they have inner struggles you don't have. They have a very different path to take than you and they've been given a totally different set of circumstances to grow up within.

Even as you walk down the street, feel that love for humanity for everyone around you. It isn't always easy. I live in downtown Toronto and I walk around the city a lot. There are angry people, sad people, homeless people, happy people, people high on drugs and others who are high on life. But it's what we all have in common that we need to tune into. This is a divine love. It goes beyond their external appearance. It is loving them as human beings.

People used to ask Mother Teresa how she could do the work she did. She replied that she always looked for Jesus in each person she encountered.

Imagine seeing the divine in each person – at home, at work, at the coffee shop, or walking down the street.

This is especially important if you have never actually experienced this kind of unconditional kindness and respect in your life (don't worry, you are not alone). This is how we start to cultivate it right now. This is how we personally create this foundation of love in our lives. It will take some effort in the beginning and slowly, it will spread to all of your relationships.

The first step is feeling agape for others everywhere you go. As you feel it in your life, people will come into your life who also love in this way. Or you will teach them. The second step is to surrender enough to truly receive it. This is a bigger challenge than feeling it for others, but it's so incredibly worth it.

CHAPTER 3

PHILIA: CREATING
LOVING SANCTUARY

"As if I would have sex without talking to my mom first!"

I was driving our 16-year-old babysitter home, and somehow we got to talking about sex. This was her response to whether or not she'd had sex yet. I was aghast. What 16-year-old talks to her mom about sex?

Luckily, I was good friends with her mom so I asked her what her secret was. Why were her kids so open with her?

She kind of shrugged and said, *"I don't know. All I care about is that they can trust me. I really never know what I'm doing in my own life. So, I can't really lecture them on theirs. Everything I do is really to gain their trust."*

Wow. My two children were very small then. I wanted for us what my friend and her children had.

From then on, my goal as a mother was to be the one safe place in the world that my kids could go to feel loved and supported. I figured that my role as a mom was unique. My role was simply to love them and keep them safe. When the rest of the world told them what to do, how to do it, and whether they were doing it right, they would always have at least one safe place to turn.

My job was to create sanctuary. My job was simply to love them.

PHILIA: TRUST AND SAFETY

Agape is the love that flows between everyone – strangers, friends, family and lovers. It is the foundation of all love between humans.

Philia builds upon agape and deepens the connection. The love becomes personal. This is the love we have for friends and family. These are the people who know us. We trust them. They are our confidantes. We have fun and explore the world together. We can drop our guards, be vulnerable and share what's going on in our lives. They are our safe places to go when things get hard.

When we have children, parents, friends, or intimate partners and we extend this kind of love to them, they will know you don't judge them and will feel free to share their innermost thoughts and fears with you. Because you know how vulnerable we all are, you will always be a safe place. We can all be ourselves.

This kind of loving openness is what truly joins us together. This is what creates life-long bonds with our children. This creates trusting confidantes with friends. And between intimate partners, we are truly able to "merge as one" in sacred union. This connection also happens when we struggle together – like soldiers, emergency workers, even colleagues. We know that the other will "always have our back."

This is the stage of a romantic relationship where you "get to know each other." You discover if there is philia love between you as well as passion. Do you enjoy their company? Can you trust them? Do you feel safe in every way around them? Do you want to share your innermost thoughts with them?

BEING 100% SAFE & TRUSTWORTHY

Let's imagine being emotionally safe and loving all of the time. Not most of the time when we are well-rested and things are going our way, but *all* of the time – 100%. Seems impossible? It isn't. We are actually made to be loving. To open our hearts and love. It's actually easier than throwing up guards and walls and defences.

Why is this so important in tantric intimacy? Because we are opening a channel between our heart and the heart of another. We want this loving energy to flow unrestricted between us. If we are unsure what might be coming from the other, then we won't be completely vulnerable. We will always have to put up walls to protect our heart.

A common response is we don't believe that 100% is possible. Sometimes we have bad days right? Some days we are tired and overwhelmed. We want to have some wiggle room, but we can't.

Let's look at an example where a woman is married to a man and everything is going perfectly. They are early in the relationship and she has no reason to expect anything but love from her partner. She is 100% open.

And then one day he hits her.

Let's assume she stays. What will change? It was only one time. Even though 90% of the time he is wonderful, she never knows when the 10% is coming. She will simply put some guards up against him.

Or maybe your partner makes fun of you sometimes, or they make passive aggressive comments in front of other people. But it's only 10% of the time; the rest of the time they are really loving. You can laugh it off, but it will always create a bit of distance between you. You certainly aren't going to share deeply personal things with them. It's hard enough being the butt of their joke. What if they used *really* personal stuff?

Imagine a child opens up to a parent about something they are struggling with. It takes only one time for the parent to berate them for their choice, treat them like their problem isn't important, or tell them what to do in a way that isn't supportive or loving. That child will simply put up a wall to protect themselves from their parent. They know not to be that open with them again.

BEWARE OF PASSIVE AGGRESSION

Passive aggression is a silent killer of intimacy because it creates invisible walls between us. If you don't recognize it in your relationships, it is because you have likely grown up with it, which means you are accustomed to having invisible armour up around your loved ones. This can be quite a challenging pattern to break, but it's certainly possible.

When someone is openly aggressive, their behaviour and feelings are obvious. They might yell, insult, be argumentative, or hit you in some way. This creates a scenario where you get to fight back. It is obvious that it is unkind, unsafe, or untrustworthy. No question.

However, we aren't always so obvious with our attacks on others. We are often not upfront about what is bothering us. Maybe we don't think anything will change, or we were taught at a young age that it's dangerous to be open about how we feel, that it's best to keep our feelings to ourselves.

Buried feelings need to be released, so they twist into something the other person can't get mad about. These feelings will sneak out in snide comments. They might be "jokes with a jab," where someone says something that is supposed to be funny, but somehow makes you feel like you were attacked. Others simply become sullen and mope around, hoping the other will ask what's wrong. Or they tell stories in a way that leave other people feeling terrible about themselves.

Of course, they don't openly say what they are feeling so they can't get in trouble. If you call them on it, they say "What? You're overreacting. You're being too sensitive. I didn't mean anything by it." It's like an abusive partner knowing how to hit you without leaving a bruise. It's your word against theirs.

Passive aggression has become so common because society is governed more by logic and rules than heart and feelings. It's as if our interactions exist in a court of law, and because the other person didn't obviously *say* anything mean, you can't prove it, so they win.

In a world where we trust our hearts and our feelings, we know deep down that it was an attack. We can't pinpoint it, but we know it wasn't kind, funny, or loving.

To avoid passive aggression, find a way to be honest in a kind, loving way. If there is no kind way to say what you need to say, you must seriously look at what you want to say. Are you being judgemental of their choices? Do you want to fix them? Do you think you know what is "better" for them? These are all your own personal issues.

To know if something is loving, we have to ask: "Does this bring us closer together or create distance between us?"

Passive aggression always creates distance. It puts emotional walls up between us. It may not end your relationship (right away), but it will keep you separate and unable to feel connected.

BRINGING OUR A-GAME

If we want to develop loving connection, then we must be impeccable with our emotional safety. We must bring our "A-Game" to the table all of the time. For some, this is easy. For others, this seems like a lot of effort when they want to be able to relax.

Let's consider that right now there are about 7 billion people in the world. Within those 7 billion people, there is a handful whom you love the most. If you lost any of these people, you would be devastated.

Yet, there is a curious habit to treat these people worse than everyone else. Some call it "letting their hair down" or "being real" at home. People can yell at and treat their closest loved ones much worse than they treat the other 7 billion strangers on the planet.

Doesn't it make sense to treat these people better than anyone? Wouldn't we want to treat them in the same way we actually feel about them? Tell them that we cherish them? That we love them more than anyone?

We want to imagine this "river of love" flowing between you and your loved ones. No matter what, we want that river to flow unobstructed. We don't want anyone to have to put up walls and dams.

With every interaction, what can you do to *increase* trust and safety between you? If there are already barriers between you, what can you do to become safe enough so that others naturally let their guards down? If there are people around you who are safe to open up to, can you let your guards down and be open with them?

It is important to only open up if the other person is safe. Sometimes the people around us *aren't* safe. They don't know how to be, and that's OK. Be discerning. The guards we hold up are important because they protect us. But we want to be able to drop them anytime we'd like. And if we find someone who can be a confidante, then it's truly wonderful to drop everything and let our whole selves show.

I will be forever thankful for that conversation in the car with my friend's 16-year old daughter. It was a turning point in our lives. At the time of this writing, my children are 22 and 19 years old and I can honestly say we have never had a single argument or fight. The bond we have is completely loving, trusting and effortless.

Through their teenage years, not only could we talk about anything, our home was always filled with their friends; some just hung out and some chose to live with us. We spent many wonderful evenings chatting about the struggles and joys of life and being teenagers. It became the joke that although I had only birthed two children, I was mom to hundreds.

They were incredibly rich years.

PERSONAL PRACTICE:
BECOMING SANCTUARY

The goal here is to transform yourself so you are *naturally* safe, loving and trusting. It's about growing *within* the relationships in our lives right now. It's about looking inside and first understanding why we struggle to be 100% safe and kind. And then, the journey is figuring out what we need to heal personally in order for this to become effortless and second nature.

Having relationships built upon kindness, trust, and safety is often a new way of living. We easily get caught in the stories about who did what wrong, our painful experiences, and our residual feelings and memories. But when we look beneath the stories, we often see that our relationships are simply lacking true love and connection.

Begin by looking at all of the relationships in your life. Is there agape and philia? Is there trust and openness? Is there anyone with whom you can let your guards down completely? (If your answer is no, don't worry. You are not alone.)

What about your family growing up? Was there kindness, trust and safety in your home? Was there judgement? Did you feel you needed to prove yourself? Were you able to be vulnerable and open? (For many people, the answer is no.)

Historically, parents were taught to be the disciplinarians of their children. How their children acted was a reflection on who they were in the community. Children were born to "help on the farm." There was no birth control. Children were often "another mouth to feed." For sure, there was sometimes love. But many, many people today struggle with missing out on true unconditional love and a safe place to be emotionally vulnerable growing up, which makes all deeper love very difficult.

If *you* have children, what would it take to be their safe place? What would that look like? Can they trust you now? Can they share their struggles and hard times with you?

How about your friends? Do you have close friends who you can be open with? Can you trust each other? Can you count on them? Can they count on you? Is there love? What can you do to create more trust and openness? Or is it even possible? (Not everyone is open to this.)

If not, that's OK. You can still create this in your life now, but it is important to be aware that you might never have seen or experienced this kind of connection of love before. This awareness is important in case we start to slip into old patterns that disconnect us.

What about your intimate relationships? Is there agape? Are you always kind to each other? Do you honour each other's personal life paths and respect each other's choices? Is there philia? Are you each other's safe place in the world? Can you be completely open and vulnerable? Can you let down all of your guards and feel safe? Do you feel like you can count on this person to be there for you?

The key here is to notice all of our relationships and understand that in all of them, *we* are the common element. If we are lacking connection in one, we are likely lacking the same connection in all.

This is a huge part of our tantric journey. Feeling love and connection is intrinsically human. Looking deeply and healing the connection in our closest relationships help us heal and truly become complete.

CHAPTER 4

EROS: ROMANTIC, PASSIONATE LOVE

My lover lies beneath me.

He is so beautiful.

His eyes... his skin... his presence... his strength.

I'm filled with gratitude that

He is here.

That we are together.

That we are looking into each other's eyes.

We are naked...

Our bodies gently touching.

I'm so thrilled.

Looking into each other's eyes

So happy

So blissful

I breathe this beautiful moment in...

THE POTENTIAL OF TRUE INTIMACY

Eros is the kind of love that feels like some kind of cosmic draw. When we see this person, we get butterflies in our stomach. We can't think straight. We miss them when they are gone and we look forward to the next time we see them.

We are made for this kind of connection. It puts a spring in our step and a smile on our face. Eros further deepens the connection that starts with agape and philia. Through this level of intimacy, we can experience each other's souls. We can explore unknown realms together. We can truly merge and experience infinity.

This is where magic happens within a couple. When we have the passion of Eros within the safety of philia and the kindness of agape, we become the energy beings we truly are. All our walls are down. The river of energy between us flows unimpeded. We can truly merge with the other. Then the passion of eros increases the flow of the river, allowing us to feel pleasure and bliss that is out of this world!!

We are often taught this magical excitement is simply infatuation and it wears off in time. We are told this is the "honeymoon period" of love and it is meant to end pretty early in the relationship.

But it isn't true. The honeymoon isn't meant to end at all.

We haven't been taught how to keep this passion alive. If we were lucky, we saw it modelled for us by our parents and naturally expect it in our own lives. But for many people growing up, there wasn't even the kindness of agape, towards the children or between the parents. In this case, we won't even believe agape is possible, let alone philia, and definitely not eros. We might still desire sexual passion, but without the loving kindness of agape or the safety of philia, it will be a volatile relationship at best.

Plus, historically in the Christian church, lust, passion, and sexual attraction were considered sinful. Marriage was for procreation and to be faithful to each other. In other cultures, marriages were arranged for economic and social purposes. And many other marriages were for less than desirable reasons; there was definitely no love or connection. The chance for eros to start, let alone continue, was impossible. Your best hope was to have agape and philia with your partner. These were considered pure forms of love. This model has been the precedent for many generations and still lives on some level within many of us.

The common reality today is that many of us create this "honeymoon period" ourselves. We start out with passion, kindness, and trust with each other. We are on our best behaviour in the beginning because we feel attracted to this person and we want to be together. But then, once we've "got" them, we stop being so careful. We aren't *always* kind. We aren't *always* there for each other. We stop feeding the fires of our passion.

We have a choice to make in every moment. This love between you weaves together a cloth that connects you. Every time we are genuinely loving towards the other, we add to the cloth, increasing our connection. Each time we are unkind or unsafe, some threads are cut.

THE TREE OF LOVE

A tree is a beautiful way to understand how each love builds upon each other to keep eros alive in your relationship.

The roots of our love is agape. This is where we deeply connect with each other. The stronger our kindness and respect for each other, the more nourishing our relationship.

From this strong foundation of kindness, respect, and connection grows philia – the trunk and branches of our tree. We are truly each other's best friend. We can confide in each other. We can count on each other to want to be there. We enjoy each other's company – a lot.

From this healthy and strong tree, beautiful leaves and blossoms can grow. The stronger the tree, the more blossoms we have.

Our relationship is a living thing. Love cannot be promised and then ignored or put on a shelf. This is like the tree never getting water or sunlight. It will eventually die.

Similarly, every time we are unkind or we disrespect each other in any way, we damage the root, which starts to systematically starve the whole tree.

Also consider that sometimes the tree is alive with blossoms and other times there are only leaves. Perhaps in the winter, the branches are bare. We experience this in our love as well. Perhaps you are going through a difficult time in your lives – job loss, a death in the family, or illness. At this time, the passion of eros might not be "in full bloom," but the roots and tree are still there. They are still alive. You can still nourish yourself in the safety, kindness, and true affection.

Plus, it is during these hard times that our root system becomes stronger. The whole tree is nourished. Because the tree is so strong, no one is worried about the lack of blossoms; you know that soon spring will come, and you will have more blossoms than ever.

DEEPENING YOUR LOVE

The answer is to stay lovers forever. Keep the play. Keep the passion. Keep the flowing love.

We can keep house and pay the bills with lots of people. We can even go to a sperm bank and have children with anyone.

But we can't be lovers with just anyone. If you find someone special, then being lovers is the greatest thing you can have together. This is the passion that invigorates us. It's what makes us excited to be alive. It fills us with joy and happiness that doesn't happen anywhere else.

When we are lovers, it is all about the flame of passion between us. It is about our connection. It's about exploring each other's souls. It's about having experiences in the world together, and the connection is the ultimate point. And so we do things to deepen it, to make it stronger, to nurture and feed it.

When we are lovers, we realize how precious it is to have this kind of connection. We are so grateful to have found his other person that we *want* to do things with them. We want to do things *for* them. It isn't work or expectation. We desire it. We want to explore more. We want to see them smile.

THE CHALLENGE OF LUST

What is the difference between eros and lust? Eros is passion *with* love and connection. Lust is passion *without* love and connection.

Lust feeds our primal wiring to procreate. We don't need emotional connection to make it happen. We can walk down the street and see someone we find attractive, and we can practically feel our hormones rise. This is not eros. It is lust. It is our hormonal reaction to potential mates.

The challenge with lust in our society, (and the reason that women tend to be more hurt by casual sex than men) is that we don't get what we wanted out of it.

In the animal world, if a female animal is in heat, the primal desire to have sex is in order to get impregnated. There are mating rituals that they go through in order to attract a suitable mate with strong genetics to create healthy offspring. Similarly, the male will seek out a female who is healthy enough to carry his offspring and care for it. Then the two animals mate. The female is impregnated. She is content. The male has spread his seed. He is content. All is well.

But of course, when this plays out in humans, it's not so good. The woman generally does not desire pregnancy. She desires love.

There are exceptions, of course. For many women who are trying to get pregnant, they might get total satisfaction out of purely physical sex. They don't care if it's good sex or if they orgasm. There is a mechanism inside that knows they want to be impregnated right now and they simply need the man to make it happen.

Yes, there are times when women may want to have casual sex. A desire for "any kind of sex" can happen in their most fertile parts of their cycle. Of course, because they don't have the desire to get pregnant, satisfaction will matter more. However, they will generally be disappointed. For the most part, casual sex tends to not be great and there is just something missing afterwards. Deep down we know that if it was going to be truly primal sex, then we should have gotten something more out of it.

It's also interesting to note how many women find their desire for sex diminishes after menopause. They no longer have that time of the month where they are satisfied with physical, procreative-type sex. If that has been the only kind of sex that they normally had in their lives, they will accurately say that they aren't interested in "having sex" anymore. But are they interested in true lovemaking or tantric intimacy? This is a whole other story.

The greatest challenge of lust is that it only feeds a small aspect of who we are. The physical desire to procreate perhaps lets off steam. Some call it "sex for sport." It is just something we do. It feels good. We like it. Of course, it was *designed* to feel good, good enough that we will crave it. But this is only for our physical pleasure in the moment.

When we meet someone who we feel passion for and are looking for something more than sex, we normally slow down to get to know them. We develop connection. We learn out about them. We develop agape and philia. We create a bond.

Somehow we know that this connection is necessary for the relationship to "go anywhere," for true eros to exist. We may not use these words. But we know that we want something more. We want the lovemaking to mean something.

LUST VS. EROS FOR OURSELVES

One cultural belief that lives on in many of us is that sexuality and spirituality cannot coexist. We are taught that sexual desires are in opposition to the desire to be "close to God." We often have shame and guilt attached to enjoying sex, letting ourselves go, and fully embracing our life force in a sexual way.

Much of the origins of the Christian belief that lust was evil came from Saint Augustine in the early 5th century. Due to his own confused and sexually-charged adolescence, he was tormented that these desires had nothing to do with love, procreation, connection, or God. He coined the term "concupiscence," which is often defined as "desires of the lowly appetites" or "fleshly desires."

He decided the lust of his flesh was working against his connection to God. This was compounded by very influential monks at the time, like Jovinian, who believed celibacy was the only way to be close to God. This became the roots of our current belief that sex is dirty, unspiritual, lowly, and only satisfies primal needs. This belief was applied to the story of Adam & Eve and how they succumbed to their desires. Lust and sex became "Original Sin." Sex and desire became "bad."

This is a belief that still flows under the surface for many of us. Many believe sex is dirty and feel guilt if we want it or genuinely enjoy it. Or on the other side, we see sex as our way of rebellion against society, so we sleep with anyone we want, even to our own detriment. This rebellion is still accepting the original belief that sex is bad; otherwise, it wouldn't be rebellious.

It's interesting to note that concupiscence wasn't just about sex. It was about anything that took us away from God and our spiritual purpose. It also could have included the personal desires for wealth, status, etc., instead of pursuing higher callings. His point was that these things take us away from our true purpose. In fact, he didn't even think sexual desire was the greatest of the "lusts" that torment us, or the most dangerous one.

St. Augustine's full thoughts on this topic are a vast discussion, full of his own personal ups and downs as he wrestled with his own lack of willpower towards lustful thoughts and his desire to connect with God. These are important ideas that continue in our beliefs today; it's good to recognize them.

St. Augustine was not aware at the time of the possibility of Eros – where love, spiritual connection, and sexual passion all existed and mutually fed each other. He separated "lusts of the flesh" from spiritual aspirations. This "Sex vs. God" perspective and the idea that celibacy is the purest way to live and be close to God turned sex and desire into a great sin and something that "good and holy" people didn't desire or need in their lives.

This is important to consider because we all have desires. We long for connection. We long for sexual intimacy. If we have any beliefs these desires are "wrong" or "dirty" or "unholy," we will always struggle because these are a natural part of being human. Being connected to God or Spirit is also a natural part of being human. To be whole, we must be able to fully embrace both aspects of ourselves without them being at odds with each other.

While studying tantra, I imagine we are doing exactly what St. Augustine would have loved to do – to combine our physical lives with spirit. To know that all of our desires for love and passion can actually bring us closer to God.

Who knows... maybe St. Augustine is somewhere smiling right now.

LUST VS. EROS IN RELATIONSHIPS

Ironically, the church's interpretation that lust didn't belong in a good marriage is actually correct. Eros is beautiful in a marriage, but if all we have is lust, this can be incredibly damaging – not to mention unfulfilling.

If two people are happy simply having physical, sexual release with each other, this is a pleasurable option in the moment. However, if there are emotional bonds or the desire for real love, lustful sex without connection can be simply unfulfilling in the short-term and subtly damaging at deeper levels in the long-term.

When we have an emotional bond with someone, we sense their wholeness. We can feel the whole breadth of who they are – physically, emotionally, mentally and spiritually. When we join intimately, we have the potential of joining 100% of who we are with 100% of who they are. Deep down, some part of us knows the incredible bliss this could bring.

When the other person walls off most of who they are so they only connect physically, we know we are being cheated. And we're not only being cheated, we're being cheated of the juiciest and most interesting parts.

It's like being beside a huge buffet filled with all of your favourite foods, and your loved one gives you a tiny crust of bread from it. Maybe you take the high road and choose to be thankful for the crust of bread. You know that there was so much more – right there in front of you! But you couldn't have it. For a million reasons, your loved one couldn't open up and share completely.

This withholding of ourselves (although mostly done unintentionally and unconsciously) can breed long-standing resentment, passive aggression, and manipulation in a relationship.

Lust feeds us the crust of bread. Eros is the whole feast.

HOW MUCH LOVE DO
YOU HAVE TO GIVE?

Sometimes we have no idea how much love we have to give.

My friend told me this story recently:

She was with her new man. After making love for a while on the beach, she fell asleep on his chest. When she awoke, she realized he hadn't moved. He had held her and let her sleep. She'd never had a man hold her in such kindness before.

She was so filled with love for this man that all she wanted to do was give herself to him. She wanted to make love with her whole being. And they did. She said it was the most beautiful lovemaking she had ever experienced. She felt wholly and completely loved.

She said the amazing thing was that she could pour love into this man and he would return even more. Then she would give more... and so on. She couldn't believe the way her heart opened and kept expanding and expanding.

She had no idea how much love she could give.

Sometimes, we are with people who aren't able to receive the love we want to give. If this happens in our early formative romantic years, we may never realize our true capacity for love.

This is commonly found out after people leave their first marriage or long-term relationship. Maybe they got together early. Maybe they were happy to find *someone*. Maybe there were children or shared property or businesses. Or maybe they are afraid there isn't anything else better out there. Even though there isn't as much love and kindness as they might like, they keep trying.

Our partner's ability to receive love could be a result of their makeup or what they were taught as children. Regardless, if your love is not received, there is some part of you that dies. It feels unseen. And if it is unseen, we may think this need isn't even real. You may end up thinking this is normal, or it might become a self-worth issue, and you think you are simply unlovable.

Then, one day, the relationship ends and you find yourself over the moon in love with someone else. You had no idea you could actually feel this way. You had truly believed what you had previously experienced was all there was.

If there is some part of you that believes there is something more, you are probably right. Keep seeking.

A PRACTICAL LOOK

So what does a relationship filled with eros look like in real life?

Passion

Passion is possible. Passion is wonderfully overwhelming. It gives us desire for living. It gives us focus that makes us want to get up each day and embrace whatever it is we are passionate about. We feel fully alive. We require no food, no drink, and no addictions. The passion is so great and complete.

When we feel this passion for another, simply kissing and embracing is wonderful. The chemistry is indescribable. It feels surreal to be in that space. We want to make love for hours. We want to smell them, breathe them. When our lips touch, the world stands still. This is great passion.

Continuous Intimacy

The connection between you is always there whether you are together or not. It's a candle that is always burning. You feel the presence of this candle when you are making dinner, going for a walk, at work, or making love.

This isn't co-dependence. It isn't a need to be always close because you are not whole without the other person. You are both whole and completely in love.

As you walk through your day, this love is felt and you both are nourished by this wonderful connection.

Full Acceptance

When we love another, we accept them. This is the agape aspect of our love. This is knowing we each have different paths to take and we respect each other's choices. True love fully accepts them. We honour them as fellow humans trying their best.

What if there are things about them we absolutely can't live with? Maybe we desire something they don't want to give. Or maybe you find you aren't compatible. All we can do is be honest with each other. Maybe your honesty sets them on a different path and your relationship deepens. Wonderful!

But if not, we have a decision to make. We could choose to move on. Perhaps that relationship is now complete. This is a good choice to make if you really aren't compatible in a way that makes both of you thrive.

For many reasons, many will choose to stay. Many of us are afraid to be alone. We would rather have someone who is "so-so" in our life than no one at all. For others, leaving means failure. Marriage is supposed to be forever.

When we stay in a situation that doesn't allow everyone to thrive, we will either let the part of us that craves passion and romance die or we will do something more devious – we will try to "fix" the other. We will tell ourselves we are doing it out of love, but this isn't love. This is creating a false reality. Fixing others always creates distance. It will block the river and eros will surely die.

Reciprocal Love

The thrill of passionate love is having it fully reciprocated. This isn't neediness. This is the only way for true merging to happen. Deep down, we desire the union of souls. And it can't be one-way.

Energy must come from both sides. Both parties must fully give to the union. Or it will be nothing but a convenient companionship.

Many have felt one-sided love, where one is all-in and the other is not. This is a very painful relationship to be in. Often this is when we choose a partner who isn't able to experience the depth of connection that we can. Perhaps they had a hard childhood and struggle to connect. Maybe they have a hard time trusting others, so they struggle to be open and vulnerable to bare their soul and go deeper.

When both partners truly desire eros in their lives, we simply have to be honest about the reality of what we are feeling and improve our communication (we will talk much more about this in later chapters). When both people are on board, there is always great potential and hope.

Freedom to Choose

Sometimes love gets very possessive. Historically, in many places marriage was a contract where we really did own each other. We promised "till death do you part," which can really feel like being owned by the other "till death." So the idea of being possessive is actually well rooted in our culture.

This feeling of possessiveness is especially acute when there are certain aspects of love missing in the relationship. Maybe there isn't trust and respect, passion, or even kindness. If this is the case, to think of our partner having this with another person is heartbreaking, so we tend to hold on even tighter.

This is not love. It is possessiveness. When we love each other, we *want* to be together. We don't need someone holding on tight to make sure we stick around.

If we are bound by anything – either a legal document or the emotional iron-grip of another – then we will not be free to love. This is more like a kidnapped person learning to love their captor.

When each person has choice, then love can flow freely. There is something magical about being in a position of choice. When we are bound and we have no choice, huge parts of us shut off. When we have choice, all parts of us are fully alive.

Plus, when we have choice, we are aware of how thankful we are for this other person. We make an effort to nourish the love between us. We stay aware in the relationship. We feed the fires of our passion. We are aware that one day, it may be gone. Eros cannot be controlled. It is either there or it isn't.

This isn't depressing. It is the same way that experiencing death makes us more aware of the joys in our lives. It makes us thankful to simply wake up and breathe in another day.

Similarly in love, we must treat it like the gift it is – ever changing and uncontrollable.

Loving Completely and Unbounded

Ralph Waldo Emerson once said, "The love that you withhold is the pain you carry." We are meant to let love flow out of us, withholding nothing.

When we love in this way, amazing things happen. Energy flows through us that we can't describe. It could be the excitement of a child running to the arms of their grandparent. Or picking loved ones up at the airport after a long separation. Nothing is held back. We are able to completely let all of our love flow out of us. This is amazingly nourishing for us!

When we are in an intimate relationship where there is complete trust, understanding, kindness, and passion, these two unbounded loves collide and it is a tidal wave of energy flowing through your bodies. Suddenly all the pictures you've ever seen of two people embracing and energy flowing all around them is totally real. They are truly floating in ecstasy.

When we can release every ounce of that love right now, *we* heal. Our spirit soars. Our spirit says "Oh my god! I'm so glad to be alive! I'm so glad we're actually on this planet! Isn't this great that I'm allowed to breathe? I actually woke up this morning! I'm so lucky because I have all this fantastic things in my life."

Love should be known as the amazing spiritual experience that it is!

EXPLORING INFINITY TOGETHER

It is within this deep connection that we can explore infinity together. Two infinite beings who desire to connect can go to places we cannot go alone. What will that look like? What will it feel like? There are truly infinite possibilities.

It is only when we have a limit to what we are willing to experience that we can get bored in a relationship. And I don't mean sexual experimentation. That is something else.

Tantra is a spiritual journey. How deep do you want to go with each other? How open can you be with each other? How vulnerable can you be? This is where the depth is. This is where the true juice is.

It's like having a best friend. Do you get bored of this person? No. Why? Because you have no guards up for each other. So your conversation never ends. You can talk and talk for hours. Sometimes about things you've talked about a thousand times. But it never gets old.

I have friends with whom I could travel around the world. We might have nothing in common and not be lovers or not even know each other for very long. But, for whatever reason, we have no guards up to each other. We are wide open. There is a kind of unspoken trust.

With this friend, you have fun whether you are watching a movie, chatting, driving bumper cars, or sitting in silence at the edge of the lake. For whatever reason, you don't get bored.

Why? Because anything is possible in any moment.

The same goes for a lover. When we don't have any guards up to each other, when there is trust and love, the exploration of each other is truly infinite. The potential of where you can go when eros is flowing freely and unbounded is truly limitless and beyond our wildest dreams! (But more about that in later chapters.)

PERSONAL PRACTICE:
TRANSFORMATION THROUGH LOVE

If you are in an intimate relationship right now, how can you cultivate eros?

First look at whether or not you have the foundation of kindness. Is there mutual respect? Do you consider each other equals? If you do, wonderful. If not, then we must start here. Nothing can grow without this foundation.

Then ask if there is trust (philia) between you. Do you feel comfortable to drop all of your guards together? Are they safe? Are *you* safe? Can you be vulnerable? Are you OK with your partner being vulnerable?

Is there passion? Did you have it at one time but it died? What happened? What blew the flame out? What caused your disconnection?

If eros is still alive, then what can you do to make it deeper? To feed the flames? To increase this connection between you and your partner?

In all of these scenarios, the question is, what would require us to *grow*? Evolution is a process of growth and expansion. It is becoming something we previously weren't. Imagine growing through intimate love.

You and your lover can grow together to move to each next step. Your relationship and deep connection can be a container for amazing healing, growth, and bliss.

If you are not in a relationship right now, you can look at past relationships to understand what happened within the context of agape, philia, and eros. Are there patterns you would like to change for the future? Is there personal healing you need to do to create this foundation of love and kindness?

Whether we are alone or in a relationship, tantra is first a personal journey of introspection and personal transformation. When we bring ourselves to a place where kindness, trust, and passion easily flow within us, then opportunities will arise everywhere around us.

CHAPTER 5

CONNECTION TO SELF

Who are you really?

The movie *The Matrix* describes two worlds. The first is the one we think we see all around us – our work, people, politics, money, and where we like to eat sushi. It seems real, but we are actually asleep. It is an illusion that has been programmed into our minds so we think it is real, so we will continue doing what we have always done without question.

The second world is our actual reality. There are still people, society, and work to do here. The difference is that we are awake. We are conscious and not slaves to what society has told us is real. We are free to explore what humans were designed for. We understand that we are so much more than our physical bodies, our work, and the pressures of society.

Our hero, "Neo," is captured by the rebels who have already figured this out. Right away, they give him the option of swallowing the "blue pill," which returns him to the sleeping world of limitations, rules, and ignorance, or he can swallow the "red pill," wake up and find out the true nature of reality.

The "red pill" is actually a tracking program to find out where the "real Neo" is. In the pretend world, he knows where he is. He works for a computer firm, lives in an apartment and buys coffee around the corner.

But where is *he*? His *soul*? His immortal, deep self that came to this planet for an experience? Where is *that* guy?

We all have this dual existence. Perhaps we have a public persona, or we work hard to be the perfect mother/wife/sister/friend/employee/boss/husband/father/son/daughter/church-goer/atheist/free-spirit – whatever it is we desire ourselves to be.

These are only projections of who we want to be and how we want to be perceived in the world. This is how we "fit into the matrix."

But who is the one who wants this? Who is the one inside?

This is who we must find.

TANTRA ACCEPTANCE IS TOTAL

To be tantric, we must accept and love every part of us. There is no option to this. We are designed to work as a whole, functioning unit. Anything less simply won't bring us to our full potential.

The healing journey means finding the parts of ourselves we have cut off, cast out or neglected and then integrating them back into the whole. Everything is right here already; there are simply parts that we can't look at for all kinds of reasons.

On the inner journey, we cannot hide from ourselves. When we meditate, we often struggle with being alone inside our minds because the "lost" and "dark" parts of our psyche continually try to rise up to be healed. They might be memories and feelings from our past that we don't want to experience again, or they might be current issues that we don't have solutions for. Being left alone with these thoughts often feels like being trapped in a room with someone you really don't want to talk to.

The integration of all of these experiences, painful memories, and struggles depends on our ability to first look at them in kindness and know we have the emotional strength to feel them. Then, over time, we have new experiences and moments of inspiration that show us how the strength we developed during the difficult times actually became our solid and enduring foundation.

LOVING WHO YOU ACTUALLY ARE

Paradise is at your own centre;
unless you find it there,
there is no way to enter.
ANGELUS SILESIUS

What if you are shorter than what you think is ideal? What if you are naturally round when the world says you should be thin? What if you are thin, when the world says you should have beautiful, full hips? What if you prefer physical labour but you were born to doctors who feel only academics are worthy? What if you believe in spirituality, but your family was all about the corporate world?

There are things in the world that we are told are really important. We often craft an ideal person in our minds of who we would like to be based on those "important" things. When we don't line up with that image, we either work hard to achieve this image, or we silently beat ourselves up for not being that way.

We cannot control our height. This is who we are. Yet if you live in a society where tall men are the lucky ones, then are you OK that you aren't one of them? What if you are a tall woman who is dying to find a man who is tall enough to look into her eyes?

For many men, the size of their penis is a big deal. Society even jokes that men with small penises get big trucks because they are "compensating for something."

But this is completely out of our control.

Whether we are given a small penis or one so big that you can't have intercourse at all, none of this tells us anything about the person or his ability as a lover. In tantric intimacy, size is irrelevant because it is the quality of the lover and the power of the connection that creates the magic.

If our deepest inner critic is saying, "I wish I was one of those popular, strong men who women can't take their eyes off of," instead we want to think, "Hmm. This is who I was born as … I wonder what this journey is all about."

We can control how we treat others. We can control how we react in situations. We can control how loving we are towards others. And we can control how loving we are to ourselves. This is incredibly important.

Self love makes the most sense when we understand there is a greater purpose for being here than to fit in or be physically attractive and successful. For some reason beyond our understanding, we were born who we are. We are a woman or man or both. We were born into wealth or poverty. We had parents who were loving or unkind. We were born into a certain body type. We were born with gifts and specific challenges.

It may sound cliché to say that we need to fall in love with ourselves, but we have to understand what love is. Love is how we connect. And if we don't truly love ourselves, then we will always be disconnected from who we really are.

When we are tantric, we have to go one step further because we don't just appreciate and love our life. We are actually excited and amazed by it. It's like truly being head over heels in love with someone. You are truly excited they are in your life. You can't believe you could be so lucky! You love spending time with them. You love all of their quirks and their uniqueness. You truly adore them and feel a special deep connection with them.

We must love ourselves this way.

We must understand just how incredible we are. We are truly divine, amazing beings. Even if, according to the world's standards, we have messed up, or we don't fit the physical ideal model, or we aren't the smartest kid in the class, we are completely wonderful.

Can you believe this?

Close your eyes and breathe. Feel the place inside your chest where you feel still. This is your essence. It is who you are. It is your connection to infinity – to the divine.

SELF-LOVE

Our desire and need for self love is such a widespread problem that it has nearly become cliché to say. But without loving ourselves, we really can't love anyone else. Here's how it works in the context of agape, philia, and eros.

Agape

Do you have agapic love for yourself? What does your inner voice sound like? Is it your "inner critic" or your "inner cheering squad"?

This is the foundation of our love in all of our relationships.

When we can truly look at ourselves with kindness and respect, we don't beat ourselves up for choices we've made. We honour that for some reason we made those choices. We know we are doing the best we can. We give ourselves a hug when we're down, not a reprimand – either for something we've done, or even for simply feeling down.

When we feel this way towards ourselves, only then can we extend that toward someone else. If we can look into our darkest parts and be kind and respectful, then we can also see someone else in their darkest and troubled moments and extend the same love to them.

When we don't have agape, we can go no further in love; no matter what happens, we will judge ourselves if anything goes "wrong" and we won't be free to be open and vulnerable. If we pretend to have agape for others, we will easily love others who are doing what we believe to be "right" but everyone else will fall into the same category of our darkest parts – unlovable, and wrong. Not loving at all.

Philia

Philia is literally being your own best friend. It builds upon agape because your friend is kind to you. (Understand that if you have never had a good friend who is always kind and respectful to you, you will have to expand into what is possible, not what you've experienced.)

This friend is also someone with whom you can bare your soul. You can drop your guards. Where agape is for everyone – friends and strangers – philia is for friends and family. When you have philia love for yourself, you truly know yourself. No matter what others might tell you, *you* are the expert here. Since you have a deep love for this friend (you), it is safe to be vulnerable with yourself.

When we don't have philia for ourselves, we keep walls up within and are unable to admit how we truly feel. Somehow, our feelings don't matter. Other people's feelings and comfort matter more. We convince ourselves that other opinions are more important.

We don't live within our own truth. We hope that other realities are the truth, but they aren't. So, we perpetually struggle in all of life because we aren't able to live within what is actually going on.

We don't understand why we are triggered by the actions of others. We don't understand why things bother us so much because our truths are buried. We can't even admit them to ourselves.

When we have agape and philia love within, we can easily bare our soul to ourselves. We are honest about our feelings. We matter.

Rollo May used to say that no matter how much counselling you do, nothing will ever work until you have your "I am" moment – that moment when *you* actually matter. Once you have this moment, *you* are important. Your opinion counts. Your feelings matter. This is when you truly are allowed to "take up space" and exist as part of the whole.

Eros

Yes, you can be passionately in love with yourself.

Can you imagine loving yourself with all of the passion you desire from someone else? What does this mean? What kind of passionate relationship do you want with another?

They long to be with you. They love spending time with you. They do lovely things for you. You love doing things for them. You are excited you get to be in their life. You feel a special connection with them that you have with no one else.

This isn't narcissism. This is gratitude for this precious human that you get to be. This is deep, unbounded love.

As deeply as you can love yourself in this way, you will find this love with others. If you think you are just "okay," then you will also find others who also think you are "okay." Of course, you don't want them to think you are simply okay; deep down, you want them to love you passionately. So, you will constantly want them to prove that they love you passionately. But it will never be enough because even if they do, you will never believe them anyway.

If you don't love yourself that way, you won't believe that anyone else would either, no matter how much they try.

Remember, this is a journey. If you don't feel all of agape, philia, or eros for yourself right now, it's ok. This is the journey of healing. We need to bring back all of the parts of ourselves that we haven't loved or couldn't handle before and integrate them. It takes time, and it is often like peeling the onion.

It's all good. We simply need to know what we are aiming for, because love always helps all aspects of our journey.

PERSONAL PRACTICE:
EYE-GAZING WITH YOURSELF

They say the eyes are the windows of the soul, and it's true. You can look at my cheek or my shoulder or my nose, and all you will see is a cheek, shoulder, and a nose. But look into my eyes and there is something else. There is something alive in there.

Let's take a look.

Take a mirror, and look into your own eyes. This might seem odd; I'll admit the first time I did it, I was very uncomfortable with the idea. I avoided it for a long time. I didn't want to do it at all.

When I finally did, I started crying. I had to look into my own soul, past my mind, past all my thoughts, past everything I was pretending to be, and really be present with myself.

Even worse, I had to look into my own eyes and apologize for thinking that who I was wasn't good enough all these years. For judging myself so harshly and wishing I was different. It was like looking at my inner child and admitting how unkind I had been.

This is so important. If we can't look into our own eyes and be at peace – and deeply love what we see, then how can we deeply share with another?

You can practice eye-gazing for as long as you like, or you can do it for five minutes. Allow your mind to turn off and experience whatever is there. Maybe you don't experience anything. Maybe you get caught up looking at your features and wrinkles. That's OK. It's all an experience. Try again another day.

Our experience is different every day that we meditate or we run. Sometimes we're all systems go and it's easy, and other days it doesn't work. So, do it a few times. See what comes.

When we don't love who we truly are, we create a persona – a false self. Then we project this persona everywhere we go so this is the person others see. Sometimes we can pull the wool over their eyes – if they aren't paying attention.

But tantra asks for much deeper connections. Tantra asks us to connect with God. Tantra asks us to connect deeply with each other.

False personas don't work here. We can't connect through a fake front. We must be able to be open, vulnerable, and real.

This is why our personal work is to truly love ourselves – inside and out. Unless we love what is under the mask, we will never show it to anyone. We will never let anyone all the way in.

Similarly in our connection to the divine, whatever you believe that to be, if we don't love ourselves, we will always feel unworthy of this connection. We will believe we are too broken. We will believe no one would ever love us enough to accept us completely.

This is the illusion.

We need to see through the illusion and know we are incredible, that there are no judges and juries out there deciding who is good or bad or worthy or unworthy. This is between us and the divine.

Everything else is illusion.

CHAPTER 6

LETTING DOWN OUR WALLS

I had always hidden my feelings from other people. I wanted to be a good kid. I wanted to appear strong. I didn't want to burden others with my problems. But of course, all of those unresolved, hidden, and very loaded feelings don't go away. They sit inside of us and fester, making us react to things more strongly than we want, keeping us at a distance from people and generally eating us up from the inside out.

Jim, my first teacher, was the first person to really pierce through my armour. To get better and heal, I had to start feeling and expressing my emotions. I had to start being honest about my truth.

And so, I would go to him for a session and he would deliberately make me angry about something. (This was quite a feat because I prided myself on the fact that I never got angry. But you know the saying – "Pride goes before a fall.") He knew just the right thing to make me fume inside. Then he would look at me with a twinkle in his eye and say, "What are you thinking, Katrina? Or more accurately, what are you *feeling*?"

I would squirm and try to keep my composure. I would try to answer him with my brain. Then he would stare at me with the annoyingly peaceful smile of a guru who can see right through you.

Eventually, I would burst. I would scream and yell and cry and swear and let it all go. The more I yelled, the more he smiled. He would even giggle to himself out loud and say, "Wow, you're *really* angry, huh?" And then he would smile, so completely happy with himself.

With him, I felt free to express *exactly* the depth of what I was feeling. All of the sadness, anger, frustration, disappointment, and grief I had been holding down for 30 years came flying out.

I wasn't directing it at *him*. I was releasing emotion. I was being honest. I was exposing my true self. To him. And to me, for the first time.

FACING MY FEAR OF EXPOSURE

The nice thing about emotions is that after we express them, they pass. It is only when we repress them that our mind gets involved and starts to analyze them. Then the stories we make up start to take on a whole new life of their own.

When I began learning to express these emotions, I communicated differently with my husband and children. I learned to say to my husband, "I am so frustrated. Do you mind if I vent for a while? It's not about you. I just need to let it out." At this point, he had the freedom to say, "Yep. Let's hear it!" or "Honestly, I can't. I'm in a tough place myself right now."

With my kids, I never wanted to burden them with my sadness or frustration. (And interestingly enough, there was always a strange correlation between the days they were constantly fighting and when I was repressing my feelings.) But I had to learn how to express my emotions no matter who was around. I couldn't hide them anymore.

One day, we were upstairs in our old farmhouse. My kids were 2 and 4 years old. I was exhausted, having a hard day, and the kids were having their typical sibling fights - "He's touching me!", "No I'm not", "Yes you are!!" I had a basket of laundry under my arm and I just couldn't keep it in any longer. I leaned against the wall; I slid down to the floor and started crying.

My 4-year-old son stopped fighting with his sister, toddled over to me, put his little hand on my shoulder and asked, "What's wrong mommy?"

"I'm just so sad today."

"Hmmm. Ya. I get that way too." And he slid down the wall (just like I had) and sat beside me holding my hand. My daughter soon came over and crawled up on my lap. My tears continued. I let my sadness flow, but there were now lots of happy mom feelings mixed in there too.

What I realized is that our kids *feel* our truth. They feel our feelings whether we express them or not. They are emotional sponges. Can you imagine the effect on them when they feel sadness from us but we only show them fake smiles? I've often wondered if this is the beginning of why we struggle to trust others.

Similarly, we feel each other's truths. We know if our partner is being open with us. We are aware if there is distance between us. We are aware when we don't feel safe to be fully ourselves. Even if we don't have the words to describe it, our bodies and emotions know the truth.

THE WALLS WITHIN US

In 1979, the rock band Pink Floyd released the album "The Wall." The songs poignantly described how fears, rules, and oppression cause us to build walls around us. Each fear getting its own brick of protection.

They look at some of the earliest influences in a young person's life – school, home, love, and society. In school, we learn "where we fit" into society based on intelligence. Whether we are at the top or the bottom, it can create limitations in our lives that distance us from others. The "smart" kids must contribute to society in a certain way, regardless of what they deeply want, thus creating a wall within themselves. The "less intelligent" kids can build walls around them to defend themselves from further embarrassment and judgement.

The song "Mother" is about growing up with an overprotective single mother who, in order to keep her boy safe, convinces him to build a wall to protect him from all the horrors that are "out there." She warns him about the dangers of war, how there are "bad" girls out there who will break your heart, how others might not like you and might hurt you. It is easy to imagine this in our own lives with parents who want to protect us from experiences they had in their past and from their own fear of relationships and society at large.

As we go through life, these bricks fit together and build walls around us. We aren't even aware the walls are being built – they just grow along with us. We have never known anything different. We barely know they are there.

Then we have our own difficult experiences. Someone says something unkind. We have a hard break-up. Things don't work out the way we planned. At this point, we start adding our own bricks.

As much as these walls might have been important to protect us at one time, if we can't see them, then they limit us in all aspects of our lives. Most of all, they effectively keep everyone out – including our loved ones and partners.

The key going forward is to listen to what our loved ones are saying. Are they saying things like: You're not listening. I can't reach you. There is distance between us. You're keeping me away. You're afraid to get close. It's like you don't see me. Why are you so defensive? Why don't you trust me? What are you afraid of?

This is our chance to hear what our loved ones are saying and start asking questions. Ask your partner and friends why they think you're like this. Pray. Meditate. Ask for answers.

Each revelation removes a brick and we are a little freer. And if we're lucky, we remove one brick and even more come crumbling down!

BEING TOTALLY VULNERABLE

We need to be vulnerable in intimate relationships.

This is a challenging topic because it can be a very difficult world out there. The idea of *becoming* vulnerable feels like we are releasing the protection that keeps us safe – and sometimes sane. And yet, it is absolutely necessary in order to be truly intimate and connect with anyone.

Consider these wise words from Archbishop Desmond Tutu, "We are fragile creatures, and it is from this weakness, not despite it, that we discover the possibility of true joy."

It isn't that we need to *become* vulnerable. We need to realize we already *are* vulnerable. We must admit to ourselves how fragile life is – how fragile *we* are. We are always only one car accident, one phone call, one illness, one freak storm from our lives changing forever. This isn't a scary or depressing thought. It is reality. When we realize this, we have a much greater potential for happiness.

In romantic relationships, imagine how differently we would treat each other if we recognized from the first moment how fragile romantic love is. What if we didn't pretend it lasted forever? What if we treated it with the love and kindness it needs to be nurtured? Imagine the happiness that would be possible.

FINDING SAFETY WITHIN

The way to embrace our vulnerability, be honest about our emotions, and let go of all of our walls, is to connect to the divine inside of us.

This is what gives us the strength to truly be open with others.

When we connect to the still, deep, timeless part of ourselves, we know our true self is always "safe." We are much bigger than our emotions. We are bigger than our pain. We don't need walls up to the world. We only need to expand into who we really are.

All of these protective walls and fears are leftovers from believing that we are limited, small people. They come from believing we are muscle and bones living by chance in this world. So, we have to keep ourselves safe.

As we connect deeper with our infinite self and our connection to the divine, we can look at our vulnerabilities and fully accept them. When we accept them, we will be able to share our deepest self with others.

When we find this internal strength, we won't need the walls any longer. We are stronger. We aren't alone. We soon know we will be fine no matter what comes our way. And we either take the walls down, or walk around in front of them and join the world.

TRULY JOINING WITH ANOTHER

When we have this inner strength, it becomes easy to join with others. It could be chatting with someone on the street. It could be confiding in a close friend. It could be having a loving conversation with a child or parent. And it's definitely easier to completely merge with a lover.

Have you ever noticed how emotions fuse us? Relationships can stay on the surface when life is easy and fun. But as soon as you go through challenges together and you are real about what you're going through, an amazing bond forms.

You can see it with soldiers who went through war together. Or firefighters, police, or paramedics who help out in traumatic situations. Or when families go through the death of loved ones or serious illness. They become bonded forever. When everyone lets down their guards (which doesn't always happen), everyone's love and connection are deepened.

It is very human to connect with our feelings and emotions. In many science fiction movies, there is often the "Mr. Spock" character who feels no emotions and is completely logical and composed at all times. They are always "fascinated by the humans" with their complex emotions and connections with each other.

This is really what it is to be human. We aren't robots. We are meant to connect. And we're meant to connect deeply with each other.

WE ACTUALLY ARE MIND-READERS!

Couples often argue because one (often the woman) will say, "You should know what I want. I shouldn't have to tell you!" This is very common, and the popular advice is, "You need to communicate properly and not assume the other person is a mind-reader.

In the beginning of a relationship, or in any relationship where there isn't a deep tantric bond, it's true that verbal communication is important because it is all you've got.

But these women aren't wrong. Deep down, they know that we have the ability to intuitively know each other's needs. This is a wisdom that we hold deep inside of us. We just need the kind of connection that makes this possible.

Within that connection, we can actually "feel" this other person. This doesn't only happen with a long-term committed partner. When we get good at dropping our guards and being open with people, we can do this with anyone (who is also able to drop their guards and join with you).

In loving relationships, how much we can intuitively know about the other is dependent on how few guards we have up to the other. There is something magical that happens when we fully drop our guards. These aren't just the protective guards around our hearts; we can also drop the guards around our thoughts. And when they come down, we simply understand things about the other person without them having to say so.

If you have close bonds with your children, it's easy to know when something is off. You might not know the exact details, but you'll know it's something at school, or with friends, or their new partner, or their job. You just know.

This also happens between teacher and student. In guru traditions, this non-verbal communication is considered a "transmission." In a teacher/student relationship, the teacher is in the masculine role and the student is in the feminine role. For students to learn anything, they must be able to drop their guards and listen and receive.

When a teacher holds great wisdom and you feel like you can trust them, it is easy to drop your guards and receive. When this happens, you will receive much more than what they are verbally saying. Your whole being will become wiser.

Similarly, in an intimate relationship, when we have a close bond and are fully open to each other, all we need is to look into each other's eyes and we instantly know what is going on. This is why when couples begin to study tantra together, they often struggle with eye-gazing. If there is distance in the relationship and unresolved issues from the past, their guards will be way up. The moment they have to connect through the eyes, there will be serious discomfort. One might start to laugh or make a joke to break the connection. One might start crying. They might keep all of their guards up or not do the exercise at all.

PERSONAL EXPLORATION: AWARENESS OF OUR WALLS

Fragility and vulnerability

Are you comfortable being vulnerable? What does vulnerability mean to you?

How differently would you live if you were conscious of the fragility of life? How would you act differently in your relationships if you knew they wouldn't last forever?

Expressing emotions

Are you comfortable expressing emotions? To yourself? To others?

Do you allow them to flow so they can come to completion? Or does your mind get involved and extend them beyond their natural time, creating long-term drama around a simple feeling?

Do you trust when something feels "good" or "bad" to you? Do you believe this is your truth?

Do you have walls up?

What are your walls? Are there parts of you that you would never want anyone else to see? Are there topics in your life that you don't want to talk about? What are they? Can you even admit them to yourself?

Did you build these walls in childhood? In previous relationships? Are they still needed now? Or could you let them go?

Connecting with your big picture

How can you strengthen your connection to source within? How different would your fragility feel when you connect with the bigger picture of your life? How easy would it be to express your emotions? How would it feel to not have to keep walls up all of the time?

SECTION II:

LIVING IN YOUR MYSTERIOUS CENTRE

This magnificent refuge is inside you. Enter!
Shatter the darkness that shrouds the doorway.
Be bold. Be humble.
Put away the incense and forget the incantations they taught you.
Ask no permission from the authorities.
Close your eyes and follow your breath
To the still place that leads
To the invisible path
That leads you home.

TERESA OF AVILA

COMBINING MYSTERY WITH OUR KNOWN WORLD

This section "sets the stage" for our personal tantric journey.

The world we live in is actually a mystery to us. When we pretend it isn't, we end up missing most of what is happening around us. Our worldview is so incomplete, we will misinterpret most of our experiences – especially the tough ones.

Our brains were designed to help us navigate, understand, and experience the physical world around us. But really, all of the greatest parts of this world are true mysteries.

This is a great challenge to our minds that desperately want to explain things and simplify the world so we feel safe. However, our tantric journey is about experiencing the world for what it truly is – physically and spiritually. It is about experiencing this incredible world with a divine perspective.

We will redefine what we understand spiritual reality to be. And we will learn how to connect to this mysterious world through breathing and connecting to our meditative and timeless centre.

CHAPTER 7

ONENESS AND DUALITY

When my dad was in his 20s, he drove tour buses through the Rocky Mountains in western Canada. One day, he was driving his bus back to the garage with a few tourists on-board. He was heading down a steep part of the mountain when he realized his brakes weren't working. These roads were right on the edge of the mountain. There was nowhere to go if something went wrong.

He also knew there was a bridge just around the next corner that was only wide enough for one vehicle. All the way down, he simply prayed there was no one else on that bridge.

But of course, there *was* a bus on the bridge. It was halfway across and coming right for him. He had people on the bus and absolutely no way to stop.

His mind went completely blank as he veered onto the bridge, heading toward the other bus.

Suddenly, he found himself safely on the other side, and the other bus was also safely on its side.

The buses weren't damaged. There wasn't a scratch. And that bridge barely fit *one* bus! This wasn't possible. It just wasn't possible.

He drove back to the garage in total disbelief. When he got there, the mechanics came running out to him. *"What happened on that bridge? The other driver just returned and he was white as a ghost. He couldn't even talk about it!!"*

To this day, my big, strong, logical dad cannot tell this story without crying. The sheer reality of what happened completely blows his circuits.

INTEGRATING THE UNBELIEVABLE

The Universe is not only queerer than we suppose,
but queerer than we can suppose.
J.B. HALDANE

What if there were things in life that we couldn't begin to fathom? What if we *can't* understand everything around us? What if the only way to find peace in this world is to integrate the impossible and inconceivable into our day-to-day lives? What would that feel like?

My dad's story is REAL. It isn't a fictional movie or a delusion. It is real. Accepting these experiences into our consciousness is the beginning of integrating the spiritual reality into our physical (and understandable) reality.

We all have moments in our lives that are beyond our understanding. We tend to call them coincidences, flukes, or miracles, and then we go back to our lives as if they didn't happen. But what if we *always* remembered? What would happen if we kept that feeling of awe and "impossibility" in our consciousness all of the time?

How would that change how we walked through each day, holding the reality that truly *anything* is possible in each moment? Knowing that we really have no idea how this world works?

When we realize each moment is pregnant with infinite possibilities, our lives become a whole lot brighter and fascinating (and maybe scary). Even the possibility of something undesirable happening wakes us up to the wonder of what *is* happening right now. We stay in a space of being completely alive.

This space of being completely alive is the essence of being tantric.

INTEGRATING SPIRIT AND MATTER

One of the greatest challenges in all spiritual journeys like tantra is that we don't understand what spirit actually is. We hear about it. We try to understand it with our brains, but our brains are part of the physical world that can only understand the physical world. So, we believe being spiritual means the act of going to church or burning incense or meditating for hours, doing yoga, or complex rituals.

All of these things are physical actions. They are all still well within the dualistic domain. They are our brain's best try. The danger is that we might believe we are being spiritual by doing these things. They can become a real distraction from the truth.

It is like taking an idea like God and humanizing it by saying that God is jealous or angry. Obviously none of this is true. We can't even fathom what God is. This is why every great religion sternly warns us not to define "God" or even name it because we will always be limiting it.

> Christianity: "My name is "I am who I am"."
> Buddhism: "If you meet the Buddha on the road, kill him."
> Taoism: "The tao that can be told, is not the eternal tao."

We will never get it right. By trying to name and simplify "spirit," we will always miss the point. We will miss the magic, the opportunity, the sheer boundlessness of what is actually possible.

For example, the physical world we live in is 3-dimensional - length, width and height. We too are all three-dimensional. Now imagine that aliens come to our planet, but they are only flat. They have never experienced height before. Everything in their world is some kind of flat surface. Could they begin to conceptualize what our world is really like? If they tried, would they get even close?

No. They wouldn't even have the language for it.

The same thing happens when our brains try to understand spiritual reality. We must embrace something our minds cannot understand, conceptualize, or describe. This is possible, but our rational, fearful mind doesn't like it.

This is the greatest challenge of tantra and any spiritual journey. Our brains always want to humanize spirit/god/consciousness. We so desperately want to explain it to make ourselves feel intelligent and safe. Cultivating the ability to allow our brains not to understand and to trust what we sense, feel, or "know" deep inside of us is a huge part of our tantric journey.

Oneness & Dualism

Combining our spiritual and physical aspects is a lot like mixing oil and water, so it is helpful to look at this philosophically. It's easy to say the words and it seems like it should be an easy thing to do, but we are actually mixing two very different ways of experiencing the world. This is why it's so magical when we accomplish it.

We begin with the concept of Oneness and Dualism.

Spiritual Oneness

In spirit, there is only "oneness." We are all a part this singularity. There is no right and wrong, up and down, or left and right. There is no time and no space. Everything "just is."

In religious traditions, this is God in all of its names. It is omnipotent (all powerful), omniscient (all-knowing), omnipresent (everywhere all of the time). This is true because spirit/God/consciousness/source is all things all of the time.

In nontheist traditions like Buddhism, this is nothingness, void, Zen, etc. This too is a singularity, full of potential and life.

We can feel this oneness within us when we close our eyes and point to a spot in the centre of our chest. This is the spot we point to when someone asks "Who are you?"

Within this point, we can feel there is a stillness. This point never changes. It is the same today as it was when we were 6 months old and it will be the same when we are very old. We might call it our soul, our connection to Source, our heart centre. Within all of the events of our lives, this point is always constant, quiet, and still.

It is oneness.

Physical Duality

However, we physically live in duality. We exist in a "space-time continuum." Although we are infinite spirit that is "everywhere at once," in our physical reality, we are definitely in one place (space) in each moment (time).

These two aspects – space and time – allow our spirit (oneness) to experience itself in all the combinations that space and time can offer – infinitely interesting ways.

If this is confusing, then it means part of you is grasping this. Our brains are part of this dualistic reality. They can't really get it. Just stay with me.

SPIRITUAL ENERGY IS ALSO PHYSICAL MATTER

So, how does this work? How can energy/spirit exist in physical form? What does this really mean?

It's all about magnetism. If we look at our cells under an electron microscope, we will see we are actually 99% "nothingness." Each atom is a collection of energy particles in orbit around "black matter." These atoms aren't even touching each other. They are being held in formation through magnetism.

In essence, we are made up of energy that is held together by magnetism creating physical form.

This is our physical, dualistic world. Magnetism, by definition, creates a two-sided charge: positive and negative, attraction and repulsion, masculine and feminine, yin and yang. This describes all motion and creation in the world – our relationships, our passions, our loves, and our sexuality.

This is the "duality" of our lives. We now have up and down, dark and light, happy and sad, hot and cold, attractive and repulsive, rich and poor, etc.

This is the world we live in.

The path of tantra is to fully integrate this divine/spirit/energy into our everyday lives.

OUR SPIRITUAL JOURNEY

What is this spiritual journey, then? It is embracing what you cannot understand. It is embracing the unfathomable. It is recognizing you don't know what is actually going on. It is releasing control and your need to feel safe.

It is no longer pretending that your brain can figure it out.

It is the end of asking "why."

It is listening deep inside and knowing you are connected to something infinite, timeless, and beyond our understanding.

As this connection strengthens, we no longer create philosophies and beliefs because we realize they are just a best guess. Instead, we still stop and listen in every moment to see what is being asked for, and what is possible.

This is foundational for our tantric experience because in the past, we have been caught in believing the physical, dualistic world is all there is. We believe the person in front of us is simple to define. We think we understand who they are. We think we know "how they tick." This leads us to assumptions and expectations of each other, which completely limit what is possible in our relationships.

We assume we know what makes *us* tick. We think we know why we are here or why we were designed the way we are, or why we were born to the parents we had or why we have had our experiences. Our brains so desperately want to feel in control, we will make up any story to make us feel safe in a constantly changing world.

Sexually, we treat each other like we are simply human bodies that desire sexual release. We are so much more than that. We definitely have our primal, animalistic sides, which may desire the deeply wired pleasure of procreative release. But we are also amazing, mysterious, infinite creatures. When we assume we are less, we will always be dissatisfied. We will always seek "more."

This requires a new kind of trust. It requires us to not just "say" we are spiritual. We must actually trust. We must trust there is more in this world than we could ever imagine.

This is what expands us. This is what makes us as big and limitless as we truly are. What would it take for you to embrace everything you will never understand about your life, how you are designed, your relationships, everyone in your lives and all of the world around you?

This takes incredible personal strength. It requires a personal centre that is unwavering – like the eye of a hurricane. *This* is your tantric journey: to strengthen this connection so you can easily trust something that you don't understand at all, while remaining involved in your life in "the village."

Imagine the titans we would have to become. Now we are getting close to our true potential.

A PRACTICAL LOOK

Pour the ocean into a pitcher.
Can it hold more than one day's store?
RUMI

Tantra is both a spiritual and a physical journey. What sets it apart from many traditions is that our goal is the full integration of our spiritual *and* physical lives. Neither is of higher value. In fact, it is when we bring them together that magic happens.

We often feel like we are missing something in our lives because we have been taught that either the spiritual or the physical worlds are not real.

For many people, the physical world is all that matters. We focus on work, paying the bills, taking care of the children, relationships, politics, and everything that needs to be done in a day. Life is a struggle. We don't know how to change it, nor do we have the energy to try. The days pass and suddenly, we wake up and we are old.

In this scenario, it is easy to get bored with life and despair about our current situation. We can lose hope that better solutions will come. We seek escape from our responsibilities and difficulties through addictions, vacations, or anything that helps us forget about our day-to-day lives.

The worst problem is we feel like automatons walking through our days. We should be happy and fulfilled, but we feel like something is missing. That life could be easier. That life could be exciting and new. We don't want to leave the life we have, but we don't know how to change it either.

Then there are many religious and spiritual communities who say that only our spiritual lives matter and all physical pursuits are a distraction from the truth. The body is filled with impure desires. Money is evil. We need to transcend the physical world to truly become enlightened.

The first challenge with this is that our bodies are absolute miracles. How they work and the subtle magic that happens within them in each moment is truly beyond our comprehension. These bodies are not to be ignored or believed to be our "grossest" aspect. They are incredible creations that we were given. Why would we think we weren't meant to fully live in them?

The greater challenge is that it is *within the world* that we have the best opportunities for true, spiritual growth. It is through our struggles in life we dig deep and really find out who we are. This is where all our philosophies are tested and wisdom is found. We can believe all kinds of things when we are in isolation, but once we are actually living in the world, we get to apply all of our best ideas and philosophy. This is where we find out the truth. This is where we manifest our inspiration. This is where we truly grow and thrive.

Both of these extremes cause us to be only a small portion of who we are. We are designed for these two aspects to work together. They are meant to build upon each other exponentially. We are meant to grow and expand in ways we can't even imagine.

PERSONAL EXPLORATION:
INTEGRATING THE IMPOSSIBLE

I invite you to write down stories in your life you can't explain. It could be an experience of a miracle. It could be a coincidence that really couldn't have been "just a coincidence." It could be a feeling you had or one of those moments when you knew something was wrong and then the phone rang...

If you don't have any examples in your own life, then ask those around you. What "miracles" have they seen? What events in their lives have they considered "flukes" or "accidents"?

Google other people's miracles. People have had experiences just like my dad for centuries. Read their stories.

Then sit with your collection of stories. Allow these stories to sink in.

Understand that your brain *cannot* understand them. It is impossible. It is like those flat aliens trying to understand 3-dimensions. It isn't possible.

But we *can* accept them as truth.

How does this change how you walk through your days? Does it open you to the idea that anything truly could happen? Does it make the small things even smaller?

It's important to understand we are made to be able to hold these two realities within us without going crazy. We can allow our minds to rationalize and feel comfortable with what it can describe and understand in the physical world. And we can also accept that there is mystery and infinity everywhere as well – and we are a part of that, too.

Tantra means "tools of expansion." This is definitely an experience of expansion.

LEARNING HOW TO BREATHE

The way of experience begins with a breath,
such as the breath you are breathing now.
Awakening into luminous reality
May dawn in the momentary throb
Between any two breaths.

Exhaling, breath is released and flows out.
There is a pulse as it turns to flow in.
In that turn, you are empty.
Enter that emptiness as the source of all life.

Inhaling, breath flows in, filling, nourishing.
Just as it turns to flow out,
There is a flash of pure joy –
Life is renewed.

RADIANCE SUTRAS

Learning how to breath properly is central to our tantric journey because it brings us to our centre, to the present moment, and gives us the wonderful chance to take a step back and access the many options in each moment (as opposed to simply reacting).

Most of us don't breathe properly at all. We often contract our stomach as we inhale and release it as we exhale. This is opposite to how we naturally should breathe because as our stomach presses in, our diaphragm is pushed upwards against our lungs, limiting how much air we can take in.

Have you ever noticed that when you are stressed out, you stop breathing? Or when you are upset, your breathing becomes very shallow? This is a natural response to keep us from feeling whatever we don't want to feel. We sedate ourselves by underbreathing.

This also happens when we are lost in our minds. When we are going through stressful scenarios in our minds, our bodies feel the stress and our breathing goes into a fight or flight mode and breathes shallowly.

This is why breathing is so central to meditation techniques. It takes us out of our minds and into our bodies and into the current moment.

Did you know that many of us hold our breath unintentionally during sex? We are often in such a hurry, or fantasizing, or worried, or so excited that our breathing is actually shallow. And this reduces what we feel! This is certainly not our goal.

When we breathe, we want to expand our lungs fully with each inhale, and press in our stomachs to expel all the used up air with each exhale.

Of course, when we start breathing deeply, we will start feeling more acutely. We will feel our sadness, grief, and anger, and we will also feel our happiness, pleasure and excitement.

This is all good. As we continue our journey, we will be happy to feel everything – to be fully alive in every moment, regardless of what that moment holds.

THE ROLE OF BREATH

The breath offers a number of important aspects of being tantric and connecting with others.

It brings us into the present moment

All infinity only exists in this present moment. Becoming aware of our breath instantly brings us "right here." Limitations only exist when we are caught in the past or the future. Here, in this moment, anything is possible.

The breath stills the mind

While we are breathing deeply, our mind will stop spinning. Breathing deeply relaxes our nerves. Our brain is part of our entire nervous system. As much as this system tells our brain when things are happening to individual parts of our body, it also works as a whole. It is an electrical system that becomes fully activated when any part goes on alert.

If our body is in pain or stress, our mind will be distracted by that pain. If our mind is stressed out and swirling on an issue, our body will be tense and tight. When our body is tense, it is not receptive. It isn't open. It is not sensitive to touch or pleasure.

Our breath calms our mind and body at the same time. This is really important today because many of us spend our days breathing very shallowly. We are in perpetual fight or flight mode. This is like running through the jungle because a sabre-tooth tiger is chasing you. Our nervous system responds by being perpetually on alert and our breathing becomes shallow.

Unfortunately, we get very used to this and believe it is normal. Breathing deeply naturally takes us out of fight or flight mode and our minds and bodies can relax. They can heal, receive and be present.

We feel our feelings

We naturally sedate ourselves through under-breathing. If we are upset, it is common to hold our breath. When we are upset, we can walk through our days barely breathing at all. Of course, we are doing this with good reason; if we breathe deeply, then all of our feelings will rise.

Deep down, we know this. Imagine that we are running around like crazy, upset about something. A friend asks us what's wrong. We say it's nothing. They sit down on the couch with us, look us in the eyes, take a deep breath and ask again. We sit still, look at them, take a deep breath and immediately start crying.

We know how dangerous it is to breathe deeply if we want to maintain a calm exterior when we are truthfully dying inside.

The path of tantra asks us to fully feel our feelings. They are our truth. They matter. Maybe we start to breathe deeply in private, allowing ourselves to cry. To feel. We honour those feelings and we breathe even more deeply.

Breathing connects us to Spirit

Our bodies are our physical incarnation, and our breath is our connection to spirit. The breath literally animates our bodies. We know that the body dies when we stop breathing. There is a final exhale, and the spirit leaves us on the breath.

When we sit and meditate, or pray, or watch a sunset, our breath is the most noticeable thing. It is what is moving. If we pay attention, we see the spirit is moving through us.

It is also the source of inspiration. "Inspiration" and "respiration" come from the same source, "respire," which means to breathe. Where does inspiration come from? It is interesting that it is connected through the breath.

Breath connects us with another

In intimacy, when we desire to connect our spirits, our breath naturally syncs together. If we want to stay separate, then our breath stays separate from the other person. When our desire is union, we naturally breathe together.

We could be sitting down with a friend or child, looking at each other and taking a deep breath. There is something about this that "puts us on the same page." We know this intuitively. When someone we love is anxious or hurting, we will hug them and breathe deeply, unconsciously hoping they will breathe with us, relax, and find some peace.

We become one body with one breath

In sexual intimacy, sometimes we start to breathe as one. As the bodies vibrate together, our breathing naturally syncs. Sometimes, as we become one, our breath will often become opposite to each other, as if there is a common breath/spirit between us. As I breathe out, you breathe in, and as you breathe out, I breathe it in. We are passing the same breath back and forth.

You can practise this intentionally while kissing or lovemaking by inhaling each other's exhales (this is described in greater detail later, in Chapter 15).

Also, in intercourse, as the masculine moves inwards, "he" will exhale, while the feminine will inhale. Then as the masculine pulls back, "he" will inhale and the feminine will exhale. This does not happen in typical sex where the masculine (vajra, dildo, finger) is pulled in and out; this kind of sex keeps you separate. Your breathing won't naturally merge.

But when you are joined and your hips are moving together, forward and back, whoever is moving forward will naturally exhale and whoever is moving backwards will inhale. Your faces don't even have to be together. It will happen naturally. You are one body, one breath.

PERSONAL PRACTICE #1: HOW TO BREATHE FULLY

Make sure your spine is straight. If we hunch our shoulders forward, or tip our lower spine, this contracts our lungs and we won't be able to get our maximum breath.

As you inhale, expand your belly. Allow your navel to move outwards. We aren't actually breathing into our stomach; we are making room for our diaphragm to move downwards allowing our lungs to open.

Do this for a while until it is easy. Then allow your ribs to expand as well. Allow yourself to exhale slowly, feeling the navel gently moving inward towards the spine.

When this feels natural, add in the upper chest and collar bone area. On your inhale, expand your belly, ribs and then upper chest. Allow your body to exhale naturally.

This is good to practise while sitting quietly, as in meditation. Having no distractions is a good thing when we are learning a new skill.

PRACTISE #2: BREATHE, BREATHE, BREATHE

All day long, practise breathing. Notice when you are holding your breath. Notice when your breath has become shallow. Notice when your posture has become slumped; relax your shoulders back and take a deep breath.

As you're walking down the street, if your mind is racing, take a few deep breaths. See how you feel. If you are struggling emotionally with someone in your life, straighten your spine and simply breathe.

Each breath brings in new energy, spirit, hope, and possibilities. This is the number one way to mix energy with matter. This is how we infuse our physical lives with infinite hope and possibilities.

CHAPTER 9

BECOMING MEDITATIVE

August 21, 2011: Goderich F3 Tornado

My daughter and I were relaxing on a lovely Sunday afternoon.

Suddenly, it got very dark, and the rain came down like crazy. Hail the size of golf balls fell from the sky. We went to the window and watched hail bouncing six feet off the ground.

"Wow! What a storm, eh?"

My daughter was about to go upstairs to close the windows, when the sound of the wind became deafening. The trees outside the window were bent over right to the ground. And then a 30-foot spruce tree flew by the window and slammed into our car.

"Oh my god! Head to the basement!"

Down in the basement, it felt like we were inside a washing machine. All the little windows were filled with leaves, debris, and sticks. We couldn't see anything; all we could hear was the insane sound of cracking, hail, and wild winds.

When the storm subsided, we emerged out onto the street. Our entire neighbourhood was destroyed.

Homes were picked up and dropped. All the trees and electrical poles were down. The streets and properties were covered in debris, trees, destroyed vehicles, you name it. Everyone was wandering around in shock.

The days that followed were a mix of shock, trauma, community-building, tears, laughter, and chaos. The whole story really deserves its own book.

But for me, there was a strange sense of calm inside the chaos.

Sometimes, we are focused on making sure our lawns are cut and our picket fences are painted white, while the relationships and quality of life *inside* the house are in ruin. In our little town filled with white picket fences, all of our "garbage" and issues were strewn across the front lawns and streets. Everything became very real, very quickly.

Because everything was on the surface, it was easier to find your centre. It was easier to remain calm. It was easier to figure out what was real and what was drama. It was easy to know what mattered, and what didn't.

My most vivid memory was wandering around the town immediately after the storm. As I walked past the flower beds up to the town square (which was completely destroyed), I could hear only sirens and crying and yelling all around me. I was stepping over electrical wires, fallen trees, and debris. What I remember most was how the sun came out and I could smell marigolds in the air.

I was so calm inside. Some might say it was shock. But really, I was shocked into reality. I was shocked out of the strange mental jungle we so often live in. I was thrown right to my centre.

To this day, when I close my eyes and take a deep breath, I can return to that moment, with the sun on my face, marigolds in the air, chaos all around me, and I am completely calm, present, and right here.

BECOMING MEDITATIVE

The eternal self dwells in eternity,
and eternity intersects linear time at only one point:
the present.
MARIANNE WILLIAMSON

To be tantric is to be fully aware. It is to be fully present. It is to be connected to the timeless aspect of who we are. This is also what it means to be meditative.

Connecting with our meditative centre is actually the goal of meditation practice. We don't meditate to become good at meditating. Meditation relaxes our minds and brings us to a focus so we can have a meditative centre throughout our day.

This is foundational for tantra because we often live on auto-pilot. We aren't present. Instead of being fully aware and alive, we go through our days as we always have, doing what we've always done, reacting in all the ways we've reacted before. We aren't living each moment; we are only repeating the past.

Tantra asks us to come into the present. It is the only place we can truly feel alive.

Each time we sit to meditate, it's about using the time and the technique to heal and transform our mind. It's about practising focus and stillness. It's about connecting our breath with relaxation.

Our meditative mind connects us to our stillness. It connects us to our hearts. It allows us to find love and kindness, even in difficult situations.

Not only does this reprogram our brains to be calmer, more focused, and kinder, it also sets up healthy trigger responses to stress. We learn to breathe deeply in times of struggle. We learn to step back, straighten our spine, reclaim our focus and return to centre.

We start to use this all day long. When faced with a difficult situation in life, our mind becomes programmed to take a deep breath. Our mind settles. We become focused, and we are much clearer as to what we can do to solve the problem.

We use this in relationships – especially where there are high emotions at stake. People are upset. Everyone is angry, including you. Instead of reacting in a way that actually isn't what your heart wants, you take a deep breath. You look at how you are feeling. You honour those feelings. You look at the other person. You are able to honour their feelings. You take another breath and you remember that you want to build a bridge between you. You don't need to be right. You desire connection.

Then you say something new. You say something clearly and loving.

And you both head down a completely different path.

EXPERIENCING WHAT IS

Feelings come and go like clouds in a windy sky.
Conscious breathing is my anchor.
THICH NHAT HANH

We meditate to teach ourselves to come back to the present moment because it is here that we experience reality. In the present moment, we are able to "be" with what's real. Our minds don't come in and make judgements or observations that twist what we see. We are able to drop everything we imagine and we experience exactly what *is*.

Life can be very confusing. We are bombarded with information, experiences, disappointments, joys, excitement, and challenges from all sides. We experience the struggles of the world, the fight between the head and heart, the "good" and the "bad."

Then we meditate. The confusion disappears. We are able to experience what is. Our stresses are gone. We are left in the moment... breathing air.

In this moment, when we have found that peaceful place inside, we can experience our beginner's mind. We are able to ask ourselves, "What is this all about? What's really going on? Why is this on my path?"

This is where true self-discovery is possible.

DEVELOPING OUR NEUTRAL, TIMELESS MIND

There are three minds in yoga: positive, negative and neutral. These three minds govern how we live in this dualistic world (positive and negative) and the oneness everywhere (neutral).

Positive & Negative Minds

Our positive mind holds all of our ideas to go and do things. It makes us want to create, meet people, go to the gym, paint a picture, and have new experiences. It gets the new job, creates the spreadsheet, decides to have children, takes us on a run, makes money, and everything else that creates and takes us forward in life.

Our negative mind is the part that asks if what we're doing is a good idea. Have we considered all the options? Is it safe? Is it what we want? When this mind is healthy, it is a valuable checkpoint that ensures we are on our path – that it is in our highest good.

These positive and negative minds tend to be the bulk of the "discussion" that goes on in our heads. They have all of the arguments for and against all decisions. They also have all the shoulds, wants, fears, and worries.

The challenge is that those positive and negative minds tend to be all we've got, and they are often out of balance with each other.

For many, the positive mind is very encouraged. They must get out there and be productive. We are taught to always improve, have more, be more, build, and grow. Our positive mind tends to be heavily developed. However, without the balance of the negative mind, we may spend too much, do too much, take too many risks, and overextend ourselves in all aspects of our lives.

For many others, their negative mind is heavily developed. We are filled with the fears of our parents and society. We fear judgement, failure, success, and the opinions of others. When our negative mind is much stronger than our positive mind, it can stop us from doing what we really want or trying anything new.

This often comes up in relationships and intimacy. We may have many heavy checks in our negative mind, which is trying to keep us safe. We've been hurt before and we don't want to be in a position where we are vulnerable. We will completely wall off intimacy and choose not to get close.

Neutral Timeless Mind

We also have our neutral mind. This is the mind that observes what we are doing without judgement. It watches from the sidelines, observing.

It connects with the oneness, that timeless part of us, the part of us that is completely still. Because this part of us is timeless, it doesn't have an opinion about what our positive and negative minds are arguing over.

This neutrality can seem like a curious thing in a world where everyone has an opinion about everything. We value having an opinion. This is a big part of how we interact with the world. "Slipping into neutral" is often a new skill to learn – to just observe what is happening without judgement.

This timeless mind allows us to observe our situation objectively. It is peaceful. There is no emotional charge. We can have a meditative presence. In this space, our mind is still so we can hear new information. This is when we hear inspiration. This is where new creative thought comes in.

It is also where we are able to heal because we are calm, and centred. Our nervous system is relaxed. We can turn off our brain. We can turn off the fears, turn off the courage, turn off everything and simply be.

Connecting Timeless Minds

As a sneak peak for later, the timeless aspect of ourselves is how we deeply connect with another person. When we gaze into their eyes, we see the timeless part of them as well. As you look at the other person, everything except that timeless part of them disappears. You are completely present with them.

This is where magic can happen. This is how we can merge together because these timeless parts of us are the same. This is the merging that creates oneness and complete bliss.

RELEASING THE DESIRES OF OUR POSITIVE MIND

Osho once described our desiring minds as "calm waters lashed by wind turning into waves and rollers."

But what is wrong with having desires? This is a tough one. We believe our desires propel us forward, that our desires are our passions, and that we must pursue them. This is only partly true.

The challenge is there is something "wanting" in the term desire. It implies a lack right now which needs to be filled, that we desire something other than what *is* right now.

For example, as I write this book, I can imagine the joy of it being finished, holding it in my hands and sharing it with you. But until that day comes, there are a couple of different ways I can experience my writing.

When my "desire" to finish is forefront in my mind, I tend to be completely distracted. I am worried I'm not writing fast enough. I'm not going to meet my deadline. The publishing date is going to get pushed off. This desire puts me into a future state.

Or, I can sit and enjoy the process of writing. I am aware it will be awesome to have it complete. But right now, I am fully enjoying sitting in this café and watching the words magically appear on the page. This is total bliss. My mind is calm and I am enjoying the moment.

The goal of writing a book hasn't changed, but my process and experience is completely different. My lake is calm. My mind is at peace.

All magic happens in *this* moment. Our minds must be fully present for the divine to be present. When we are in a desiring state, we are placing our happiness in a future time when our desire has been realized.

It might seem like a subtle play on words, but the difference is vitally important.

RELEASING THE FEARS OF OUR NEGATIVE MIND

Our negative mind is meant to act as a healthy checkpoint to make sure that what our positive mind wants to do is a good idea. The negative mind is intelligent. It is useful. It keeps us on path and safe from wrong choices.

However, when our mind is filled with fears, it becomes dysfunctional. These fears stop us from making the right choices. They stop us from speaking up and standing our ground. They stop us from moving forward on our path. It is imperative that we look at them if we want to find balance and real fulfillment in life.

Everyone has fears. In fact, we tend to have fears layered upon fears which is why many people struggle with anxiety today. Sometimes we are raised in environments that taught us to be always waiting for something bad to happen and now we just don't know any different.

We must become aware of our fears. On the one hand, our fears will drive us to make decisions unconsciously as we try to avoid everything we are afraid of. These fears will put us in a holding pattern, we will fear change, and we will abandon our true path in life.

On the other hand, our fears can be useful tools to wake us up to the miracle of the present moment.

The clues to this part of our journey lie in our everyday lives. Where do we struggle in life? Relationships? With whom? Parents? Children? Partners? Colleagues? Neighbours? Friends? What's going on here?

What if you are unhappy in your relationship? Are you afraid to speak up? Are you afraid of them leaving? Are you afraid of being alone?

Then go deeper. Why are you afraid to be alone? Does it mean no one loves you, or that you are not lovable? I know that when I was alone for the first time, I realized that I was definitely afraid that if there was no one sharing my bed, I was somehow worthless. I really had to look at the roots of that belief and let it go.

Are you afraid of criticism? Will you do anything to make sure everyone likes you? What would you do if your boss criticized you? Maybe your first feeling is embarrassment. What is underneath that? Perhaps a fear of others thinking that you are less than great. What's under that? Fear of rejection? Under that? Fear that you are not good enough. Under that? The truth that you don't love yourself – and the fear that others will find out?

What if we are afraid of death, even if only on a deep, subtle level? We could spend each moment we were alive worrying and thinking about not being alive. So, essentially, we die right now.

This is a very strange program.

It's actually a funny fear since it is such a gift to be alive at all.

Every day, we wake up in this magical world. We are walking miracles having new experiences and adventures every day. It's like being on a roller-coaster. While we're flying around the ride, we are fully enjoying each thrill and dip and drop. Of course, the ride must end eventually, but it's a lot of fun in the meantime.

This is why tantriks always want to wake us up to the present moment! To break us out of our patterns, to wake us from the spells we are under.

If we wake up and truly embrace each single moment we are alive, what will happen? Each moment will become rich. That moment might be looking at a sunset, reading a book to a child, giving a presentation at work, or receiving the Nobel Peace Prize.

All of these experiences are only as rich as we are present – in perfect proportion. All things are equal. It is the quality of our presence that makes them totally wonderful or completely empty.

STRENGTHENING OUR NEUTRAL MIND

This is where strengthening our timeless, neutral mind is so important. The more time we spend in this still, quiet place, the less of a hold our negative mind will have on us.

The wonderful thing about meditation is that it naturally loosens the grip of the negative mind through healing our nervous system. Our brains are part of the same nervous system as all of the nerves in our body. When we breathe deeply, our body relaxes, and so does our brain.

As our bodies learn new ways to relax, our worries, fears and stresses start to become less common. They aren't as strong. It is easier to take a deep breath, slip into our neutral mind and see what is *really* happening in each situation. In this silent place, we hear new solutions.

As we continue on our tantric journey, we strengthen our connection to the divine within. The inner courage to trust our deepest wisdom and intuition soon takes over, and the fears that once held us have no hold at all.

PERSONAL PRACTICE: NOTICING THE BREATH

At the end of the exhale,
Breath surrenders to quietude.
For a moment you hang in the balance –
Suspended
In the fertile spaciousness
That is the source of breath.

At the end of the inhale,
Filled with the song of the breath,
There is a moment when you are simply
Holding the tender mystery.

In these interludes,
Experience opens into exquisite vastness
With no beginning and no end.
Embrace this infinity without reservation.
You are its vessel.

RADIANCE SUTRAS

This is a foundational tantric practice we can use sitting in meditation and in all moments of our day. The practice helps us to experience our duality and our oneness and how they can effortlessly flow together.

Step One: Notice your natural breath

Simply breathe naturally. Be aware of your breath as you inhale and as you exhale. Do not change your breath in any way.

This is a discipline itself – to simply allow ourselves to be whatever we are in any moment. In a world where we are supposed to be improving all of the time and changing how we are, it is quite a gift to learn how to simply notice "what is" and be happy with it.

Step Two: Experience the gap between two breaths

As you continue to breathe naturally, notice there are "gaps" in your breathing at the end of your inhale and at the end of your exhale. This is where "nothing" is happening. They are still points between the movements of your breath.

Imagine that as we inhale and exhale, we are fully engaging in this physical world. We take in air, oxygen and prana with each inhale, and we release back into the world on each exhale. In the gap between the breaths, we are neither inhaling nor exhaling. This is a stillpoint. This is our connection to oneness.

Feel the breath moving in and out of your lungs. Feel it as it goes through your nostrils. Feel each inhale as a birth, a new moment. Then there is the gap, the stillpoint – our connection to spirit.

Our exhale is like a death. It is the end of that moment. Then we have the gap in oneness.

It is difficult to describe the full effects of what happens when we do this technique. It is blending the indescribable with the physical world. It is best to practise it and allow it to do its magic.

This *will* naturally help us become present, which is so important in relationships, in lovemaking, and in all of life. It also allows us to observe what *is* and *is not* what we desire. We practise how to flow with the breath instead of forcing it. We can have such a tendency to force, to impose ideas upon the simplest exercise, and in life.

Mastering this technique allows us to experience glimpses of pure stillness. It allows us to practise the bliss of allowing the mind to still. To feel the space between the thoughts. To allow ourselves the freedom of *being*.

Section III:

The Magic of Masculine & Feminine Union

The masculine and feminine
do not exist in isolation.
They play together
Building upon each other.
Most powerful when they polarize
Uniting in the bliss of oneness
And new creation.

KATRINA BOS

Due to power struggles over the eons where the "masculine" overpowered the "feminine," we have become either afraid to be the "masculine bully" or the "doormat feminine," or we have decided that masculine and feminine are the same, creating a confusing androgynous culture.

Both of these options leave us emasculated and de-feminized, with little idea how to interact with each other.

We need to completely redefine what masculine and feminine means.

Understanding our true masculine and feminine nature is important to our tantric journey for three reasons:

1. We find spiritual bliss when we fully unite masculine and feminine.
2. We find happiness, peace, and fulfillment when our personal masculine and feminine are balanced.
3. We have a dynamic, passionate life when we understand how these two forces play and move each other.

Masculine and feminine refer to energies present within all of us, regardless of gender. Sometimes we may take on a masculine role in an interaction and sometimes the feminine role. However, what is interesting is the polarity in which you are the most comfortable.

In same sex couples, this is often clear. One is naturally more masculine and the other is more feminine. However, in heterosexual couples, there are times when the man takes a very feminine role and the woman takes a masculine role. Sometimes the male partner has been emasculated growing up and learns it is simply easier to fly under the radar, follow, and keep the peace. He is then attracted to a woman who has learned that the only way to protect themselves or get anywhere in life is to take charge and never give up control.

In many cases there isn't anything wrong with this, but it is important for each partner to look within and be sure they are OK with this switch in gender roles. Although this may work on the surface, it's important to be aware if this is truly what each person wants on a soul level.

CHAPTER 10

MASCULINE & FEMININE UNITY

We were fully clothed. We were kind of dancing, but there wasn't any music. We were embracing in a door opening. I had read a lot about surrender between the masculine and feminine, so I asked if we could play a game where I would surrender to him completely. I would simply follow his lead – whatever he wanted.

We continued to embrace and he started gently swaying. I could feel my body trying to anticipate what he was going to do. I could feel my mind analyzing what was happening, so I repeated to myself, "surrender, surrender." And my body released to him.

When I released to him, something shifted within him. His body strengthened; he knew he had to support me. Something came alive in him. As I felt this strength, my body surrendered even more, and I wondered how much I could let go. Each time I released, he got stronger and stronger.

He gently moved my hands while our bodies swayed. Once in a while, he kissed me. We became one unit moving seamlessly together.

It was absolutely euphoric. There was no time or space. I lost track of whose body was whose.

I don't know how long it lasted, but by the end, I felt completely drunk (and no, there were no substances used). It was like I was floating on air, and I'm sure my eyes were rolling back in my head. My whole body was vibrating. Eventually, I sat down on the floor and allowed the world to spin in the most wonderful way. And all we did was dance... kind of.

MASCULINE & FEMININE INTERPLAY

Our lives are made up of the interplay of masculine and feminine energies. Each of us has both masculine and feminine within us that need to be balanced for us to have personal peace and happiness, regardless of our gender. The yin-yang symbol is a representation of this principle, and represents all balance and creation in life. The white part is called yang (masculine), and the dark part is called yin (feminine).

We can find bliss and stillness within ourselves when we are alone, and we can also find it with another by combining the masculine and feminine to create a new whole creation.

The masculine and feminine are always two parts of a whole. When we are truly creating, they always compliment and balance each other.

MASCULINE/YANG	FEMININE/YIN
Giving	Receiving
Talking	Listening
Teaching	Learning
Movement	Rest
Leading	Following
Manifestation	Inspiration
Structure	Flow
Logic	Intuition
Assertiveness	Passivity
Order	Chaos
Protector	Vulnerable
Known	Mystery
Seen	Unseen
Energy	Matter
Expansion	Contraction
Rising	Descending
Creator	Created
Light	Darkness

In all interactions, both masculine and feminine energies are necessary or there is no unity and no creation.

MASCULINE & FEMININE CREATION

It's important to understand there is no masculine or feminine in isolation.

Individually, we are completely whole. We are balanced between masculine and feminine. We listen *and* we talk. We create *and* we meditate. We give *and* we receive. We are complete.

It isn't until we interact with someone else that we can be masculine or feminine. The table above describes how we interact with another.

We tend to think of certain people *being* masculine and others *being* feminine, but the reality is we are not masculine or feminine *until we interact with someone*. It is how we *act* within that connection that is either masculine or feminine. This polarization creates the magnetic bond. The masculine and feminine energies act upon and with each other.

Let's say you are sitting with a friend. You are both individual and complete people. You are both equally yin and yang – feminine and masculine – perfectly balanced. You are simply two individual whole people sitting side by side.

Let's say you turn to your friend and ask them a question. You have now done something "masculine." You have chosen to interact with your friend in the hopes of creating something – a conversation. You are coming out of your individual wholeness to unite with another to create a new whole.

Your friend chooses to engage in this new union. She listens (feminine) and then responds (masculine). While she responds, you listen (feminine). Now the two of you are fully engaged with each other. If the conversation is to be a fully balanced and harmonious union, then one person will always be masculine and the other feminine. This dynamic creates a beautiful new experience.

So what if both people start talking (masculine) at the same time? There is no more union. You have now become separate again. There is no giving and receiving. Both are dumping their thoughts into the air between you.

What if both of you become feminine and stop talking? Then the conversation will end. There is no motion. You have retreated back into your individual wholeness.

Leading & Following

There are many examples of wonderful leading and following. However, historically, the desire for power has shown us people who simply desire control, which is not leading. This dynamic has caused us to fear "leaders" and being a leader. Because of this, we often struggle to follow as well.

Some people are born leaders. These people have vision. They have integrity, and people *want* to follow them. There is no need for control or power over anyone. Everyone acts within their own truth.

Bosses are great leaders when they genuinely know and care about their team. They know the strengths and weakness of their employees and they organize what needs to be done so everyone gets the assignment for which they are best suited. They enjoy the pressure and challenge of responsibility. It makes them better and helps them grow. People love being a part of their team.

People who couple dance know the blissful magic of joining with another person and moving seamlessly together with the music. There is no power struggle. There is a *joy* in following a good leader. The leader chooses moves their partner loves to do. They are constantly reading their follower to see what would flow nicely. There is great joy in leading someone who is completely relaxing into the dance with you. The feeling of trust from the follower increases the confidence of the leader, which increases the trust of the follower, which deepens the connection. The dance gets more and more dynamic and blissful.

It is through this dynamic of the masculine (leader) and feminine (follower) joining that we find happiness and bliss. Being on a dynamic team with a great leader is truly exciting for all the team members and the leader. Dancing in a couple where you have joined into a unit causes time to stand still, and your feet barely touch the floor.

But if the goal of the participants isn't union, then nothing joyful is created. If the person in charge isn't a good leader, the team members will not drop into their feminine role of follower. They will question and argue with their boss because they do not feel a healthy lead. They will have nothing to follow. There is constant strife.

Similarly, if the follower can't relax and follow when dancing, the leader won't try to lead them. Or if the leader is doing their own thing and paying no attention to their follower, the follower won't be able to trust and surrender into the dance. These two people will hold each other and co-dance to the music, but there is no blissful union.

Order & Chaos

Even order and chaos work together to create life. Masculine energy is stable, calm, and orderly. The feminine is chaos, wild, and mystery. Logic is masculine, where intuition is feminine.

We like to joke about the chaos of the feminine – women having scary thoughts when they are pre-menstrual or changing their minds constantly "on a whim." However, it's important to look at this because in society we only understand the masculine. We want stability. We want to be assertive. We want clarity. Logic rules. This is masculine energy.

And what about chaos and wildness and intuition? These are not aspects we have historically deemed important. Who wants chaos? Isn't it a bad thing? We often think of chaos as the aftermath of a tornado or war. We think of it as something negative and destructive.

Chaos is simply the lack of order. The reality is that nothing new is ever born out of order alone. We can make all the spreadsheets in the world and all the pros and cons lists, but nothing new will ever be created out of it. It's not until we do something completely outside the box that we have a sudden "Eureka moment". This is where something new is born.

Everything is born out of the feminine, in all of us. Physically of course, women have babies. God knows if you've ever had children, if you can't handle chaos you're going to go crazy. Embracing the feminine energy allows you to let go of the logic, let go of the order, and embrace the chaos. Then everyone is happier.

The feminine, wild, chaos can be really scary. We are so unaccustomed to feeling chaos and having unknowns in our lives. We want stability, even if it's not real or good for us. We will take any answer as long as it makes us feel safe.

This is where we really need to be able to embrace the feminine and say that chaos is OK for a while. It's OK to be wild. It's OK to not know what's coming next.

Sexually we have been raised with rules. Here's what's right. Here's what's wrong. Here's what's acceptable. Here's what isn't. What about wildness? When do you get to do whatever you want? When do you get to access the part of you that isn't civilized? That part that hasn't been told what to do? That part that still knows how to play?

In tantra, it's important to be able to be wild, to let go of the stops and to feel free to allow our soul to play, without any rules.

Of course, we need the masculine as well. I've talked mostly about the feminine because it's so underdeveloped, but only where we have stability in our lives are we free to be wild. It is from the calm and stable times that we then can choose to let loose and feel freedom. In the reverse, when we have had times of real chaos, our soul will seek stability.

It's all about balance. If your life and relationships are filled with stability and commitment, you have a home, you go to work, you are responsible, then spontaneity and a little wildness will "colour in your picture." Similarly, if we find ourselves desiring chaos, flow, and wildness, choosing to create commitment and have responsibilities can bring real meaning into our lives.

It is the flow within the stable structure that allows for incredible creativity and bliss.

Giving & Receiving

There is great joy in giving, and there is great joy in receiving. But the true bliss of union happens when we give to someone who truly desires what we are giving. Similarly, when we need something, there is great joy in receiving it from someone who truly wants to give it.

I love hosting Christmas dinner. I love cooking and creating a space and having family and friends over. There is great joy in this for me, but it's no fun unless I have people to receive my gift. There is a natural joy in the union of me as hosting and my friends and family enjoying themselves as guests. I desire no reciprocation. My joy is truly in the experience.

Yet, in giving and receiving, we have strange dynamics today. We are told we *should* give, which can easily take the joy out of it. On the other side, we are told we should be independent and have no need for other people to do things for us. We end up in a society of people doing things they don't want to do and silently resenting the ones they are doing it for. On the other end, there are so many people who could really use some help but won't ask for it.

The bliss of union only happens when both deeply desire to give and receive what is given. If the person giving is only doing it because they *should*, there will be no union. They will stay separate from the receiver. Similarly, if the receiver doesn't want what they are being given, they will also remain separate. In these cases, giving and receiving might have happened on the surface, but no union, bliss, or joy was created.

The Protector & the Vulnerable

Imagine you are sitting on the bus. You are completely whole and balanced – both masculine and feminine.

Suddenly you see another passenger trying to take an elderly woman's purse. She is visibly upset and she can't defend herself. You are watching her, and your focus on her is creating a connection between the two of you. You are energetically "getting involved."

Because you are focusing on her and she is vulnerable (feminine) and in trouble, this will send you into protective energy (masculine). You go over and tell the offender to back off, to leave her alone. You now have a relationship with her where you are the masculine and she is the feminine. Something new was created in that moment. Once you know she is safe, she is no longer vulnerable, so your masculine energy recedes. You return to your seat. You are again your balanced, separate self.

Now, I want to qualify this because I know the idea that the feminine is vulnerable and weak can trigger many people – women are not weak or helpless. However, we are not talking about women and men. We are talking about the polarities of masculine and feminine.

There is a reason why one of the primal roles of the masculine is to protect the feminine. The feminine has children. If she is in danger, she cannot fight or escape because of them. The masculine must protect her. Together, they make a natural, perfect whole.

This dynamic could be seen in a parent defending their child. It could be a child defending a parent. It could be a woman defending a man.

This is an important dynamic to understand because sometimes we identify masculine as someone who is big and strong and a protector. However, unless they are actually protecting someone, they aren't masculine. They are only themselves, both masculine and feminine.

Similarly, being meek, quiet and subservient has historically defined being feminine. This isn't healthy. Everyone is meant to be whole. Unless we are truly being attacked, overpowered, or we are unable to stay safe because we have children or others in our care, we are not weak, nor do we need protection.

The Hunter & the Hunted

The spark goes out of relationships for many reasons, but a common reason is the masculine partner stops pursuing the feminine. As one man said, "Why keep running to catch a bus you've already caught?" But to create magnetic energy to nourish the bond between us, the masculine must perpetually pursue the feminine.

Some might say that it should go both ways. And yes, when you look at the yin/yang symbol, there is a dot of masculine within the feminine and there is a dot of feminine within the masculine.

The question is what stimulates *your* life force? What makes you dig deep within and access the true power within?

The challenge today is that we have confused equality of the sexes with the sexes being the same. This has resulted in losing our polarity with each other. When there is no polarity, we can be very comfortable, but there will be no life and dynamic union between us.

If you identify as a man or you are the masculine partner in your relationship, then you will naturally be stimulated by expressing masculine energy, like pursuing the feminine. You will enjoy giving to others. You will feel complete when you are protecting and providing. This is pure masculine energy.

If you identify as a woman or are the feminine partner, you will thrill in being pursued. You will happily receive and appreciate the giver with all of your heart. You will enjoy feeling safe so you can pursue the inner chaos and wisdom that flows through the feminine. This is pure feminine energy.

Yes, we must all be completely balanced within ourselves and we must not require having others in our lives to complete us. But if we choose to join with another, the polarization between us creates the excitement and joy in our relationships.

Healing Unhealthy Polarity in Relationship

There are two main ways that relationships become dysfunctional. Either there is no charge at all between you, or there is charge but it is damaging and unhealthy.

No Charge

This happens when we are together because we are "really comfortable with each other," or some reason besides being passionate love. There is nothing wrong with choosing to be with someone because we are super comfortable, but it often feels more like a relationship with a sibling or friend than a passionate lover.

In this case, there has never been any magnetic charge. You both looked at each other and realized you like being around each other. Maybe you also get intimate. Maybe it's lovely. You don't fight. There are no real problems, but there isn't much going on energetically, either.

This may also happen in a couple where both people are gender-neutral. Neither desire that big passion and excitement. They like the calm and knowing what to expect. Awesome.

If you would like to explore tantric union, this is a nice partnership to expand yourselves within because it is so safe and loving. You can explore polarizing together. Even in a gender-neutral relationship, there will be one partner who is more masculine or identifies as a man, and the other will be slightly more feminine or identify as a woman.

Explore what it would feel like to play up these roles. Explore what it feels like to put more energy in these directions. What happens between you? What subtle shifts do you notice? Do you enjoy the new energy flowing inside of you?

We are all able to polarize 100% in both directions. The process of figuring out how to do this causes incredible personal expansion and growth. This is when we truly approach the potential that we are all capable of.

Broken Masculine & Feminine Union

We all recognize the broken masculine and feminine. We've seen the partnerships where one is overbearing and the other is a doormat. We've seen where one "protects" the other to the point of complete control. We've seen where one gives to the point that there is nothing left to give and the other never receives it, and therefore doesn't appreciate it.

Even our broken, dysfunctional versions of the masculine and feminine fit together in union. This union isn't healthy and it doesn't create new life. It doesn't create happiness, and it doesn't energize the partners.

These unhealthy unions slowly destroy both people in the partnership. They only drain each other and make both ever more unhappy.

We come into these unions broken ourselves. If we want someone to love us because this will show us we are worthy, we will fall for someone who says they love us, and it won't matter how they act. Maybe we believe excessive attention means they really, really love us, so we accept controlling or abusive partners.

We will repeat unhealthy relationships from our childhood. If we were controlled as a child, then we may go the other way and become over-controlling of our partner. We become afraid to listen to the other because this might feel like a loss of control. So we do what we want, regardless of those around us, to maintain control.

There are many versions of the unhealthy masculine-feminine balance. Notice that whatever is going on, everyone balances each other. We don't exist separately. If we have a union of any kind, we are both playing a role.

If you find yourself in one of these relationships filled with control-issues, power struggles, resentment, lack of trust, and real distance, you can still study tantric intimacy together. But you will have to step back a bit and do some personal healing first.

You will have to find your personal centre, meditate, and see the programming driving your actions. You may not be aware of what you are doing. We have to bring ourselves to a place where we love ourselves completely (this is a big deal). We need to cultivate our witness mind so we can observe our actions and the dynamics in our relationship with an objective eye. This way, we can have conversations with our partner about what's happening without attacking each other in anger.

This will require you to cultivate 100% kindness right away. You will need it for you and for your relationship. The sooner you can become 100% kind and fully commit to it, the sooner you and your relationships will heal.

Once this is possible in your everyday life, you will be able to move into more deep and intimate work.

PERSONAL PRACTICE: CREATING TRUE MASCULINE & FEMININE DYNAMICS

As you walk through your day, notice the masculine and feminine interactions around you. Are people engaged with each other? Or are they separate, and only *look* like they are engaged?

We can see this easily in conversations.

If we want to "have a conversation" between two people, these people are actively involved in it. One is sharing and the other is actively listening at all times. There is intention with their verbal communication. This active talking and listening creates a dynamic conversation where we can learn, share ideas, come up with new solutions, or simply enjoy each other's company.

However, many of our conversations do not create wholeness or unity at all. Often we are completely separate. There is no actual energy dynamic, no union.

Here are some dynamics to watch for in your conversations:

Union: Sharing ideas on a topic (both masculine and feminine in turn)

If you are both intrigued with the topic, you will eagerly listen to the other person's perspective on it. Listening will be authentic because you genuinely want to learn more about it. As one person speaks (masculine), you will actively listen (feminine) and vice versa. You will not be aware of anyone else around you. You can always tell when two people have great respect for each other's thoughts because they easily listen and don't interrupt when the other is speaking. This can be a beautiful back and forth dynamic resulting in new ideas and solutions.

Union: Learning from Another (one masculine and one feminine)

In this conversation, the listener (feminine) asks the other about a topic they want to learn about. They are holding out a bowl and asking the other person to fill it with their knowledge. If the other would love to fill that bowl, they will start to speak. The more intently the listener listens, the more the teacher will teach. This also exists in a classroom where the students are intrigued with the teacher and the subject. It's a beautiful harmonious union where true knowledge is passed on.

Separate: Forced Listening (forced masculine, unwilling feminine)

Let's say one person wants to *tell* you something. Maybe they want to tell you about their latest trip to Italy, or what their partner did last night, or what they saw on the news, or whatever new exercise program they are doing. If you are interested in any of these topics, you will be happy for the update.

However, sometimes, people like to talk and it doesn't matter if the other person wants the information being given. This can be seen in classrooms and meetings where the teacher/leader is talking without connecting with the group. In these cases, one person is talking and the others are silent and polite, but there is no dynamic. Everyone remains separate. There is no union.

Separate: Forced Talking (forced feminine, unwilling masculine)

Of course, sometimes people want information or attention from another that the other doesn't want to give. An example would be a partner asking the other about their day or about what's wrong. It could be a parent trying to get their child to talk to them, or the desire of a child to get their parent's attention. It could be a friend or co-worker prying and asking personal questions.

In this case, the one who asks the question or desires the attention is not connecting to the other person because they are not reading them. They are forging ahead with questions, which of course drives them further apart.

Union: Enjoying Each Other's Company

In this case, you simply desire the joy of the union. The masculine and feminine interplay isn't required for you to "create something." You want to hang out together. You enjoy the friendship that already exists. If one person happens to talk, then the other listens, and vice versa. Even in silence, there is still a connection. You have united into one and are receiving (feminine) from the Universe together.

Observe all interactions in your day. If you talk to someone and they aren't listening, ask yourself why you are telling them about this topic? Is this a forced conversation? Would changing the topic create a better dynamic for everyone?

If you are caught listening to something you aren't interested in, why are you there? Could you ask this person a question that you *are* interested in? Were you raised to believe you always had to be polite and weren't allowed to excuse yourself?

CHAPTER 11

BALANCING THE MASCULINE & FEMININE WITHIN

There was a time that I chose to be celibate for six months.

It was a very difficult time in my life. I had no idea how much I had depended on having "my other half." I was recently divorced after having been married for over 20 years. My two children had both grown up and moved away for school and travel. I was alone for the first time in my life.

Previously, when I felt alone, I would simply go on a date and find someone to fill the empty space, but now I didn't have that option. I had to start enjoying my *own* company.

The demons kept rising in my head. They whispered, "Why are you alone? Nobody loves you," "If you were prettier/thinner/etc, you would have someone," or "People need to have sex. This is stupid."

Most of the whispers were about my self-worth; if there was someone sharing my bed, I was somehow a more lovable and more worthwhile person. And yes, it is nice to share a bed with someone, but I knew that there was something I needed to solve here.

I had the inspiration that I had to become my own best boyfriend. I realized my personal masculine side was very weak. I was good at being masculine in the world – teaching, creating structure, running businesses, taking care of others. But personally, for me? I had never really been there for myself.

I asked myself what I was looking for in a man. What would it mean to have that masculine energy around me? What would that protection, structure, action, caring look like? Once I figured it out and actually put the effort into it, my "boyfriend" turned out to be amazing.

He would take my cell-phone away, draw me a bath and ask me to lie there and take care of myself. He protected me and said "No" to others to protect my time and space. He took me out to restaurants, bought me flowers, and did crazy nice things for me all the time. He also created structure in my life that made me so much more efficient and relaxed (my bohemian feminine side just had to agree to see it through).

I felt so loved and honoured, even though I was all alone.

Soon, there were no whispers in my mind about my worthlessness. There were no longings to have sex or masturbate. I was strangely content and happy. In fact, it was a bit unnerving to be so content without any sexual contact or loving connection to another.

People often asked me whether I masturbated all of the time, but I never had the desire. I was completely sexually satisfied. In fact, I was having spontaneous orgasms all of the time.

My masculine and feminine energies were flowing so beautifully within me that every so often, a thought would cross my mind or I would read something or see a painting. Then I would take a deep breath and this wave of orgasm would flow through my body.

I wasn't doing anything to make this happen. There was no special breath. There were no exercises or yoga postures to practice. I was becoming spontaneously orgasmic. It was beyond anything I could have imagined.

During this time, Jim, my first teacher, called me (he always has impeccable timing). I told him about my celibacy revelations and the spontaneous orgasms. He laughed and said, "Yep! Just like I always said. You know you've arrived when you can have an orgasm by looking at a salt shaker!"

Did I lose my interest in others forever? No, but I was no longer searching for someone else to fill me or balance me. I was all I needed to be. I could choose to be with someone because I enjoyed their company, because I loved them, but they didn't have to *be* anything in particular to fill any void within me.

Hey, I didn't even need another person to fulfill me sexually... Apparently all I needed was a salt-shaker.

BALANCING THE MASCULINE & FEMININE WITHIN

We must each be balanced between our masculine and feminine. This is the core of our wholeness. This allows us to talk and listen, work and rest, protect ourselves and be vulnerable, and be logical and intuitive.

The beauty of being balanced within is that each side feeds and strengthens the other. The more we rest, the more we can create. The more we create, the deeper we rest. The more logic and structure we have, the more we can be free and spontaneous and still have safety.

These concepts often seem to be opposite of one another, but they actually work together in a symbiotic relationship.

Logic & Intuition

Logic (masculine) is considered to be governed by our left-brain, and intuition (feminine) by our right-brain. What joins these two hemispheres is called the corpus callosum. Our brains are made up of neurons which are considered grey matter until they are used a lot, in which case they form a myelin sheath around them and become "white matter."

Did you know that Albert Einstein's corpus callosum was nearly all white matter? This means his left brain and right brain were in constant communication. His logic and intuition worked seamlessly together, building upon each other.

There is some truth that certain people tend to be more "left-brained" and logical and others tend to be more "right-brained" and artistic. But what if we also cultivated the other half of ourselves? What if we could integrate them so they worked together? Imagine how much more multi-dimensional we would be. Imagine how expansive we would become. What would be possible then?

Order & Chaos

We often tend towards either chaos or order. If we are very left-brained, we will tend to desire order all of the time. If we are more right-brained, we will prefer the freedom to "stay in flow." We won't want the restrictions of discipline and order.

We need both. We need to know there is food on the table and the bills are paid and then we can have all the freedom in the world to expand, create, and do whatever we want.

Similarly, if all we have is order and structure, there will be no life. We will need to add some new colours to our world. These new colours come from the chaos and mystery within. They come from trying something that doesn't make any sense. They come from talking with someone you wouldn't normally talk to. They come from making choices you can't explain and following your intuition instead of logic.

This is what creates a beautiful balance in our lives.

"Living in the World" & Introspection

Our minds can be compared to an iceberg. The small part that can be seen above water is our conscious mind. Below the surface is everything we are not aware of. This can be what we naturally learned from our parents and society, pain we have "pushed away" and tried to forget, unconscious fears, and hopes. Perhaps this is also where karma and memories from past-lives live.

Our conscious mind is masculine. It is above the ground. It is sun energy. It is light. It is seen.

What lives in our unconscious is the feminine. It is beneath the surface, connected to moon energy. It is the unseen in the darkness. It is mystery.

The balance here comes when our conscious mind notices a glitch in our lives. Maybe we reacted too strongly to an event. Maybe we aren't achieving the goals we set out for ourselves. Maybe we are having a string of difficult relationships. All of these things might trigger us to go deeper and look under the surface for a solution.

So we go inwards. Perhaps we learn how to meditate to quiet the mind. Maybe we learn to feel our emotions and give them more worth. Maybe we pay attention to our dreams at night. Maybe we pray for help and listen for an answer.

This is how we access our feminine wisdom. This is where we "go deep" to find out what's really going on. When we discover what is going on, perhaps the awareness is all that was needed.

Then, our masculine side can take action and make the necessary changes.

This allows us to live very consciously and allow our life experiences to help us grow and expand in deep and meaningful ways.

Protector & the Vulnerable

One day, I went for a healing session with an energy healer. At one point she looked deep into my eyes and said "You sent your little girl [my inner child] away. She wasn't safe. And now, you don't know how to be a care-free child anymore."

Later in the session, she asked me, "Would you like to bring her back? If she comes back, do you promise to listen to her and keep her safe?"

This describes the beautiful balance between being a protector and being vulnerable. At some point in my life, I stopped protecting myself. I allowed myself to be treated badly. I allowed others to walk all over me. If there was a problem in my marriage, my family, or my husband's family, I would "throw myself to the wolves." I would be the "sacrificial lamb" if it meant finding peace. I didn't protect myself at all and my inner child was hurt – a lot.

Of course, sometimes we go the opposite direction and are so afraid of our inner child being hurt that we become over-protective of ourselves. We don't let anyone close. We don't confide in anyone. We are defensive both verbally and physically. We can even be defensive intellectually, distancing ourselves with logical, rational arguments so we never seem vulnerable.

Neither of these situations allows us to have any fun. Our inner, happy child never gets to play. In the first case, the child is always afraid of getting hurt because they know there is no one there to stand up for her. In the second case, she never gets to play outside at all.

The balance comes from clarity. Let's say that our life was a house. Within the house, we have rules. First of all, we *choose* who is allowed to come into the house. Second, within our house, there are rules for behaviour (how we are treated). Our inner protector makes sure everyone is following the rules. The protector doesn't have to be violent or mean. They just need to know what the rules are (the masculine likes rules and structure). They will have full strength and power as long as they simply enforce the rules.

Our inner, playful, child lives in the house. Within the house they are safe. They can play, laugh, cry, be angry, relax, and do whatever they want. Most of all, they can be honest. Children are naturally honest with their feelings when they know they are safe from ridicule, criticism, or punishment. If your inner child is upset, do you send her to her room to keep the peace, or do you listen because her feelings matter?

When our inner masculine, protector side is strong and confident, our inner feminine, vulnerable side is also strong and free to be honest. We are able to be honest with ourselves about how we are actually feeling. We can admit when we are hurt, disappointed, or angry. We are also free to be so excited about something that we can't contain ourselves.

Sometimes it's as simple as our protector saying "no" to others and enforcing healthy boundaries. It is allowing ourselves to be vulnerable and open to new ideas. It is protecting our time, attention, and energy from those who might want more than we want to give. It is our inner self being honest when we are tired, discouraged, and wanting a new direction in our work, personal lives, and relationships.

Seeking Wholeness Within – Not With Another

We often say that opposites attract, and this is true. We seek in others what compliments our personal gifts. If we are naturally shy, it is nice to have an outgoing partner who allows us to expand into the world in a safe way. If we are very outgoing, then it is a beautiful balance to have a quiet place to rest in our intimate partner.

Sometimes we literally choose this other person to "complete" us. We know we are looking for this "completion" when we need the other person to be a certain way. Maybe they need to make a certain amount of money or look young and beautiful to fill our own lack of self-worth. Maybe we need them to be subservient to make us feel strong. Maybe we need them to be controlling to make us feel safe.

All of these are clues to help us look inside and develop the aspects of ourselves that are lacking. In this way, we can become whole.

We can see this particularly in the masculine and feminine dynamic. When you are the masculine partner, you will often seek a feminine partner who displays feminine traits that are weak in you (regardless of gender). Perhaps you like that they have emotional empathy and are intuitive. Or maybe they have a wild and creative side that you lack.

On the flipside, maybe you admire in your masculine partner their structure and order, their assertiveness and quick-thinking, and their ability to make a plan and get it done.

These are all naturally attractive traits in another person. However, our true journey is to be well-rounded ourselves.

Our partner is not there for us to lean on their gifts. If our partner is intuitive, then we need to learn how to be intuitive from them. If our partner is excellent at completing tasks, then we can learn from them, too.

This is the path to wholeness.

If we don't, we will *need* this other person to be a certain way because we haven't done the work to learn the gifts they have. We may even resent the other person and mock the very characteristics that our soul is drawn to. For example, if we are always late, we may call the other person compulsive and overly strict about timeliness. Or if we are closed to other people emotionally, we might label our partner over-sensitive and too emotional.

We must take this journey on our own. We must become whole so that each of us is free to be whatever we want in any moment.

PERSONAL EXPLORATION: EXPANDING OUR SMALLEST HALF

When we look at the yin-yang symbol, the masculine and the feminine parts are perfectly equal. Yet, most of us are not perfectly balanced at all.

Let's consider some personal dynamics. On which side are you most often in the following dynamics?

- Talking or listening
- Logic or intuition
- Structure or flow
- Being the protector or being the vulnerable one
- Giving or receiving
- Order or chaos
- Leading or following
- Moving or resting
- Embracing the Known or the Unknown

We all naturally tend towards one side or the other. However, if we aren't balanced, our "strong" side will weaken. We can maintain our current "imbalance" for a time, but eventually, it will burn out and collapse to the size of our smallest side.

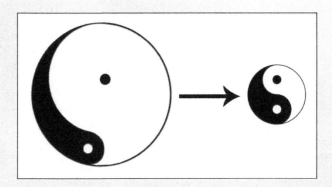

SHRINKING OF POTENTIAL, FROM OUT-OF-BALANCE TO IN-BALANCE

Let's imagine you are more of a talker (white part/masculine) than a listener (black part/feminine). You could go years talking and never listening to others. But what will happen eventually? People will stop listening. You will not get any feedback from others. Plus, people don't like to be "talked at" forever. Over time, your audience of people who will listen to you talk will shrink to the size of your "listening" part of the symbol above.

Let's say you are always "doing" and never resting. What happens? You eventually burn out. Your whole potential shrinks to whatever amount you are actually resting.

We can maintain all of this for a time, but eventually, we feel the imbalance and our world shrinks accordingly.

We must cultivate our "smaller" part. This is our expansion. If we are a natural leader, use this gift but also find opportunities where you can be a great follower. If you love to tell stories and share with others, be conscious of learning to listen and hear the experiences of others as well. Or if you always want flow and embrace chaos, then work on embracing structure and logical thought.

As we increase our "smaller" side, this increases our ability to use the side we are actually gifted with. This increases and expands our entire experience in a beautifully balanced way. As we attract others into our lives who are the "opposite" of our natural tendencies, we will easily unite with them because we won't be uncomfortable with who they are. We will embrace their "opposite" qualities in the same way we have embraced our own.

SECTION IV:

SEXUAL INTIMACY

Rivers of power flowing everywhere.
Fields of magnetism relating everything.
This is your origin. This is your lineage.

The current of creation is right here,
Coursing through subtle changes,
Animating this very form.
Follow the gentle touch of life,
Soft as the footprint of an ant,
As tiny sensations open to vastness.

Power sings as it flows,
Electrifies the organs of sensing,
Becomes liquid light,
Nourishes your entire being.
Celebrate the boundary
Where streams join the sea,
Where body meets infinity.

RADIANCE SUTRAS

We had known each other for quite a while and had crazy mojo, but there was more to it. There was a twinkle in our eyes when we saw each other that was magical. We had the kind of connection where looking into each other's eyes was the most amazing place to be. We had consciously decided not to get sexual right away, so we simply enjoyed each other's company for a long time.

One night, we went on a bit of a "sexting" spree. We were in different cities, so this was all we had. By the time we went to our separate beds that night, all that sexy fun had nearly put us both over the edge. Luckily, we would be seeing each other the next day.

When he walked into my place, he was about a foot off the ground with a smile he could barely contain. I was exactly the same. As we embraced, our bodies were already vibrating.

We kissed for a while as we slowly undressed each other. We had not even so much as touched shoulder skin at this point. Every tiny movement that exposed skin sent us both over the top.

Eventually, we were totally naked and pressed against each other. He sat down on a kitchen chair (we never even made it to the bedroom). Our bodies were screaming for each other and completely ready. I straddled him and we gazed into each other's eyes as we breathed in what was happening. My yoni could feel him long before we even touched. As soon as my yoni felt the tip of his vajra, our whole bodies started quivering and vibrating.

I slowly descended, aware of every fraction of an inch. His whole body shook. It was like we were plugging into the biggest electrical socket in the world. All we had to do was to hold on and let it flow – without losing our minds.

I thought that I had had orgasms before. I thought I had felt pleasure before. This was totally different. It was like being inside a hurricane or an atomic bomb. It was all pleasure, bliss, release, love, and swirling energy.

For me, as my body felt this overwhelming experience, another part of me actually floated above, like I was encompassing both of us. I was blissfully all of it and also fully within the pleasure explosion. It was absolutely amazing.

For him, his whole body was in convulsions – his legs and arms were shaking uncontrollably. He couldn't understand what was happening. He was freaking out. So I whispered to him, *"Just come... let it go."*

Well, he came all right. We both rattled, shook and flew to another planet.

Afterwards, he simply stared at me.

"What was *that*? That wasn't normal. That wasn't even *human*. What the f@#k was that? Oh my god... What just happened?"

Deep down I knew this was *exactly* what humans were meant to do.

This wasn't just the excitement of the first time being together. This experience repeated itself for us in a hundred different flavours for years afterwards.

WHAT WOULD HAPPEN IF WE BECAME AS BIG AS WE ARE?

What would happen if we combined everything we have learned so far in this book and applied it to sexual intimacy?

Let's say we find someone and we genuinely feel all the levels of love with them. We respect and trust each other. We feel safe to drop our guards and let ourselves be completely seen by this person. Plus, we also feel incredible passion and excitement around them.

We also understand that when we join with another, we can merge and actually experience infinity. Even if we can't fully imagine this, we can hold it in our minds as a possibility.

We are completely present. All that passion and love is fully focused on the other and we are thrilled with exploring our connection deeper and deeper.

We enjoy polarizing and playing with masculine and feminine energy together. We speak and move through inspired thought.

This is an amazing experience fully-clothed. Imagine what happens when we add the thrill of sexual exploration. Unending possibilities, and infinite pleasure and bliss!

THINGS TO NOTE

Heterosexual Stories

Most of the stories in this book have nothing to do with sex. They have to do with becoming tantric, so they apply to all people of all genders and orientation.

The stories of love-making that follow are stories from my life. I am a heterosexual woman and the stories are about intimate encounters with men, with the exception of one short story from a male friend of mine in the "subtle magic" chapter. (He wasn't studying tantra. He just had an amazing experience and shared it with me.)

The majority of the following chapters fully apply to all genders and all orientations because it is always the power of the intimate connection that creates the energy and magic between us. Touch physically connects our bodies, and it is our intention that increases our magnetism.

Intercourse

Although I do cover what is possible within heterosexual intercourse, we can still learn a lot about what each gender is capable of within the beautiful intimacy of same-sex couples. Regardless of what we do with our genital parts or how we fit them together, they are completely magical. Most of this magic has been lost and so there is a lot to explore here.

I feel there is a greater lack of understanding in the heterosexual world of what our bodies are capable of doing. Because of the long history where procreative, obligational, and unsatisfying sex was so normalized, there is considerable "unlearning" required.

TERMS USED

We will be calling the penis and vagina by their Sanskrit terms. Not only are they nicer words to say, but they give us clues as to their actual roles within tantric intercourse. Our bodies are capable of actually playing together.

Vajra

Vajra is a Sanskrit term meaning "thunderbolt" and refers to a man's penis. I love this term because it truly reframes the penis for what it is – the giver of unlimited and powerful energy.

In procreative sex, the vajra must go in and out to create excitement to cause ejaculation, which is wonderful. However, it tends to portray the vajra more like a battering ram. We become obsessed with the importance of size, length, girth and hardness – all of which are important for a battering ram.

But the role of the vajra is different. It is the source of divine masculine energy fuelling the feminine. This shifts our entire consciousness around its role, which is half the journey in tantric sexuality.

Yoni

This refers to the female genitals – the whole area, not just the vagina. All the parts of a woman's genitals play together to stimulate her incredible orgasmic response.

Her clitoris is actually an entire system that extends in an upside-down V from the spot we know as the clitoris under her labia. Her G-spot is actually an entire system of erectile tissue that engorges when a woman is turned on – when her whole being is aroused from her heart outwards.

Even a woman's uterus contracts and expands and participates. All of these parts, plus all of the muscles, veins, and sensory cells dance together to create the magical yoni – capable of giving life and other wonderful pleasures.

CHAPTER 12

WHAT ARE WE TAUGHT ABOUT SEX?

My lover and I would go for romantic walks in the moonlight. We were the kind of lovers who were simply thankful to have found each other. Every moment together was special.

One time, before we went out, he sent me this text: "My beautiful goddess awaits me. As I approach her, a gentle rain falls upon her breasts while her face glistens in the moonlight. She is so beautiful and I will be lovingly kissing her soon."

What made this text so special is that he wasn't the "artistic poetic" type. He loved to play sports, drink beer with the boys, and had a pretty tough exterior with the rest of the world. Receiving a text like this pretty much put me over the edge.

Later, as we wandered down the path through the woods, we held hands. We said all of the mushiest things. We told each other how we felt with total presence. We really meant it, and we held nothing back.

And then we walked in silence for a while.

Most of the time when we held hands, it was normal, happy hand-holding. But sometimes our hands felt alive. It was like all the love and excitement we felt for each other flowed through our hands and into each other.

On this night, a vibration flowed up our arms. We breathed deeply as the orgasmic vibration slowly moved through our whole bodies. We stopped walking and stood still and gazed at each other, as if we were both plugged into some invisible electrical socket and staring at each other was the only way we could breathe through it.

The response was, "What was *that?* Wow!"

We hugged and kissed for a while and then kept walking... Of course, the longer we walked, the less our feet touched the ground.

MOVING BEYOND OUR PRIMAL WIRING

We learn nothing about sex. We learn how to drive a car, use a computer, balance our books, and play the piano. But for most of us, the most advice we got about sex was "Don't do it," and "If you do, use protection."

Knowing nothing, when we enter puberty and become sexually aware, we default to our primal wiring to procreate.

This primal wiring creates our desire to ejaculate to create new life. We are attracted to someone, one person inserts one part of their body into another part of the other person's body, and we do various things until one or both people ejaculate and/or have orgasm. This is often called "friction sex" because the orgasm is created from the movement or stimulation of various genital parts.

The procreative model doesn't mean we are literally trying to have children every time we have sex, but the model is the same. We "play" until orgasm or ejaculation. These are the signs that we are finished, and achieving these is the goal (similar to wanting to conceive).

Today, young people have a new model where they can learn about sex: porn. It is easily available on their phones as soon as they become sexually interested. This model is partially based on this primal wiring since it is still focused on eventual ejaculation, but it lacks all the exploration we naturally do when we know nothing. It creates a foundation for our future sex lives that satisfies less people than ever before.*

In truth, there is a whole other world where we don't just have orgasms – our entire bodies become orgasmic. We actually deepen the bonds with our partner after each experience. We develop constant intimacy, in and out of the bedroom. We discover the potential of these miraculous, multi-dimensional bodies and the magic that happens when we bring them together.

WANTING TO BE "GOOD" AT SEX

After a while, we realize that simple procreative sex isn't satisfying. With the sexual revolution (and the realization that women could actually feel pleasure and orgasm), we wanted to be "better" at sex. We wanted to explore more pleasure for ourselves and for our partners.

For the most part, this is a good thing. We want to bring the one we love pleasure. We want to see them scream in ecstasy. This is a wonderful thing and it is much better than having mechanical sex, where the pleasure of both partners isn't important.

Yet even within loving relationships, this can still get old, and the fact that it gets old makes us feel badly. We love this person. We are doing everything we can to please them (and ourselves), yet it isn't enough to keep the spark alive.

* I receive emails all the time from young men around the world who started watching porn when they were 12 and are now addicted and don't even know what *they* enjoy. Many young girls also start here because they want to look like they know what they are doing. Of course, it's a very limited view for them to base their future sex lives on.

So we read sex books (which is a great idea; learning about our bodies is always a great idea). However, when we learn technique after technique, they reinforce the idea that we are separate. I am doing *this* to you or you are doing *that* to me. This can definitely create fun and pleasurable experiences. But there is always the giver and the receiver; it isn't about union.

In the study of tantra, we have to watch out for anything that further separates us. Because the truth is that we *are not separate*. We are connected. Not only are we connected simply because we are all humans, we have loving connection with this person. Because of this loving connection, we can feel a pull towards them – a longing for full merging. So, when we do all these "tricks" to each other, although they are pleasurable in the moment, they maintain the separation. What our souls want is to feel the deep connection that we not only know is possible, but is already there.

The other challenge is when we learn techniques meant to ensure pleasure for our partner, we now have a goal we want to achieve. This immediately brings our brains into the bedroom. Now we must perform. We must be good at what we are doing. Now we have pressure. What if we fail? What if it doesn't work? This stress can lead to performance anxiety, erectile dysfunction, premature ejaculation and many other subtle issues.

This also creates stress in the receiver. It is no secret that women are famous for faking orgasms. Why? One reason is because they want their partner to think he's a great lover. This isn't necessarily a bad thing. If their partner feels like they are doing a good job, this increases their "masculinity," which may lead to better sex next time. However, if they don't fake it and their partner realizes what they are doing isn't satisfying her, this could be a knock to their masculinity, which could cause performance anxiety in him the next time, creating a vicious negative spiral.

Unfortunately, in this scenario where we are separate from each other and we are supposed to be "good" at pleasing each other, we create all kinds of tension, expectation, and stress, and we are simply supposed to be making love.

THE MAGIC IS IN THE CONNECTION

The meeting of two personalities is like the contact of two chemical substances;
if there is any reaction, both are transformed.

CARL JUNG

We knew that orgasmic experiences are not of this physical world the very first time we orgasmed. Orgasms are something completely different... they are of the infinite.

Our bodies can connect us through touch and playing together can deepen our connection.

But ultimately, all mind-blowing pleasure and ecstasy comes from your energetic connection. It comes from love. It comes from intention. It comes from a desire to experience something beyond the physical.

The magic of sexual intimacy happens as we deepen the connection between us. The connection between us is like a river. The deeper and wider it is, the more energy can flow through it. Love is the mysterious power that flows between us and it has the potential to put us into highly orgasmic states.

This loving, sexual energy will take us to places we have never imagined. This exploration alone could make us happy and bring new sexual experiences to last us a lifetime.

As we deepen our connection through life and intimacy, once in a while, we will actually merge. In this merging, we will experience the bliss of "oneness." From here a whole new adventure happens within it where you lose track of the bodies, you have no sense of time and space, and you float in indescribable bliss.

This happens because we are more than our bodies. We have infinite energy coursing through our beings. We are physical, emotional, mental and spiritual (and likely even more). If we limit our experience to our physical bodies, we will always feel like we are missing something.

Instead imagine that our bodies are like physical keys that fit together so we can plug into a universal energy socket. Our touch makes our bodies alive with energy. Each touch connects us energetically. Each touch brings us into a similar "vibration."

It is this "vibration" we want to tune into. It is all of the unseen connections between us that will take us to another world, because when we add in the "energetic" sides of ourselves, we are now in an infinite playing field. We become aware that the energy running through us is endless. We have no idea where it is going or what it is going to do. So we trust, because it is always wonderful.

As we connect with another person in every way, we start to feel *their* energy as well – which is also infinite.

Everything we do deepens this connection and the energy flows more within you and between you. Soon, you are barely aware of the bodies at all. They know what to do. Our bodies know how to make love without us. We allow the bodies to connect and the energy continues to flow.

What happens in this space is different every time; you have two souls meeting and we are different in every moment of our lives. Sometimes you have pleasure flowing for hours and hours. Sometimes we cry because something is unearthed and we are able to heal it in this loving, safe intimacy. Sometimes we are playful and we move between monkey sex, love-making, and sacred union. It's all good.

This is the joy when we let infinity in. This is what elevates all experiences when we include spirit in all aspects of our lives.

RELEASING WHAT YOU ALREADY KNOW

My invitation to you going forward is to release the ideas you have about "doing" different things during sexual intimacy – even our belief that all "successful" sexual intimacy results in intercourse. We must release these ideas so we have a chance to experience something different.

Perhaps it is helpful to return to a time in your youth when you were still exploring. Maybe intercourse wasn't a given. Return to the thrill of "just fooling around" to create a whole new foundation.

This is incredibly important for everyone. However, it is slightly different depending on your orientation.

The heterosexual world is at a bit of a disadvantage when it comes to true pleasure and connection because pleasure, connection, and love simply have not been the most important part of sex. Historically, the patterns have been "sex for procreation," "sex for obligation," "sex to make someone happy," etc. Because opposite genitals tend to fit together easily and coincide with the primal wiring of procreation, many heterosexual couples fall into old patterns that never get past the goal of ejaculating. Eventually, everyone gets bored.

In the LGBTQ community, there is often a higher awareness of personal pleasure and desires. Right from the beginning, you must be creative. You must explore. You often figure out what you like and what your preferences are early. There isn't the historical precedent to fall back on, which is a great bonus.

For everyone of all orientations, we want to use tantra to find the powerful energetic connection. Orgasms and ecstatic experiences can happen fully clothed, without any sexual touching at all. All the energy comes from the energy flowing between you.

We achieve this by increasing our connection. If you are heterosexual, then perhaps it leads to yoni/vajra intercourse, which will be talked about more in a later chapter. If you have similar genitals as your partner, or any situation that doesn't fall into the vajra/yoni intercourse category, then this chapter creates the foundation for your intimate experience.

As you connect intimately with each other, the energy builds. The key is to do only what maintains and increases that connection. Everything we do, whether it is oral sex, touch, intercourse, kissing – can be done in ways that separate you into giver and receiver or they can also be done in ways that maintain your connection, where you sink into the experience and connect deeper and deeper with each other.

Personal Exploration: What Does Your Soul Already Know About Sex?

I waited until I was 20 years old to have sex for the first time (I was waiting for marriage. I know, kind of ironic). By the time I actually had intercourse, I was ready for explosive fireworks. I was ready for pleasure beyond my wildest dreams.

Alas, that's not really what happened. Actually, not at all. I lay there after the whole 15 minute experience and wondered why I had built this up to be such a big deal.

Of course, some of the build-up might have been the result of ideas placed within me from the media. It might have been heightened from the whole adult world telling us not to have sex, so I assumed it must be incredible beyond belief.

However, I think our souls actually know the pleasure that's possible because when I discovered true tantric intimacy, I had all of the fireworks and excitement that my 20-year-old self had imagined.

What does *your* soul know? What do you think sexual intimacy is meant to *feel* like? This is not about what you enjoy or your wildest fantasy. It's about how true intimacy is meant to make you *feel*.

Close your eyes and breathe deeply. Really come into your centre. Then ask the question, "What would infinite sexual pleasure feel like?"

Don't analyze it, try to describe it, or wonder if it's possible. Just trust that your soul knows the truth.

If nothing comes to you, then let the question live within you. Perhaps when you are lying in bed one night, you will be completely relaxed and suddenly a feeling will come over you.

Or maybe you will be making love and you'll experience something new.

Just ask the question.

And trust that somewhere in your life, you will receive an answer.

CHAPTER 13

TANTRIC TOUCH

The monkey took hold of my finger,
and I had never been touched like that before.
Her touch was incredibly alive and electric.
There was so much concentrated feeliness in her hand
that I felt this warm glow travel from her hand to mine,
on up my arm and then I felt a nice electric rush up my body...
I knew that my hand, and everyone else's too,
was potentially that powerful and sensitive,
but that most people think so much and are so unconscious
of their whole range of sensory perceptors and receptors
that their touch feels blank compared to what it would feel like
if their awareness was 100%.

I call this "original touch" because it's something
that everybody has as a brand new baby.
A baby born blind doesn't lose his original touch
because he can't afford to pull his attention out of his skin
and out of his hands
when he gets so much of his information from the Universe this way.
Many of us lose our "original touch"

ORIGINAL TOUCH

This is what touch is meant to feel like.

When babies are born, we naturally touch them. We don't even think about it. We know that's what you do. We caress their hands, feet, arms, head, and fat little knees. We know this is normal.

Touch feeds us like food and sunshine. It heals us inside. When we touch a baby, it receives the touch completely and melts into it. There is no intention in the person touching them, and there is no intention in the baby receiving. The touch simply goes deep into their system, nourishing them.

Yet we seldom experience touch this way because we have become walled off to it – almost like armour to the outside world.

Are you willing to become this sensitive?

One of the blocks to feeling this deeply is that we don't want to feel all of our emotions. What we do physically is connected to what we do energetically, emotionally, and mentally. We are all one system. If we are physically de-sensitized, then we are likely emotionally de-sensitized as well.

This is where it is helpful to explore the previous chapters about letting down our walls, becoming vulnerable, and unearthing any pain, trauma, and difficult emotions that may be driving us unconsciously in our lives. They may also be affecting our ability to feel pleasure physically as well.

This kind of healing goes both ways. As we heal where we are shut down emotionally, our body becomes more sensitive. Also, as our body is able to relax and let go, we may unlock old emotions that are ready to be released.

RE-SENSITIZING OUR BODIES TO TOUCH

We need to re-sensitize our bodies to this touch. Through rough handling or shallow experiences with people, we can end up feeling only on the surface. It doesn't go deep enough anymore.

Our skin is our largest organ and filled with touch receptors, and we are capable of experiencing touch with our entire nervous system. These receptors are connected to all of the nerves that are connected to every cell in our body, including our brain. In fact, when we are touched, it is our brain that interprets whether it is pleasurable or painful.

When you think of how the nervous system is designed, we realize that every cell of our skin, our muscles, and our organs have nerves that go all the way to our spine. Right from the tip of your finger, there is a nerve that travels all the way to your spine, sending a message to the brain. There are millions of these nerves all over our body.

This touch can connect us to our infinity. Our nervous system runs on energy, and it is a complete system. It is whole. We think touch is localized because that is how our brain separates our experience. In truth, the effects of touch in one area instantly spreads throughout our whole body (and mind) immediately.

Think of the first time someone kisses you and you feel it all the way into your toes. Or perhaps they just touch your shoulder as they walk by and your whole body reacts.

We also feel pain this way. When you bump your knee on a chair, your entire body collapses. You feel it in your whole body.

Our nerves are receiving information all the time. It is not only happening on the skin. After touching the skin, the energy shoots through the body, turning even the smallest amount of contact into a full body experience.

RE-SENSITIZING THE GENITALS

We often call regular sex "friction" sex, since the pleasure and excitement come from the rubbing together of various body parts.

Through this, our genitals can become desensitized. Because we focus on physical stimulation to find pleasure, everything needs to be tight, hard, and tense.

But what happens in our bodies when there is tension? We *feel* less. It's like a boxer tensing his muscles to receive a punch. The tension lessens what he feels. Over time, it creates a kind of armour. The less we feel, the more we need to amp everything up to find the pleasure we desire.

Yet, our genitals have a high density of nerve endings. We are designed to feel immense pleasure here. And this heightened pleasure is capable of flowing through our entire body.

The key is to be able to relax. The vajra can still be firm, but it doesn't have to be rock hard. When we stop using it as a battering ram and instead as a masculine energy source, it will fluctuate between hard, firm, and soft - and it's all perfect.

Similarly, women have to practise relaxing their yoni during sex. You can imagine the effect of "friction" sex on a delicate yoni. She must be always on guard. She becomes like a hard cylinder, ready to be entered over and over again. This creates an armouring to the point that many women feel almost nothing in their yoni. They become completely numb (we discuss this in more detail in the chapter "Sexual Healing").

Relaxation is the beginning of increasing our sensitivity and bringing our genitals to the pleasure they are truly capable of.

TOUCHING EACH OTHER

Let's begin with the fact that we each have infinite energy running through our bodies. Many people can "see" energy all around us. We have "auras" of energy that can interact with people close to us. There are electrical currents coming out of our fingers when we touch someone.

When we touch, we want to increase the connection between us. Our intention is to connect these two energy fields together. (Yes, I know it might sound a little weird.)

Because our bodies are designed to enjoy pleasurable touch, it's easier than we might think. If we simply allow our bodies to intuitively touch each other in pleasurable ways, this will create energetic connections between us.

Of course, we must slow way down, keep our minds out of the game, and let our bodies flow together, exploring this touch. As soon as our minds become engaged, we will no longer be feeling with our bodies and we will lose our connection.

This is why it's so much fun to go back to "just fooling around." We have long ago forgotten the joy of simply touching and being touched. We think that because we "graduated" to having intercourse, touching is almost immature or a lesser pleasure. This is completely backwards. We can experience incredible pleasure through touch. (I once had a lover who could have a full-body orgasm when I very gently touched the inside of his elbow... No kidding.)

PERSONAL EXPLORATION:
EXPERIENCING TANTRIC TOUCH

Solo Practice

Let's experiment with our nervous system and touch in a non-sexual way.

You might choose to start by touching your face. Touch lightly and see what it feels like. Do it slowly enough that you actually experience every inch. It's not about going over all the skin. It's about the experience in the moment.

Then touch your hands. Even if you hold just one spot, see if you can feel that touch going through your entire body. Visualize the nerve endings starting in your fingers going all the way through your arms and into your spine. Breathe deeply and be present.

You don't want to have a plan as to how you're going to touch yourself. Stay present. Close your eyes and simply allow your hand to move where it wants without any thought. Allow your mind to rest and follow your instincts.

Do it for as long as you'd like. Do it in a very relaxed way, the same way you would caress a baby without any intention. Be aware of your whole body. You can touch anywhere you want, just not sexually. We don't want any kind of goal of orgasm to be involved here, only gentle touch.

With A Partner

Now let's experience this with someone else. It could be your romantic partner or a friend. The intention is to heighten the sensitivity of our nervous system through the experience of non-sexual touch.

Sit across from the other person and decide who will go first. One person will give and the other will receive. The person receiving the touch decides where it's okay to be touched. In a public class, the touch should be from the fingertips to the elbows. I don't recommend using the whole body because this exercise is about experiencing flow *through* the body when it's touched, not about touching the whole body.

Set a timer for how long you want to practice (5-10 minutes). If you are the receiver, close your eyes to get rid of all other stimulus around you. Then, allow your partner to touch you. If at some point you don't like what they're doing, you can ask them to give a lighter touch or change what they're doing. This is not about guiding them in how you like to be touched. It's about you feeling what happens when someone else touches you and experiencing the energy within your body.

For the person who is touching, release your mind and simply touch without any intention and as slowly as you can. Breathe deeply and be completely present. This other human has allowed you to touch them and be in their space. They are trusting you. That's a huge deal. We want to be conscious of that and allow it to be a sacred experience.

When you're done, switch roles and let the giver become the receiver and vice versa. You don't have to do it the same way the first person did it. Just practise however you feel called.

Tantra is about following your inner calling and trusting your intuition, moving with spirit and instinct as opposed to your mind. Close your eyes and touch, be touched and relax. Forget about everything you have ever experienced and fully explore this brand new moment.

CHAPTER 14

RELEASING GOALS AND EXPECTATIONS

He was such a great guy and he *loved* sex. He had read every sex book ever published. He had practised and honed his skills like a master. He could pleasure a woman for hours and hours.

But he had never experienced anything like tantra.

He read all of my books, and we chatted endlessly about it. He wanted to try it so badly. However, I was concerned that he wouldn't be able to leave his tricks at the door. I worried they would distract him from the experience.

One day, we made a date. He wined and dined me and eventually we ended up back at his place. Everything was lovely.

Yet once we were there, something didn't feeling right. I couldn't feel *him*. He was physically excited and totally attentive, but I could sense his brain was going a mile a minute, like he was constantly creating and adjusting his game-plan. He finally had me there. He was going to make sure it was awesome.

When I told him something didn't feel right, he offered to give me a massage (I love massage). That was nice, but I still wasn't feeling *it*.

I asked him if we could just sit on the bed for a while. We sat cross-legged and stared at each other. I wasn't sure if this would work, and at the same time I wasn't sure what else to do. Unless the energy was real, nothing interesting was going to happen.

We eye-gazed with each other for a long time. It felt like two titans staring at each other wanting to bring all of who they are to the experience but not wanting to drop who they are, either. It wasn't a battle *between* us. It was more like two strong people having no idea how to be vulnerable.

Finally, *that* magic point happened.

There's often a point in meditation when your brain gives up control. You have set a timer and you are going to sit there for the whole time, regardless of whether you want to or not. For a time, your brain argues with you and tries to convince you to give in, but then *that* point occurs where your brain realizes you *aren't* going to give up.

All of our shields dropped. Our brains stopped planning. We let go of all of our skills and strengths. We sat in front of each other completely open, vulnerable, and as innocent as children.

Like a magnet, my body flew onto his lap and we began kissing. Honestly, from there, everything is quite a blur. From the outside, I imagine we looked like one of those scenes in the movies where there are two bodies rolling around the bed, completely oblivious to everything around them. Between us, on the inside, it was like we were flying down a wormhole for hours and hours.

My next memory is straddling him as he lay on his back. The energy was flowing up my back and out the crown of my head. When I feel this sensation, my whole body is so orgasmic that I always get concerned because it's hard for a man not to ejaculate. It's like the magnetism of my yoni practically pulls it out of him.

I looked into his eyes and saw this unwavering strength and determination. Once I saw that, I was free to completely release to the energy. He wasn't going to lose it. He totally had me.

RELEASING GOALS & EXPECTATIONS

Wandering re-establishes the original harmony
which once existed
between man and the universe.
ANATOLE FRANCE

Imagine having no goals in lovemaking. This can be a very foreign concept since we are taught to have goals for everything. This is how we accomplish and get done what we want in life.

However, this is the most important thing to let go of if we want to have a tantric experience. In fact, if you did nothing else in this whole book, the next time you make love, simply try letting go of all goals and expectations – especially ejaculation and orgasm. Simply be with and explore each other like it's your first time.

This experience alone will open you up to a whole new world and will cause you to ask yourself why you even want to make love. It will ask you to trust your body to move as it desires without your brain telling it what to do. You will be present in a whole new way.

LETTING OUR BODIES MAKE
LOVE – MOVING INTUITIVELY

Making love isn't actually something we have to learn. Our bodies know how to do it. We just have to relax our minds, let go of our expectations (especially of performance, orgasm or ejaculating) and let our bodies make love. They desire the connection. They can feel that another body is close. They naturally know what to do.

Of course, to do this, we must be able to turn off our minds. We must be able to be meditative, present, focused, and let all of our thoughts go. This is quite a journey in itself.

Tantra is an exploration of the unknown. It is about closing our eyes and trusting something that perhaps we've never trusted before. Maybe we've talked about having higher guidance, believing in spirit or God, or knowing we are so much more than physical bodies and a brain.

But do we trust that other aspect to guide us in our lives? In our relationships? In the bedroom?

We can learn all kinds of things, but the tantric path teaches us how to respond uniquely and allow for the infinite possibilities in each moment. There are no books or training that can tell you what to do in any moment. We must simply be present and listen.

There can be a fear in being intuitive. It is unknown. What if nothing comes? What if the wrong thing comes? Can we trust it? Do we trust it? That is really the question.

Our minds do a lot of work in life figuring out the best plans, the safest bets, and optimal solutions. It's no small thing to let all that go and trust the wisdom that springs from the unknown. So we must cultivate listening inside for that little voice that whispers... and then trust it and enjoy the ride.

To release this in the bedroom can be especially challenging because we are often sensitive about performing well. There can be a lot of fear, shame, and guilt. In the end, when we release the mind, we release all of the fear as well. It can be scary, but when we step outside of our comfort zone, that's when we truly live.

When we relax our minds and begin to connect, ideas will come – thoughts of touching them here, or kissing them there or breathing with them. At first, it might not be clear because this is new. You are strengthening a new system. You are releasing your mind and all its ideas, memories, and fantasies and trusting the rest of your body and spirit to sense the other person and what is real in the union.

Experiment with this intuition. Perhaps passion takes over and you ravage each other for a while – wonderful! Perhaps you slow down to gaze into each other's eyes. Perhaps you caress slowly or firmly. There are no rules. What matters is your constant connection – your total union.

You Can't Step in the Same River Twice

In tantra, the goal cannot be to repeat amazing experiences. We can have a mind-blowing, amazing experience once, and the next time, we do all the same things and it doesn't create the same experience.

Don't get me wrong. There are positions and techniques that seem to have somewhat repeatable results... but not exactly.

This is one of the important ways tantra reflects the true nature of reality. If we are paying attention, each day is completely different. We want to think we can repeat success. We want to think we can come up with the perfect plan and it will always work out.

This isn't reality. The world is not a simple system made with limited parts. There are infinite moving parts. There are forces beyond our sight moving everyone in every moment.

If we are paying attention, our partner is different than they were yesterday. Our friend is different. Our child is different. They have changed and grown. We are different. Yesterday, we had thoughts, experiences, lessons, emotions, and "aha" moments. We are different. We have grown.

When we make love, the players are different than the last time we made love. When we connect with someone, *we* are different and *they* are different.

This is the adventure. What will happen *today* between these two infinite bodies? Where will our unique energies take us in *this* experience?

If it is the same as last time, then our brains are simply moving through an old pattern. This is fine too, if it's what you want. I have my favourite restaurant where I like to get my favourite meal. It's my ultimate comfort food. Sometimes sex can be like that too. However, each intimate experience is an opportunity for adventure into the unknown. Ecstatic experiences are spontaneous. We can't plan them. All we can do is relax and see what happens.

Sometimes it takes us to places we didn't imagine. It could be healing. It could be the warmest, nourishing hug we've ever experienced or it could be crazy sexual ecstasy.

We can't force it. We have to stay with what's real. We can't control reality.

This is the beautiful surrender of tantra.

PERSONAL EXPLORATION: INTEGRATING RELAXATION INTO LOVEMAKING

Let's bring no goals and expectations into our intimate playtime.

First, we need to relax. Ecstasy only happens when there is flow. Tension is the opposite of what we want. Tension contracts and makes us small. Relaxation opens and expands. We want to be in an expansive, relaxed state.

In order to relax, we want to bring in that meditative space, we want to know we are safe. We want to feel deeply connected with our partner – truly open, warm, and loving.

We want to be completely present, with no goals or expectations. What new things can happen? What can happen that you've never experienced before?

We want to go back to that childlike state of exploration. Many great spiritual teachings say we must have a beginner's mind – that we have to come to it as a child.

We want to begin like we've never done it before. We've never touched skin before. And we've never touched *this* person before. It's a brand new experience.

In reality, this *is* a new experience. We are different today. Our partner is different today. We need to be open to what *this* experience will be.

Enjoy your exploration!

CHAPTER 15

CLIMBING MYSTERY MOUNTAIN

We had been together for a while, and I loved making love with him. The only challenge we had while lovemaking was his deeply ingrained desire to thrust his hips, like in "friction" sex. I preferred that he stay deeply inside and connected, our hips gently rocking together.

One day, he hurt his back. He was barely able to bend in any direction, but that didn't change the fact that we still wanted to make love.

He lay down on the bed and I happily took the lead. As we played and made love, I crawled on top, straddled him, and placed him inside. Oh my god, it felt good. Because I knew he couldn't move, my yoni completely relaxed and then pulled him even deeper inside of me.

I could see the frustration in his eyes because he couldn't move his hips. He had to lie there while I sat on top, squirming with pleasure. Every so often, my yoni vibrated with crazy energy, which would make him nearly lose it. When this happened, I stopped moving and whispered, *"Just breathe all the excitement up your spine - as high as you can."*

"OK... "

He would breathe deeply, the energy would subside and I would continue enjoying myself.

This happened over and over again until eventually, my entire body was so orgasmic, I thought I was going to explode. I vibrated from head to toe. He contracted his PC muscle and breathed for all he was worth, trying desperately not to come (when a woman starts to orgasm like that, she can absolutely pull the ejaculation right out of him!).

As he lay beneath me, his whole body went into convulsions. When they stopped, he looked at me wide-eyed.

"Holy crap! I just orgasmed eight times right up my spine! And I didn't even ejaculate! Oh My God!"

I bent forward and lay on top of him with him still deep inside. Our bodies melted into each other, humming.

From then on, he would shake his head and say, *"If men only knew what that felt like, they would never care about ejaculating again!"*

CLIMBING MYSTERY MOUNTAIN

When ejaculation is the ultimate goal of sex, it's like standing at the foot of the most magnificent mountain and only seeing the foothills. As soon as you get to the top of the foothills, you *think* you've reached the summit. You grab a parachute and jump (in the most pleasurable way) to the bottom of the mountain. We think this is awesome because it's all we know.

Of course, all of our friends only know about the foothills too. We can read books and magazine articles about the most pleasurable ways to climb them. After a while, we get to know them pretty well, so we try to make it more interesting. We start bringing new toys up the mountain or we bring different friends. Each new addition creates a slightly new experience, but in the end, we are still only exploring the same old foothills.

There is so much more beyond the foothills.

All we have to do is skip the parachuting spot and take a few more steps through the mist up the mountain. Then, something completely new and unimaginable opens up. The mountain extends up beyond the clouds. We can't begin to see all of it. All we can do is keep exploring.

Each time we make love, if we don't jump off the mountain (ejaculate), we get to start where we left off. We don't have to climb the foothills again. We simply connect with each other and continue where we left off, climbing higher and higher, having brand new experiences each time.

NON-EJACULATORY SEX

We have a lot attached to ejaculation.

For many men, ejaculation is one of the reasons they have sex, because it's all we know. Ejaculation is often seen as a sign of success by both parties. Men feel like they didn't "finish the job" if they don't come. Their partners might also feel that if there is no ejaculation, they aren't attractive enough or they did something wrong.

This makes perfect sense within a procreative structure. At a primal level, the only reason for the interaction was for the male to ejaculate into the female to create offspring. Both parties will believe the interaction was a failure if this doesn't happen.

This is only one option. We are able to do many other things with sexual energy besides releasing it outwards. We can direct it inside, moving the orgasm through our whole nervous system. We can connect the orgasmic energy with our partner and create a larger orgasm we can both ride together.

We can use the energy for healing. This is our life force that we generate and share.

Intercourse can be truly a spiritual experience. The joining of two people can bring us into incredible states of ecstasy. You can actually "feel the divine." You feel one with the universe. It can be a totally transcendental experience.

EJACULATION AND ORGASM ARE NOT THE SAME

It's important to understand that ejaculation and orgasm are not the same thing. When we say non-ejaculatory sex, we don't mean non-orgasmic sex (quite the opposite). You can orgasm without ejaculating and you can ejaculate without orgasming. They are separate. We tend to think they are the same because in the heat of regular sex, they tend to happen together, but they are different.

Orgasm is a function of our nervous system, our energy meridians, our spiritual connection, everything. It happens throughout our entire being. You can orgasm for hours (both sexes). You can have multiple orgasms (both sexes). None of this has to lead to ejaculation, which is really only a powerful outward release of all of this energy (again, very important when making babies).

Instead, when ejaculation is not the goal, this powerful energy can flow through our entire beings, making us fully orgasmic.

CREATING NEW PATHWAYS FOR ORGASM IN THE BRAIN

There are no rules as to what we *always* do in tantric intimacy, except that we are to always listen inside to what is real in the moment. There will be many times you will want to move your bodies as in regular sex. There will be times when you definitely want to ejaculate. It's all great.

However, in the beginning, it is good to take some time where your goal is to keep from ejaculating at all. We want to experience something new. We need to retrain our brain and nervous system to move energy through our bodies in different ways.

The neural pathways to ejaculation are very strong, especially in men. All sexual activity can easily end up on the super-highways that have been created in our minds. It's almost like a vacuum that sucks us there every time. To practise *not* going down that path can be challenging in the beginning, but every time we do it, new pathways are formed. We might simply last longer. We may discover pleasures in other parts of our bodies. Perhaps our bodies register pleasure on a much broader and expansive scale.

Once this energy travels throughout our bodies, this will become second nature. Each time we are intimate, when we breathe, the energy will flow this way. New pathways will form. With each experience, we become more sensitive, more aware and able to feel pleasure throughout our whole bodies in the most natural and effortless way.

MOVING ORGASM UP INSTEAD OF OUT

Our pelvis is like a power-generating station. Here, with just a thought, we can start our engines running. With breath, they will heat up. With touch, even more so. Then, we can add another person with whom we can polarize, join together, and really get the energy flowing.

Now we have this power station going at full steam. We have a choice as to what we want to do with this energy. We can release it outwards, or we can move it in the opposite direction up the spine and let our nervous system deliver the sensations to our whole body, using the breath to help us.

You can do this while sitting and reading this book; you don't have to be sexually aroused. You can practise while self-pleasuring or while making love. Simply feel your breath carrying the energy up your spine as you inhale and then relax everything on your exhale. With each breath, feel the energy rising up. Don't try to control what happens with the energy. Your body will take it where it needs to go. It will be different every time, because *we* are different every time.

HOW TO PRACTISE NOT EJACULATING

Relaxing

We are often the same in life as we are sexually. If we are very hyper and nervous in life, we are likely the same in the bedroom. Meditation practice will be helpful in learning what it feels like to be calm and to train ourselves to relax in all situations.

Turning off our minds is no small thing if we've never done it. To practise meditation with the intention of teaching our mind to release all of its fears and worries is incredible practice that will affect our day-to-day life, as well as our experience in the bedroom.

Deciding

For some men, they simply decide they want to control their ejaculation. At first, it is a challenge, but many men say it's like a switch flips in their brain and "now they can just control it."

It depends a lot on what *you* want. If your partner tells you that you *shouldn't* ejaculate, that probably won't work. But if *you* personally want to experience this and it is absolutely what you want, the universe will conspire with you and help you flip that switch.

Self-Awareness

You have to be fully self-aware, especially in the beginning. You will recognize the point where the excitement is building and ejaculation is coming. You can play with relaxing at that point and then starting up again. This creates the necessary neural pathways for new abilities.

Don't Worry

There is definitely a "point of no return" where it is nearly impossible to stop. If it happens, great! Rejoice in the wonderful pleasure. The last thing we want to do is make ejaculation "bad." The intention of this practice is to create other options. Getting rid of ejaculation opens doors to many other possibilities, but there's nothing wrong with it. It's fun and it feels good.

We want to have a relaxed attitude about the whole thing. We are learning something fun. Sometimes it works. Sometimes it doesn't, and it means we need more practice... and who doesn't like this kind of practice?

Contracting the PC Muscle

Men can practise tightening the muscle between their vajra and anus to help control ejaculation. You can practise this any time. If you are doing it correctly, your vajra will dance around a little. This is especially fun to practise at work, in the car, or anywhere really.

HOW CAN TANTRIC ORGASM LAST FOR HOURS?

This can be one of the most alluring things we hear about tantric intimacy – how to be orgasmic for hours. As we understand more about moving this energy through the body, it's helpful to look at the differences between the energy of regular sex and tantric connection.

We want to look at two aspects: how we *create* the energy, and how we *experience* it?

In regular sex, the energy comes from excitement and friction resulting in eventual release. This can only last a few seconds. It's like taking two pieces of wood and rubbing them together to eventually make fire.

We experience this exciting energy like a roller coaster; going around all the corners and the banks and the ups and the downs is exciting and thrilling. In the end, we rise up, up, up, heading for the final plunge. We gain excitement and potential as we climb, getting more and more excited. Then we fly over the top, screaming and filled with joy! As we wind around to the end, we feel totally fulfilled and think "Ahhh.. That was awesome."

However, tantra is based on the concept of union. Where regular sex is about how the bodies come together to create friction and release, tantra is about what happens when we come together and become one.

The energy is more like nuclear fusion. When two subatomic particles come together and unite, the energy created is like an atomic bomb. We can't even fathom it. It's like an infinite explosion, except in this case, it's not destructive. It's invigorating, revitalizing, and phenomenal.

How can this limited human body experience that kind of infinite power?

Let's imagine that our bodies are like the banks of a river. The energy is the powerful water flowing between the banks. You can't control how powerful it is, how fast it's going, where it's going, or what it's going to do. You can only sit there feeling this incredible energy flowing through your body.

This is why we must *become* tantric. It is no small feat to allow this infinite energy to flow through us. We have to *be* those banks of the river. We have to contain it and completely release it all at the same time.

This is why we do breathwork, why we meditate. This is why we must be completely open and trust each other and allow the energy to flow between us. This is why there are no tricks in tantra. *We* are the vessel for the experience. *We* are the ones who must be prepared.

This is when incredible magic can happen.

PERSONAL EXPLORATION:
MY FAVOURITE GAME: SETS OF NINE

This is a very pleasurable and fun game to play. It helps us practise feeling excitement and relaxation at the same time. It's wonderful for learning ejaculation control. Plus, it plays between the g-spot and other exciting pleasure points.

Most importantly, it forges the bond between us. As we gaze into each other's eyes and play, energetic magic happens. We connect deeply. Energetic strands form with each movement, each breath.

How We Do It:

This can be done in any position where you are facing each other.

I am going to describe this exercise in a heterosexual union between vajra and yoni. Two males could use vajra and anus. Two women could use a finger or dildo and yoni.

First, make love for a while. Bring yourselves to a place where there is plenty of sexual energy and excitement between you. This isn't an exercise that you want to jump into; we want to have a lot of sexual excitement for both people.

Decide who is the mover and who is the receiver. The mover will be on top. The other simply receives and enjoys the experience.

Let's say the woman is on top. She will bring her yoni to the head of his vajra and put him inside of her to the base of the head and count "one." Then she will pull out just a little, but not so much that you lose contact. Then she will allow him inside her again, just the head, and count "two."

Continue this until you reach "eight." Then, gently plunge the vajra all the way in and count "nine." At this point, feel free to stay in this blissful pleasure for a bit before continuing.

That was round one.

Then do the same thing, counting one, two, three, up until seven. Then two deep plunges.

Then one, two, three until six, then three deep plunges.

Continue until you are in the final round, doing nine deep plunges. I leave what comes next up to your imagination.

It is beautiful to maintain eye-contact. Perhaps one or both of you counts out loud. Play with this in whatever way is the most pleasurable and wonderful for you.

This is an excellent exercise to do when premature ejaculation is a challenge. It allows us to play with stimulation and rest times. It teaches us how to be completely present.

If you get to the point where you think you are going to come, stop and take a break. Breathe and then continue.

Maybe you only get to the third set on the first try. Maybe the next time you get to the fifth. It is a wonderful way to create new neural pathways and teach us to gain full control with different sensations.

I intentionally call this a "game to play" because we really need to be light about this. The first time I played this was with a man whom I adored who struggled with ejaculating too soon. Early in our relationship, I asked him if he wanted to play a game – *this* game. And of course, he did.

We played it with the joy of two friends. This is when I realized I was as much of a player in the game as he was. His body was reacting to me as well. I started to feel it as his excitement rose. I could tell when he was heading to the edge at the same time he could. At that point, we would look at each other like two crazy kids ready to do something fun and then we would stop moving, breathe and work together to try to stay in the game. This bonded us in the deepest, most joyful ways. It was definitely our favourite game.

And let me tell you, it was a very good day when we were able to make it all the way to the ninth round.

CHAPTER 16

POLARIZING TO BECOME ONE

My lover is young and lovely.
We are hours into beautiful play,
But there is an impatience in him.
A worry that things aren't going well.
We sit in yabyum.
I hold his face
And look into his beautiful eyes.
"Imagine there are no goals."

He breathes deeply
And gently lays me on my back.
He slides deeper into me.
Holding my hands over my head.
He gazes into my eyes.
We move together.
And then it happens:
We become one

Deeply connected,
He moves me in complete surrender.
The look in his eyes

Changes from playfulness to concern.
I am totally open.
Totally vulnerable.
He is fully in control.

I can see the questions in his eyes.
Does he want this?
Does he want this responsibility?
I surrender a little more.
He knows I trust him.
And then I see his answer:
"Yes!"

Sweat falls from his brow.
He shakes it away.
Keeping our connection,
He moves me.
I surrender more.
We breathe together.
We moan together.
We move together.
Such bliss and wonder.
We are one.

Afterwards, as we lie together
He says, with a twinkle in his eye
And a thick accent,
"I think I'm really getting this tantra thing."

POLARIZING TO BECOME ONE

In regular sex, we can become intimate while staying quite separate from each other. Each of us has our own thoughts, desires, and internal balance. We know what we want to do with the other person. We have the chance to unite with another person. Together, we can create a new whole. This is where true bliss is. This is where we polarize into two halves and then unite back into the oneness of God/divinity.

We can do this through playing with the magnetism that naturally occurs between us.

We are magnetic creatures. We say things like "I am attracted to her" or "I am repulsed by him." Intrinsically, we know there is a magnetic charge between us, either drawing us in, pushing us away, or perhaps there is no charge at all.

To have energy flowing through us as a unit, one of us must be positive and the other must be negative. This is how electrical energy flows through a circuit. In regular sex, we are often "doing" things to each other, which puts both of us into a masculine role. We are both positive, in our own worlds, doing our own thing. This is why we end up having "friction" sex – two masculine energies moving against each other, creating excitement and orgasm.

And if we are both negative, then nothing happens at all.

In tantra, we know the masculine and feminine are very different energies. When we add them together, we can create something completely new and different: flowing energy within a whole.

Let's imagine that you and your partner are holding each other creating a new whole. Within that whole, you get to polarize into different roles. Through this polarization, we get to play with the magnetic energy flow between masculine and feminine. Ironically, by polarizing into masculine and feminine, we increase our connection and become united into one.

Let's see how this works in two major polarities: Giving & Receiving and Structure & Chaos.

Giving & Receiving

Let's say I look at my lover and I want to caress his skin. Once I know that he wants to be touched, I touch him gently. For us to fully unite, the greatest thing he can do is to completely surrender and receive me. As I feel him relax, let down his guards, and fully trust me, my hands practically start moving all on their own. My masculine desire to give is energized by his willingness and appreciation to receive.

I turn my mind off and let myself melt into the experience. My fingers seem to know where to go. The more my mind disappears, the more I can feel what he is feeling. My fingers stay in certain places longer and my whole body vibrates with his pleasure. Then they find other tender places. He doesn't tell me this. My fingers simply know.

The more we both drop into the experience, the line between giver and receiver completely disappears. We truly become one.

Of course, this can happen in sexual intercourse as well.

Imagine the thrill of the masculine of being *completely* received by another person. The receiver trusts you completely and has dropped all of their guards to you. They *desire* to receive everything you've got. Imagine what that feels like.

Imagine the thrill of the feminine for someone to trust *you* enough to show all of themselves to you. To give themselves completely to you and trust that you will receive them all. To actually feel the power of someone who is "all in" moving inside of you is an amazing feeling.

This creates an interplay where it doesn't matter who is giving and who is receiving because you slowly become one unit. The energy flows between you. It is absolutely blissful and wonderful.

Structure & Chaos

This classic picture shows Shiva and Shakti in the posture of yabyum. This shows us the dynamic of mas-culine structure/stillness and femi-nine movement/chaos.

In Hindu philosophy, Shiva and Shakti are the two aspects of God. Shiva is the masculine (sitting facing us) and Shakti is the feminine on his lap.

Notice what Shiva is doing. He is sitting tall, strong, and still. He is "holding space" for Shakti. He is protective, attentive, and strong. He isn't moving.

Shakti, on the other hand, is writhing in ecstasy. She is moving. She is fol-lowing wherever pleasure and ecstasy take her. She goes deeply into the chaos and mystery that is the feminine. She doesn't have to worry about structure or stability. She is fully held by Shiva.

The wilder she becomes, the stronger he becomes. The stronger he becomes, the wilder she is free to be.

Physically, his vajra is inside her yoni, but he is not moving. His vajra is the "thunderbolt" activating and energizing the feminine. She will shift and move intuitively to find the pleasure points that want to be activated. The more energy he sends into her, the wilder her orgasm.

As in the previous example, as they polarize into these two extremes, the powerful energy flowing between them unites them. They become one unit. As he activates and energizes her orgasmic state, he joins her there. His energy and her orgasm become one. They combine to ride the same orgasmic wave together.

This is where we misunderstand orgasm in regular sex where the man, generally, orgasms once and women can have multiple orgasms. This is what happens when we stay separate. However, when we join these energies together, we ride a much greater orgasmic creation.

POLARIZING COMPLETELY

The more we can polarize, the more heightened the energy dynamic. Yes, you could each go half way, but the energy and flow created will be much less than half. The more we polarize, the flow and connection increases exponentially.

What about the dot?

It's important to see that within each side of the yin and yang whole, there is a dot of the opposite energy.

Within the yang, there is a bit of yin and within the yin, there is a bit of yang. This means that even when you're being fully masculine, you also are a little bit feminine. We want to give completely, and yet still be aware of the other. We are still listening and observing and receiving feedback from our partner.

Similarly, when we're being feminine, we're not just being passive; we are still fully awake and present. We are fully following and listening and aware at the same time.

The masculine is structure and stillness, but there is also a part that responds to the feminine. Similarly, the chaos of the feminine has a little consciousness to be aware of the masculine. It's like holding hands within the experience.

GIVING COMPLETELY
DURING LOVEMAKING

When we make love, we want to let go and love completely – holding nothing back.

Lovemaking is a natural movement based on our desires to connect with another. There is no room for thoughts or fears. These will only put up barriers and turn lovemaking into something it isn't, something we want to accomplish, get something from, or be satisfied by. This might be sexual intercourse, but it isn't lovemaking.

We are made for love. We are made to give it without abandon and we are nourished to receive it. Love-making is literally the physical experience of that love.

So, why would we hold anything back? Well, for the same reasons that we hold back in everyday life: will they give the same amount? Will I be embarrassed? Maybe we've never experienced flowing love before. We don't even know what this feels like, so we go through the motions because we can't imagine letting our guards down enough with anyone (including ourselves) to love completely.

However, the joy comes in the flow of love. This is palpable. You can feel it. It is like an energy force drawing you together, flowing between you, and guiding your motions all at the same time.

PERSONAL EXPLORATION:
MAGICAL SOUL BREATHING

We were dancing very close – rumba, the dance of love.

We were kind of kissing, kind of looking at each other, mostly nose to nose, sometimes mouth to mouth. Our bodies were pressed together and as we danced, our bellies moved together. As my belly expanded, his contracted and vice versa. It wasn't intentional; our bodies were just that close together.

We naturally began to inhale each other's exhalations. Everything started feeling very different. We had entered an altered state, total bliss and peace-like nirvana. We had totally merged, lost in each other. He used to call it "going to *our* planet."

Soon, we could do it any time – walking down the street, sitting together, making love. All we had to do was touch noses and breathe a little and there we were. We would be instantly, deeply connected, like our souls had blissfully merged.

This breathing technique truly connects your spirits. Or perhaps when your spirits connect, you start to breathe this way. It works both ways. Like all techniques, it can't be forced. It has to be in flow with what is happening.

The technique: Simply inhale each other's exhalations. Sometimes this happens naturally. Sometimes, it's easier if one person takes the lead and breathes according to the other.

This breath becomes a powerful connecter when it syncs during intercourse. As the masculine energy moves and the feminine energy receives, the masculine exhales while the feminine inhales. Then the masculine retracts with an inhale, and the feminine releases with an exhale. When this happens, you are one organism moving and breathing together in ecstatic pleasure.

CHAPTER 17

HEALING THROUGH INTIMACY

One night I was lying naked with my lover, his hands caressing the sides of my body. We hadn't seen each other in a while. I was looking forward to making love with him.

But truthfully, I was upset about personal things – nothing to do with him. I wasn't in a sexy mood at all.

I had a choice to make. I could shut down what I was feeling inside and hope that our lovemaking changed my mood, or I could be honest, relax and allow whatever feelings to come up.

I decided to be honest. Instead of making love, I looked at him and almost immediately started to cry. I spoke about what was bothering me. He held me as I let it all flow out. He stroked my hair and kissed my tears, and I felt cherished and loved.

Nothing sexual happened at all, but we sure experienced tender intimacy.

Afterwards, he told me he was touched and honoured that I was so open and trusting with him. It blew him away that I felt he was safe enough to do this with and let down all of my guards.

The beautiful hug we lay in afterwards was as blissful as the most ecstatic love-making. To this day, I will never forget the feeling of him kissing my tears away.

HEALING THROUGH TANTRIC INTIMACY

The body is like an ocean, rich with hidden treasures.
Open its innermost chamber and light its lamp.
MIRABAI

Someone once asked the question: "How can I go to bed completely in love with my husband and then wake up in the morning furious at him for leaving crumbs in the bed?"

The answer is: "Because the love made you feel safe enough to drop your guards and begin a healing process. Things that have been bothering you are now rising to be resolved. You now feel safe enough to share."

This is how we can heal through intimacy.

Imagine being intimate and vulnerable with someone whom you trust completely. You can reveal your deepest self and they won't run away. What could you reveal? What would come up? What could we release from our consciousness?

Sometimes unwanted thoughts come into our minds – secrets that we don't even want to admit to ourselves. However, when our goal is healing and moving forward, they must be said.

The healing begins when we summon the courage to say it out loud. It is when we look into the eyes of another and allow this part of ourselves to be witnessed in the real world. This is scary because when we keep it hidden, we can pretend it isn't real. Once we tell someone, it is now in the world and has been witnessed by another.

This is where the loving connection is so important. When we know that the other respects and loves us, there is nothing that cannot be shared. Everything you might have done or thought or feared is only your past experiences and choices. They have nothing to do with the present moment.

However, as long as it is hidden, it wears on us. It follows us like a constant shadow. Expressed in the safety of tantric intimacy, it can be owned as part of your experience. Perhaps it can be forgiven, or maybe not judged at all. Maybe it is finally feeling deep sadness and grief.

In this space, maybe it feels right to be sexual (or maybe not). Maybe the loving touch is very healing. That your partner still desires union with you *even though* you've shared this hidden truth sends a deep and loving message to your soul.

HEALING OUR GENITALS

Our genitals often carry a lot of trauma, physically and emotionally and there are few opportunities to heal this area. Massage therapists can release tension in our shoulders and release scarring from injury, but there are very few professionals who are allowed to access our genital trauma.

Many women hold a lot of tension and trauma in their vagina from childbirth, from sex when it happens before she is fully aroused, or by anything entering her when she's not ready (or willing). They can be hurt from surgery and medical procedures, not to mention the emotional trauma from past experiences and the pressure to orgasm to please their partner. Many women feel completely numb in their yonis – they feel nothing at all.

Men can have trauma as well. I have one friend whose memory of his circumcision as a baby is so implanted in his mind that every time he gets aroused, he feels pain and fear. He identifies the end of his penis with pain and people celebrating, because that's what happened to him when he was a baby. Men have all kinds of trauma, everything from prostate exams to being kicked in the scrotum. Emotionally, they might experience performance anxiety, erectile dysfunction, etc.

Healing can be done during slow, conscious intercourse, or it can be done through gentle touch where both people are totally present and aware. There are many books and trainings that can teach you how to do healing yoni and lingam* massage**.

After a healing like this takes place, we will feel peaceful in our whole lives. The stress we carry in our genitals stresses us out all day long. Once it's healed, something very deep is restored – a certain sense of calm and peace. We might also have increased sensitivity. We will feel all kinds of new feelings. The act of being relaxed allows the tissues to be more receptive and alive and we can have new kinds of pleasurable sensations.

YONI HEALING STORIES

One of the first great tantric healings came through relaxing my yoni – this was during my trip to Jamaica with my husband. He was deep inside of me. We were still and I was trying to relax. (I talk about this experience in a previous chapter where the relaxation resulted in ecstasy, but there were a few of these types of healings that took place first.)

As I tried to relax, I realized how much I didn't *want* to, how *afraid* I was to relax. I didn't know what I was afraid of. I couldn't identify what my walls or issues were. All I knew was that the idea of relaxing my vagina brought up all kinds of fears and anxiety.

So I breathed. I quieted my mind. And I prayed for help.

---

* Lingam is another Sanskrit word often used to describe a penis or phallus, meaning "wand of light"

** There also is a growing field of people studying sexological bodywork who are learning to do this genital healing work.

Eventually, I was able to relax the muscles, and the tears started flowing. I cried and cried. I didn't know why. There wasn't a specific trauma being released that I can remember. Whatever it was, it was releasing out of me. This was all within slow, gentle, connected intercourse.

WHY DON'T WE LISTEN TO HER?

Once at a retreat, the women had to sit in circles of three and listen to our yonis "speak." I was really nervous. I was very new to all this at the time, and I was strangely uncomfortable with the nudity.

But most of all, I didn't want to hear what my yoni had to say.

And I was right to be worried.

When it was my turn, I had to put one hand on my yoni, close my eyes and say whatever came into my mind. One woman held space for me and the other wrote everything that she (my yoni) said so I could read it later.

Well, my yoni was furious. She told me she was sick of me using her to make men happy. She wished that I would listen to her. She wished that I would take her feelings into consideration. She didn't want to be hurt any more just because I didn't want to hurt a man's feelings if I wasn't sexually turned on or stimulated enough. She was sick of being used and sick of me not listening to her.

I couldn't believe I had ignored her for my whole life and that I was carrying so much anger towards myself inside.

Once I internalized the idea that nothing was to enter her until she called for it, a great peace rose inside of me. This was *my* body. Nothing would enter it again without my personal desire to draw it in. I was not here to be entered at the whim of someone else.

Within me was now truly sacred space.

ENTERING THE TEMPLE GATES

A woman's yoni is often called the "Temple Gates." There is something truly sacred about being allowed to enter. This is one of the greatest shifts that we need to make, in regular sex as well as tantric intimacy.

The feminine must not be entered until she is absolutely ready. Period.

Many people say that after someone breaks into their home, they feel a new discomfort. They truly feel violated. Someone broke in and entered their sanctuary without being invited. It takes time to heal and feel comfortable again.

Now let's imagine that our bodies are even more sacred than our homes. Our bodies hold all of who we are: dreams, gifts, challenges, divine callings, pain, struggle, joy, hopes, everything. We are each very sacred ground. This is where we *actually* live.

Is someone allowed to barge into to all of that?

This should be obvious, but the very fact that there is such a huge industry in sexual lubrication (long before same-sex relationships became so common), tells us, historically, it has been unimportant that a woman be aroused enough to be naturally lubricated before she is entered.

Every time something goes into a woman that she either doesn't want or isn't ready for, it does damage – mostly emotionally – in quite subtle ways. It also creates a physical "armouring" of the vagina. Many women feel very little in their yoni. This isn't simply due to childbirth or unwanted sex. It could result from having sex with someone you love but your body wasn't fully ready. It can also result from aggressive fingers or sex toys.

Understanding the connection of magnetic poles is a perfect solution.* When the lovemaking has truly stimulated her, her yoni will become engorged and wet. There will be a natural negative charge at her cervix and she will become

---

* This is fully described in the next chapter.

"magnetically ready" to be entered. In the same way that when a woman is aroused her yoni will become very wet and ready, this often happens for "bottoms" in anal intercourse.

Unfortunately, there is often an obligation to let someone inside of us, whether we want them to, or whether we are ready or not. This is so commonplace that we barely think it's something worth talking about. We are often in too much of a hurry to actually wait until they *desire* to be entered. If the other person isn't "ready," then we think we simply need to apply more lubrication.

This applies to all genders and orientations. We are all sacred. If the receiver comes to a place where they totally want the other to fill them, then they will know it. There is no question.

It is the same for oral sex. It is a completely different experience to have something shoved or put into your mouth, as opposed to you desiring to put something into your mouth because you are dying to do it.

The key is to slow down and be conscious of the amazing experience. When we realize it is an *honour* to be allowed to physically join with this other beautiful human, this adds a whole other level of awe and amazement to our experience.

The moment of entry is very exciting and the more highly charged it is, the more amazing it will be!

EXPERIENCING ONENESS

When sexual union is spiritual, it is very healing. It opens us up to something we can't describe. It isn't simply becoming naked and sexual; it's the process of dropping all of our guards, being completely vulnerable, and allowing ourselves to merge with another.

This creates a state of being beyond description. Every time we have this experience, we change inside. We experience divine oneness. We become everything in the world all at once, and yet we are still ourselves.

This experience creates a "pause" inside. It causes us to stop for a moment and look around. We have to integrate this new experience. We are no longer the same.

The physical world doesn't have the same hold on us. We deeply understand that there is more out there that we simply can't explain.

This is one of the greatest gifts of tantric intimacy: to relax, trust and merge with ourselves, the divine or another. When this happens, it heals us in ways that we not only can't describe, we aren't even aware of.

All we know is that afterwards, we are totally different and so much more peaceful.

EXERCISE: HOLDING SPACE FOR EACH OTHER TO HEAL

Being there for someone you love in a healing, intimate way is as equally euphoric and wonderful as the greatest sexual playtime. This is where we can bring all of who we are to a very real and intimate situation where both people can leave renewed, healed, and feeling deeply loved.

Many of us have old sexual wounds that need healing. Sometimes it is important to seek professional help. Often, we can do a lot with a trusted, loving partner. Oftentimes, choosing both is the best option.

To begin, it's important to understand that *we* don't heal other people. Each of has our own immune systems, nervous systems, physical and energy systems. Each of us has our own karmic paths to walk and our own connection to the divine. All true healing comes from within us – never from anyone else.

Our goal is to create an environment where we feel safe enough to let our guards down and truly go into the dark parts of ourselves where we have stored pain, guilt, shame, and trauma. We store them away in a strong box which is kept firmly locked with powerful and painful emotions. This is how we keep them buried so effectively and can walk through our day as if nothing happened.

Over time, what we have hidden away grows. Those things interfere with our daily lives and create barriers to connecting with ourselves and each other. When we get the chance, releasing them and healing is the answer.

Sexual healing is so powerful because energetically, our sexual organs are connected to our first and second *chakras*. These energy centres hold everything in our lives about safety, security, trust, and relationships. These are very fear-laden aspects of our lives. To open up sexually is to expose these aspects of our lives that cause the most fear.

In the following exercise, we'll assume we have partner A, who would like to heal, and partner B, who would like to help.

Step One: Complete Trust

This exercise must be done with someone you trust completely. Partner B must fully embrace agape and philia love from the first chapters of this book. You must do this on a strong foundation of 100% kindness, trust, safety, and respect.

This is not about Partner A needing to trust the other in this moment. The trust must already exist. If Partner B needs to say, "Just trust me," then don't do this exercise yet. This shouldn't be a forced trust. The trust must be the reality of your relationship, all day long. If it has to be said, then it isn't there right now.

Step Two: Holding Space & Witnessing

Partner B is there to simply "hold space" and witness the other. They take no active role in the process. Partner B must follow the A's lead. Partner B can follow intuitively. However, be careful of taking on the role of "healer." You give no suggestions. You trust the intuition of A. Partner B is only witnessing the healing journey of Partner A and the divine. You are holding space in this physical world for them.

Step Three: Listening for Guidance

The entire exercise is guided by the intuition of Partner A. Especially if you are trying to heal deep trauma from the past, you must always move at the speed of Partner A's psyche. It might take 30 different "sessions" over a long period of time, but each session will result in real and lifelong healing. It might be the most subtle change, but it will have ripple effects throughout their life.

Step Four: Holding Each Other Afterwards

Whatever your experience is, it's important to spend time holding each other afterwards. It is especially nice to lie like spoons with Partner B on the outside holding Partner A. Lay together for as long as feels right. This is the time where whatever happened will consolidate and become permanent. Plus, it is loving and wonderful for both of you.

Possibilities:

You could choose to do something very specific in order to heal from the past.

You may simply choose to make slow, beautiful love together when one of you is feeling very vulnerable. The act of lovemaking in a difficult time can be incredibly healing – tears mixed with pleasure often end in laughter... and then more tears and more pleasure.

You could choose to do simple lingam and yoni healing massage. You can read books about various techniques to try. Remember that you are intuitive and fully connected to the divine.

Simply being present with your partner is the first step. Then, just as in the above three steps, allow Partner A to guide your fingers. Perhaps they want a soft touch "here" or press deeper there. This could be inside or outside of the yoni. It could be anywhere on the vajra and scrotum. Simply set your intention, trust your intuition, and allow magic to happen.

A Personal Story:

I was sexually abused as a young girl by a neighbour. As a result, I had very specific triggers that would make me go wild. If you grabbed my wrist to move me – even if we were only playing around – I would panic and punch you... hard. (I was a very shy and peaceful person. This was way outside my normal behaviour.)

For the first part of my life, I didn't think about it much. I just knew that I didn't like to be grabbed like that, and that I would hit you if you did.

When I started doing personal work, I realized I didn't have to live with this trigger. I also discovered I had deep trust issues with men. I didn't know how to deal with them.

At one point (before I discovered tantra), I was going through a dark night of the soul and I prayed for help. I got a vision of myself lying on the bed and my husband was holding my hands over my head while making love to me.

The idea filled me with fear, so I left it alone. The vision kept coming back, over and over again.

One night, I shared my vision with him. This wasn't something we would ever have done. He couldn't hold my wrist walking down the street; there's no way I would have allowed it sexually. He knew this, so he had some misgivings about it. This was in the midst of my healing from the breast lumps, so he was open to doing anything that would help me get better.

I told him that I might cry – but that it was OK. I needed to cry. Obviously, he would stop if I asked him to. I asked him to hold my hands over my head and make love to me in whatever way he felt called to. I had to learn to trust again.

And we did it.

I cried and cried and cried. I give him such credit for being able to be present and to hold the space for me while I did. It's incredibly hard for partners to witness us in pain, but he was able to and I am so thankful. Afterwards, I was truly different. I wasn't "fully healed," but it was definitely a step forward in my journey.

Note: I am not recommending this as any kind of technique to heal from sexual abuse. It is simply the vision that came *to me*. It was exactly the medicine that I needed in that moment.

What's important is what *you* see in this moment for you. If you see nothing right now, then *that* is your answer. Perhaps you need to find professional help. Maybe you need gentle lovemaking if you're comfortable with it, allowing it to go wherever you need. It's all about following your guidance. It's there and it's perfectly specific to you.

CHAPTER 18

CONNECTING THE YONI AND VAJRA

We went to Jamaica for some quality time together. It was the perfect chance to explore tantric lovemaking. We had each read some books and were ready to try some of the ideas – mostly non-ejaculatory sex and playing with deep sexual connection.

We'd been married for a long time and truly had a wonderful sex life. If it hadn't been for this deep knowing within me that there was more, we could have easily continued having "regular," ejaculatory sex forever. But we were in Jamaica and we were going to explore what else was possible.

As soon as we took ejaculation off the table, everything changed. Our love-making slowed way down. We spent more time fooling around. We kissed a lot. We explored each other as if we'd never done it before.

Of course, by the time he entered me, I was incredibly wet, aroused, and dying to have him inside me. *This* is when things got wild.

He lay on his back and I climbed on top. I slowly lowered myself onto him and let him go deep inside. I had read about relaxing my yoni in intercourse and wanted to try it. So we tried to stay relatively still.

My yoni came alive. It was like her deepest part reached down and grabbed the head of his vajra. I wasn't doing anything. Her muscles were doing it all on their own. Her walls started pulsing and massaging the shaft of his vajra. Our genitals were having their own little party and we were just along for the ride.

If I shifted a little bit, it would stimulate certain "sweet" spots deep inside and my entire yoni would pulse like mad. Crazy orgasmic energy flowed into my whole body. It was all I could do to keep breathing. As it subsided, I would shift somewhere else, and the orgasmic energy would fly through me again.

Each time it happened, my husband would say, "Oh my god. Do you feel that?!" He could feel it through his whole body, too.

This is when lovemaking truly became an adventure. We realized that even after decades of sexual experience, neither of us had *any* idea what these bodies of ours were actually capable of.

Needless to say, our vacation was filled with six to seven hours of love-making every day. In between, we had the most beautiful, intimate connection. It was like there was this loving candle lit between us all of the time, in and out of the bedroom.

Pure and complete bliss.

RULES ARE INTERESTING - WITH EXCEPTIONS

Our bodies can connect in many ways. This chapter describes the wonder of what can happen in heterosexual union. It is the opposite of how the majority of people have intercourse and is quite a shift from friction sex to the magnetic flow of tantric intimacy.

I want to add an important note.

Human beings are all incredibly unique and special. The danger in sharing a philosophy like this is that it simply does not apply to all people in all situations.

Sometimes, life has shut us down in ways that have closed us off to certain kinds of stimulation and pleasure. Sometimes, our masculine and feminine polarities are thrown off due to being overly-controlled in our lives by partners, parents, and authority figures. This can wreak havoc in our physical bodies, relationships, and our sexuality. This chapter might open new doors of healing for you.

Sometimes, the theory simply doesn't apply to you. Although this chapter covers what happens when a vajra and yoni are magnetically connected, there may also be important ideas for all orientations.

It may tell you something of the magic of vajras and yonis. Within same-sex couples, it might be interesting to see how this magnetic dynamic works within your union. There is a lot of discussion about the feminine since it is by far the least understood. If you're into yonis, there will be lots of food for thought here.

In the end, we want to explore everything in a tantric way. We want to connect with our partner authentically in this moment and with the most love possible. There are no rules and no ways that we *should* be.

There is only love, connection and exploration.

Feeling Magnetic Energy Flow Between Us

Previously, we looked at how we can play with uniting masculine and feminine energy into one unit. We also looked within our bodies to find masculine and feminine polarities as well. We can also play with this in sexual intercourse.

Visualize each of us being magnetically charged like a battery. One pole is masculine – it pushes outward and away. The other is feminine and it draws everything inward and towards itself.

The masculine positive pole is the end of the penis. His heart centre is his negative pole.

For the feminine, her heart centre is her positive pole and her cervix is her negative pole.

We can feel this emotionally when the feminine wants to pour her love out to everyone, especially her lover. The masculine energy wants to give strength, stability, and power to the feminine. The more energy flowing from both people, the more energy flows between them.

Stimulating the Polarities

Intuitively we know that before sexual union happens, both partners must be "ready." Simplistically, the man must be hard and the woman should be ready and wet. In fact, we know the harder he is and the wetter she is, the *more* ready both are.

Now we can take this a step further by bringing our whole beings into this "readiness."

We now want to increase the charge in the entire electrical circuit. To do this, we must stimulate the *positive* poles.

When we stimulate the positive pole, it becomes more energized, more masculine, more giving, more outward and excited. As this happens, our negative pole becomes more feminine. It becomes more receptive, relaxed, and inward. The two poles are completely connected like two ends of a battery.

We often stimulate in the other what *we* like to have stimulated, which doesn't work in a heterosexual couple. For example, because men like to have their vajra stimulated (their positive pole), they will naturally stimulate a woman's clitoris. Because women like to have their heart and breasts stimulated (their positive pole), they will want to love up their partner. There are times when both of these are lovely, but they are having the opposite effect we want in order to have magnetic, tantric union.

STIMULATING THE FEMININE PARTNER

Let's discuss how we stimulate the woman's positive pole both physically and energetically.

Physically, we want to stimulate her breasts. There is a direct internal line from the breasts to the yoni. When breasts are caressed, this makes her yoni more relaxed, receptive, and magnetically negative. Her yoni will become engorged and wet. and the negative charge creates a vacuum-effect where she will desire something to enter and fill her.

It's important to note that many women have de-sensitized breasts for many reasons – could be breast-feeding children, or it could be harsh handling. It may take some time and gentle loving to bring them back to a place of sensual sensitivity.

If we stimulate her clitoris, we are stimulating her negative pole. This causes her yoni to tighten and become more masculine. The more she is stimulated here, her body will start to desire release through orgasm, much like a man. Then, when she is entered, we will have two positive poles coming together, resulting in "friction" sex. This is fun, but we won't be able to circulate the energy between us because the magnetic flow has been stopped. However, her genitals can still be caressed and played with. When we are gentle and slow, it arouses her whole being.

What we want is to stimulate her heart centre energetically. This is the key to opening her yoni to desire union.

How do we do this?

Love her like crazy. Do things that make her feel loved. When the feminine is cherished, her heart will literally pump harder. When you simply love her and are happy to be with her, regardless of whether you are going to have sex or not, you might not have to do any other "foreplay" at all.

Can you picture it? A man takes his love out for dinner, opens her door, buys her flowers and treats her like a queen all night. Then they get home, and what happens? She practically rips his clothes off and begs him to be inside of her!

Everything we do must be authentic. If he wines and dines her because he thinks it will make her want to have sex later, this doesn't work. He has to do it because he loves her and wants to honour her and treat her like the exquisite goddess she is.

STIMULATING THE MASCULINE PARTNER

Most men love having their positive pole, their vajra, stimulated physically. It could be fondling, oral sex, or any attention at all. In the same way there is a direct line between a woman's heart centre and her yoni, there is a line connecting his vajra with his heart as well.

It's too simplistic to say that when you touch a man's vajra or have sex with him that his heart opens. However, when we genuinely love and spend time with him sexually, this can melt away a lot of the guards around his heart. His physical, sexual excitement opens his whole being for deeper connection in more ways than sex.

We also want to look at how we stimulate the man energetically.

In the same way that many women don't feel "loved enough," many men don't feel they are treated like the man they are inside. Most cultures have no rites of passage that allow men to step into their true manhood. In fact, many men have been very emasculated throughout their lives and made to feel like they aren't good enough. This has caused huge challenges for us in the bedroom.

We want the man to know he is more than enough. We want to honour him and make sure he knows that he satisfies us completely, that he is absolutely "man enough." We want them to know we are thrilled to be with *them* and we totally trust them to hold us and be there, no matter what. It is respecting their masculine power. It is honouring it and being thrilled to receive every ounce of it.

REFLECTIONS ON THE NATURE OF OUR RELATIONSHIP

You can see how these energetics are quite dependent on the nature of our relationship.

It is easy to show love and affection towards the woman when she looks at you like you're the most amazing man that ever walked the Earth. It's easy to buy her flowers when you know she will appreciate and receive the gift completely. It's easy to spend hours caressing her when you know she is absolutely thrilled to be near your masculine essence.

Similarly, it is easy for her to be excited to be with this strong masculine power when you have shown her all day long that you always have her back. She will look at you like you are all she will ever need when you genuinely give everything you've got to the relationship.

It all only works when it is actually our reality. When we don't feel this love, respect, and honour for the other person, they know this deep down. Tantra asks us to be honest and real – no faking it or creating a fantasy around it. What is the truth? This truth is always what will appear in our lovemaking.

We need to realize the truth and then move towards where we want to be. It's all a journey. We don't have to be perfect right from the beginning.

FINDING THE SECRET CHAMBER

Did you know there is a "secret chamber" deep within the temple gates?

When a woman's yoni is fully relaxed and negatively charged, the head of the vajra will be magnetically drawn deep into a place that is not normally reached during friction sex. It's called the Secret Chamber.

Just behind the cervix, the vagina continues. This spot is not normally accessed because it would hurt if touched in regular, friction sex. However, when a woman can completely relax her yoni, the head of the vajra will be naturally drawn upwards toward it. This definitely doesn't happen all of the time, but it is super fun when it does.

This is extremely pleasurable for both partners. When the woman is on top, she can manoeuvre and control the angle and movement to allow the vajra to put pressure against these spots. Describing this pleasure is impossible.

For the man, there is a phenomenal sense of being "so deep inside." Often, she will vibrate with orgasmic waves. These vibrations will vibrate his vajra, causing pleasure waves through his whole body. Soon they are moving together as she guides him to just the right spots.

THE MAGICAL YONI

This relaxation of the vagina is a big shift from regular sex. In regular sex, there is the goal of being "tight" so the male has heightened sensation. This is a very common thought today; some men will even say they prefer anal intercourse because it is tighter than their partner's vagina. However, this desire to be like a tight cylinder for the penis to pump in and out of is only interesting in procreative-style sex.

The vagina is in no way a cylinder. It is an intricate womb of sensory receptors, luscious folds, and subtle pleasure points. When relaxed, she can expand wide enough to birth a child. This is how elastic and fluid she is meant to be.

When she is fully relaxed she comes alive. This is when we find out she is not a static cylinder. The more we relax into our lovemaking, the more alive our yoni becomes. She has fingers and tongues that drive any man wild who is blessed to feel it. This is often called "milking" the vajra.

This is one of my favourite moments if I'm with a man and she suddenly "comes alive." Every single man's eyes pop wide open and they take a sharp breath in... It's so much fun!

The woman does not do this actively. She is simply relaxing and moving gently with her partner. She is positioning the vajra in the deep places within her that stimulate her greatest pleasure. As these points are touched and pressed, she relaxes deeper into them and the fingers and tongues do their magic.

It is important not to set this as a goal. As with all infinite things, we cannot predict what will happen. When we try to predict or repeat something that has happened before, it will often elude us.

BATHED IN AMRITA

It has become a common goal in regular sex to get a woman to "squirt." In the tantric world, this fluid is often called "amrita." Amrita has many meanings in Sanskrit, including God's food and immortality.

In tantric intimacy, the release of amrita is a natural part of the deep connection experience. As the woman's yoni holds the vajra deep inside and various pressure points inside are stimulated, amrita can flow. It isn't like the quick rise and fall of a "squirting orgasm." It is just a long, slow, constant flood of happy fluid flowing out of her.

MOVING AS A UNIT

Once connected, the goal is to remain connected. You don't want to break the circuit. If the man starts to move in and out, the woman will not know what is happening and she will tense. Her yoni will become positive with the tension.

Once connected, allow your genitals to become a unit, like you've just "plugged in." Leave the connection strong and focus elsewhere. Kiss. Caress each other. Breathe together. Moan. Scream. You are free to explore in any way you want with the rest of your bodies.

Within the connection, it may feel good to rock your hips together. When the man and woman stay connected, his hip bones actually stimulate her entire clitoral area. The clitoris extends like a "V" down under the labia from the clitoris. This pressed-in connection and rocking stimulates the woman's entire orgasmic system. There is no need to stimulate her tiny clitoris point. Depending on your connection and angle, this can stimulate her entire clitoral system.[*]

---

[*] For a brilliant understanding about how women are sexually wired, please read *Women's Anatomy of Sexual Arousal*, by Sheri Winston.

Tune into the natural movement of the *two* of you. Because you are a unit, all movement of the hips will be together. You become super-conscious of the point where you are joined, tuning into that place and moving from there. This is very different and extremely enjoyable.

One of the reasons men often want to move in and out is because they are concerned they are getting soft. This is fine. Being hard or soft isn't as important as we think. It is more important when we are having regular sex for 20 minutes. However, we are connecting intimately for hours. There is no need to be super hard or hard at all. Flow with what is real. There may be times you are inside and your erection is completely gone, but you are still connected. This is perfect. You can still feel everything, and your partner can still feel the connection – physically and energetically.

That being said, there are no hard and fast rules. If you want to come out a bit and play and then come back to deep connection, it's all good. We always want to trust our intuition.

PERSONAL EXPLORATION:
ENERGY FLOW EXERCISE

Let's picture a man and a woman sitting in front of each other. Picture their positive and negative energy poles. The man's heart is negative and his vajra is positive. The woman's heart is positive and her yoni is negative.

Imagine a circle of energy flowing from her heart to his and his energy flowing from his vajra to her yoni.

You can play with this energy anywhere. Sit in front of your partner and see if you can feel the energy circulating between you – from vajra to yoni, up to her heart, over to his heart and then down to his vajra. It is especially fun to visualize and feel this circuit while having intercourse.

You can play with this energy between people of all sexes. I once did this at a retreat where I was the one with an energetic vajra and the man in front of me had an energetic yoni. We could circulate this energy just as easily as the other way around. In fact, I actually learned a lot from this exercise because I realized that, at that time, I was *much* more comfortable being the masculine one with the vajra. I was comfortable in the giving role and I had a much harder time relaxing and receiving. This led to lots of interesting thought and definitely added to my journey.

CHAPTER 19
SUBTLE MAGIC

We often think about movement in sexual intimacy, but there are also magical sensations and experiences to be had within stillness.

I remember the first time it happened. We had been making gentle love for quite a while, moving intuitively, totally in our own world. He was on top and deep inside of me.

While maintaining our connection, he slowly stretched his legs out to lay them on top of mine. He held my hands gently on the floor over my head. It felt like every inch of our skin was touching each other. Our bodies had completely melted together.

As he gazed into my eyes, our lips gently touched, and we fell into a peaceful stillness. Our bodies were throbbing, sweating, and vibrating, even though we were completely still, like we were effortlessly holding each other in the eye of a hurricane.

We stayed like that for the longest time, gazing at each other while our bodies hummed together.

Not only were we in total ecstasy, we were being bathed in it.

THE MAGIC IN THE SPACES

As the sun goes down in its well,
Lovers enter the seclusion of God.
Late at night we meet like thieves
Who have stolen gold, our candlelit faces.
RUMI

What makes music beautiful and compelling is the dance between the musical notes and the silent pauses. The spaces in between are equally important and filled with charge, just like the physical notes.

This is the same in life. Within the spaces of our lives there are many wonderful things to discover.

When we change our lens, we see everything in the world, plus everything in between. We hear the notes and the rests. We feel the movement and the stillness.

This is especially true in lovemaking. There is great pleasure in the movement and excitement of intimacy, but have you noticed the quiet times as well?

Our genitals are filled with the most erogenous sensory receptors of the body. However, those receptors don't have to be sliding against each other to be stimulated and alive.

It's like shaking hands with someone. There is a certain quality to a firm handshake. Then, if we gently touch someone's hand, you can feel a little more. It is a bit more personal. If you lightly place your hand on the other, just being there and breathing, something else passes between you. An energy? An awareness? Something.

It's very similar sexually.

Sometimes, when we connect with each other, fireworks go off inside. Other times, there is only great stillness. This deep connection seems to "still your soul," like you are floating in a calm lake, completely relaxed and peaceful.

Think of the moments where you find yourself looking at each other and smiling. How long can we stay there and enjoy that happy bliss? We often feel it in the "afterglow" of sexual play, the time that we spend spooning or chatting afterwards. The energy is quiet and we are connected and loving with each other.

We can have these moments during our intimate play. When we make love for hours at a time, it is not all feverish movement. The energy rises and falls naturally. There are peaks of crazy excitement and movement, and then the energy falls and you simply hold each other, caress each other's skin, chat a bit, or relax.

These moments in the quiet are incredibly nourishing, healing and bonding. You can almost feel your soul smiling.

THE CALM IN THE VALLEY

When we are deeply connected in intercourse, there is another kind of magic that can happen that is hard to explain. The best I can describe it is what I imagine it would feel like to fly through a wormhole. Our bodies deeply connect and plug into each other and our "infinities" connect. This can take place through physical intercourse between a male and female, two males, or through energetic intercourse between women.

This happens spontaneously. You can't plan it or do it as an exercise. It often happens in between energetic love-making. As you naturally come down after a peak of energy, in the valley there is a beautiful calm. It's as if you have been blissfully climbing and now you've found the most beautiful green meadow to rest in together. You are still deeply connected. You are still one. Not only do you feel the bliss of that union, your hearts are pounding together, your sweat is intermingled, your breath is synced, and you float between being aware of the stillness and getting completely lost in it.

Strangely, it takes some discipline to allow ourselves to stay in this bliss. Perhaps it's because we aren't accustomed to relaxing and enjoying the quiet in life, so we are also unable to be still in lovemaking.

The key is to be fully present to our reality in each moment. If there is energy moving, then flow with it. If the air is still, then bask in the infinite stillness.

I once asked our friend from the story in this chapter what it felt like for him. How would he explain that deep stillness to someone who had never experienced it before? He responded, "When I am inside you and still, it's like the feeling of submerging yourself into a nice warm bath. Everything feels so relaxed and warm; except it's like that warm feeling starts around my vajra and then enters my entire body that way. You don't have to jump around and splash in the tub to make it feel good. You just want to relax and go with the feeling."

One day, I was talking to a friend of mine who had never studied tantra and something about this came up. He kind of looked at me sideways and then said, "It's so weird that you say that. Last night I was with this guy. We had been enjoying sex for a while but then we both got tired. I hadn't ejaculated, so I just stayed inside and spooned with him from behind. And it felt so unbelievable! I can't explain it. I felt such love and closeness and peace flowing between us. I'd never felt anything like it. And we were only lying there, totally still."

SLOWING DOWN

The first thing we need to do is slow down. This allows us to feel everything that is happening in the moment. We notice how soft our partner's skin is. We notice their breathing and the heat of their body. We notice whether they moan when we touch the small of their back, so we might explore more there.

We are aware of ourselves, our excitement, our nervousness, and our thrill to be with this person. We are aware of the other person. We look into their eyes. We feel their breath, their skin, and we sense all of the emotions they are feeling.

This slowness allows us to truly merge – like two dancers playing with each other, experimenting with each other's energies. It's like wandering into each other's energy field, not knowing how the connection will happen, just enjoying the process and the dance.

You'll spend more time kissing and looking into each other's eyes and each breath shared, each moment spent looking at each other deepens your connection. The magic lies in the depth of that connection.

TUNING IN TO SUBTLETY

A friend of mine once compared tantric intimacy to smoking cigars. A cigar connoisseur will allow the smoke to enter their mouth and then savour the flavours, the bouquet, and the subtle nuances of the cigar. They enjoy each second, searching for a new taste and experience.

Part of the journey of becoming tantric is tuning in to the subtleties around us. There are subtle feelings you will notice with your lover. You will start to know how they feel, without them saying or doing anything to tell us so. You will naturally respond to them. Your mind is easily quiet and your other senses are fully aware of everything happening around you.

When we are relaxed and our guards are down, our subtle energy channels open and connect with each other. It's like all the walls that hold our energy in and protect us open, and we have an infinite amount of energy connecting us. All of those energy channels communicate with each other. We pass love and bliss back and forth, building upon each other.

When we add all the joys of physical intimacy and pleasure to this, it's like we "amp up" those energy channels and go on a crazy adventure together. We have no idea what is coming. All of these channels are open – each of them with infinite power and possibilities. Our physical bodies are simply the power-generating station fuelling our space-ship into other lands beyond our current imaginings.

PERSONAL EXPLORATION: MAGIC OF STILLNESS ALL DAY LONG

At various times in your day, I'd like you to practise experiencing the magic of stillness. I'd like you to feel the subtleties all around you.

Let's say you're walking down the street. Find a bench or a patch of grass to sit on. Sit completely still and experience everything around you. Without moving your head, look around you. What do you see? Look at the big things. Look at the very small details.

What do you smell? How many smells can you identify? Let these smells fill you.

What can you hear? Are there people talking? Dogs barking? Can you hear the wind? Cars? Crickets? Are there very subtle sounds? Allow yourself to open to all of the sounds around you.

What do you feel? Can you feel the earth beneath you? Can you feel the sun or the wind on your skin? Are you cold or hot? How do you feel inside? Are you nervous? Upset? Happy? Content?

What do you taste? How many things can you taste in your mouth right now?

Then, take a deep breath and let all of these sensations flow through you. No thoughts. No goals. Simply notice all of them.

Now, imagine being *that* present while making love. Imagine incorporating this level of awareness lying naked with someone you love and adding the excitement of passion.

There are infinite sensations you could experience in stillness, in movement, in connection, in simply being together.

Endless possibilities.

SECTION V:

EXPERIENCING TANTRIC HAPPINESS IN OUR EVERYDAY LIVES

The winds of God's grace are always blowing.
All we have to do is raise our sails.

RAMAKRISHNA

TRULY BECOMING TANTRIC

One of the amazing things about writing a book is the personal transformation that it brings. We can have all kinds of ideas throughout our lives, learn great philosophies, and draw conclusions from our life experiences. Then, when you write it all down, you realize your logic isn't quite right. It doesn't apply to all people and all situations. Plus, our philosophy often displays our deepest woundings. (Kind of like someone coming out of a bitter breakup with the opinion that "all women/men are crazy...")

As I came to these "holes in my understanding," I would meditate, pray and chat with others, and then a realization would hit me. Aha! I knew how to write that part of the book. More importantly, I had discovered the answer to the hole in my *own* personal logic. I had found an answer to something that I was struggling with.

Whenever this happened, I would feel euphoric. During one of these moments of happiness, Jim (my previous teacher) called me out of the blue. I happily told him about what an incredible process writing this book has been and how great life felt.

He said, "That is so great to hear! Well, it's like I used to tell you, life isn't about saving the world. It's about saving ourselves."

This is the wonder of *becoming tantric*. It is the path to our *own* personal happiness. It moves us from confusion to clarity. From fearful to confident. From hiding our truth to complete and kind honesty. From limitation to openness.

All we have to do is live and explore our everyday lives. We bring all of who we are to every moment whether we are making love, leading a board meeting, or taking the kids to soccer. Every moment has the potential for happiness and contentment.

Ironically, this is also how we end up "saving the world." You may not notice it, but you will have a ripple effect on everyone with whom you come into contact. People will feel happier when they are around you. They will tell you things that they don't tell anyone. They will walk away inspired and they won't know exactly why.

If you're lucky, you will never know the full effect you have had on those around you.

In the bible, Matthew says, "Let not the left hand know what the right hand is doing." If we think that we know the effects of what we do, we will easily be taken out of our blissful happiness. It becomes easy to get caught up in a saviour mentality, thinking that we somehow have things figured out more than others. Not only is this an ego-trap, but we will act to have a certain effect on others instead of listening inside for guidance. We will get attached to the outcomes of our actions and we will not enjoy the process and experience of our life.

Our journey is to save ourselves. In doing so, we have a natural and beautiful effect on the world around us.

CHAPTER 20

ANCHORING IN ECSTASY

Many years ago, I found complete bliss flying through the air as my car was about to crash.

I was 24 years old, six months pregnant, and on my way to work. I lived out in the country and the roads were icy. I was driving along and suddenly my car started spinning on the ice. I realized I was completely out of control and I was heading towards a nine-foot ditch.

As my car spun in circles on the icy road, I thought I was going to die. I put one hand on my baby and one hand on the steering wheel, closed my eyes, and prepared for the crash.

I should have been terrified, but I felt quite the opposite. Time slowed down. I felt a kind of love like never before. The car was flying through the air in slow motion and I was completely at peace. There was no stress or tension in my body. I was totally happy and blissful. I will never forget that feeling.

After what seemed like hours, the car hit the ground. The windshield smashed, the entire front end of the car was caved in. Yet there I was, and my baby and I were just fine.

I had no idea what I experienced until the next day when I was listening to the radio and, strangely, they were talking about the 23rd Psalm in the bible. This was strange because it wasn't a religious radio station. It was beautiful serendipity.

The Lord is my shepherd; I shall not want.
He makes me lie down in green pastures:
he leads me beside still waters.
He restores my soul: he leads me in paths of righteousness
for his name's sake.
Even though I walk through the valley of the shadow of death,
I will fear no evil: for you are with me;
your rod and your staff comfort me.
You prepare a table before me in the presence of my enemies;
you anoint my head with oil;
my cup overflows.
Surely goodness and mercy shall follow me all the days of my life:
and I will dwell in the house of the Lord for ever.

The man being interviewed spoke about how when we release control to God, we experience peace and tranquility like never before. This was what I experienced. I felt I had the whole world at my fingertips. I felt love and joy and bliss. There was no fear, no worries, even in the possibility of dying. I was "lying beside still waters," totally at peace.

ECSTASY IS NOT DEPENDENT ON CIRCUMSTANCES

One of my favourite stories is about the sage, Saraha, who left his life of luxury with the king to study with his teacher in a little hut on the cremation grounds. As he studied with her, he transformed. He found such immeasurable bliss that he would dance around the funeral pyres in pure ecstasy.

Can you imagine? Dancing in pure joy between the funeral pyres? This seems to be impossible. We generally assume we can only be happy in happy situations. It's almost considered rude to be happy when others are suffering. How is this possible?

Our true joy comes from within and is not dependent on our circumstances. All kinds of events can happen in our lives that seem to make us happy or sad. When the effects of these experiences wear off, we return to whatever our "resting state" is. If we are generally happy, sad, ecstatic or angry no matter what happens, at the end of the day, we will return to our "resting state."

The goal is to create a resting state of ecstasy.

WHAT IS ECSTASY?

I am not a collection of incantations known only to experts.
I am not a ladder to be climbed,
a sequence for piercing energy centres in your body.
I am not found at the end of a long road.
I am right here.
RADIANCE SUTRAS

What is ecstasy? We imagine ecstasy is all about crazy orgasms and fireworks and exalted states of consciousness, but it can also exist in our everyday life when "nothing" in particular is happening.

Ecstasy literally means to "stand outside of yourself." We are standing outside of our physical existence and feeling our infinite self – our oneness – when we are in ecstasy. We are not consumed by our physical lives. We do not feel trapped and limited. We feel our timeless "oneness" as well as this world.

Any time we connect with this timeless aspect of ourselves, we can't help but feel blissful. Oneness is blissful by nature.

When we experience this in our lives, we become filled with an incredible gratitude for everything. It's like looking at our lives through the eyes of the divine. We see the smallest flower and we realize what a miracle it is. We become so thankful for the food on our table. We realize there is a gift in each simple breath.

Then we look at our loved ones. If we have children, we look at them and can barely believe what we see. We realize the absolute miracle they are. When we look at our intimate partner, we become overwhelmed with the gift that we have found this person and get to be together.

When we walk down the street, we are thrilled with all of the different people we see. All the different sizes, shapes, emotions, and states of being are simply a sign of this incredibly complex and interesting world we live in.

When we feel like this, there are no thoughts. There is an emptiness, and yet a complete fullness at the same time. This makes no sense to our rational mind, which believes that we need to attach ourselves to something to feel anything. Yet, when we detach and feel our complete "nothingness," there is an amazing sense of freedom and happiness.

We've all had glimpses of ecstasy. You wouldn't be reading this right now if you hadn't had glimpses of it, because these moments are the seeds that open us up and tell us there is more in the world.

BECOMING EMPTY

Become like a hollow bamboo... nothing inside.
And suddenly the moment you are the hollow bamboo, the divine lips are on you.
The hollow bamboo becomes a flute
and the song starts.

OSHO

Moments of ecstasy happen when we are empty. In this state, there is pure bliss.

We often struggle with being empty. In the West, emptiness tends to mean a lack, a void. We feel like we are missing something. Emptiness means nothingness. This is unnerving to our western minds.

Emptiness in Eastern thought is different. Where there is nothing, there is pure potential. Emptiness allows us to hear what is within the void. The emptiness is not nothing. There is great presence in the emptiness, and we just have to shift our senses to experience it.

In order to become hollow, we must set aside everything that is filling us right now - all of our thoughts, our issues and everything with which we define ourselves. We set it all aside in order to allow divine energy to fill us - to allow the divine lips to play music through us.

What this feels like is impossible to describe. **We just have to do it.** We have to simply release everything and breathe something different into us.

NEW REFERENCE POINTS FOR LIVING

Our challenge is that we have attachments in this world. We want to keep our world like it is. We believe all the "stuff" in our minds will keep us stable and secure in a world that is constantly changing.

Let's imagine we are ships in the harbour, anchored to hold us still. What we are attached to in life act like those anchors. Perhaps we are attached to health, youth, marital status, or being a parent. Maybe we are attached to our status in the community and how we are perceived by others.

When being healthy, married, employed, wealthy, etc., are what bring us stability, we are in trouble because all of these things can change overnight. These are the attachments the Buddhists say are the source of all suffering. Not only do we spend a lot of energy trying to maintain them, we live in constant fear of losing them.

We need to find new "reference points" in our lives. We need to find new "anchors" that never change, that can never be taken away from us. Can you imagine having deep anchors into the stillness of the universe? Being connected to a place you know will never change, that will always be there for you?

This is how we find true peace within a constantly-changing world.

These new anchors are moments in our lives that connect us deeply to what is *real* and unchanging. These are moments when we feel oneness and stillness. There is no opposite to this feeling. We cannot lose this. It doesn't change. It simply *is*.

They can be very profound moments that break our rational minds, or they can be very small things.

They could be small things, like the timeless feeling of watching your children sleep, or the inner stillness of watching the sunrise. Or the peace of relaxing into your chair with a cup of tea and a good book. Or they can be experiences your rational mind can't understand at all.

One of my reference points comes from being a mother. When my son was born he was a tiny little baby in my arms. Today, he is a tall man who towers over me. My mind can't put these two humans together. How can this very tiny baby and this great big man be the same person? (Both of my children enjoy making fun of me if they catch me getting emotional and "without words," just by looking at them.)

In the Zen tradition they would give you a koan, a saying to contemplate that makes no rational sense. Why? Because when our brain tries to think about it, it will run in circles and implode. The moment our brain gives up trying to understand it, it will come to stillness and we will experience tranquil bliss and ecstasy.

Reference points can also be sad moments. My Uncle David was a wonderful man. He was a choir director, teacher, loving father, and friend to many. When he died, hundreds of his students and choir members gathered in a mass choir at the front of the church and sang songs he had written. They sang in the most beautiful harmonies with tears flowing down their faces. Their open hearts singing out their grief together combined with my own grief caused the entire world to stand still. There was nothing in that moment except unbelievable love, grief, sadness, and happiness all at once.

REFERENCE POINTS AS NEW ANCHORS

When these are the points that anchor us in the world, we always have these places to go when things get hard. We can still be sad, disappointed, and confused in life. We are still humans living in this world. We can have difficult times.

When we allow ourselves to go to one of our reference points, the world slows down again. These anchors connect us to the world that doesn't change. We feel the stillness. We somehow know there is more going on in the world than we can ever understand or imagine. Our current struggles don't magically disappear in that moment, but we are able to be the still centre in the storm. It doesn't consume us because we are now back in our centre.

What are reference points for you? When have there been moments that you can't explain? Moments when infinity touched your physical world, when you've felt this "oneness"? Are they big stories that blew your mind? Or are they simple moments like watching the sunset, or lying on the grass looking up at the stars and being unable to comprehend the vastness before you within the context of our little lives.

All you need is one moment, one memory.

PERSONAL EXPLORATION:
MEDITATION TO BECOME EMPTY

This is a gentle meditation that comes out of the Kundalini Yoga tradition. You can use it any time to help your mind stop spinning and bring you to a wonderful, peaceful centre.

You can do it sitting as meditation practice as written here, or you can simply use the breathing pattern any time in your day. I've had students tell me they use it as they walk through the woods, drive their car in traffic, breast-feed their baby, sit at their computer – basically any time they are upset and want to find stillness and emptiness.

Posture:

Sit comfortably with a straight spine, chin slightly tucked in.

Hands:

Rest the back of one hand in the palm of the other with the thumbs crossing each other in one palm. If the right hand is resting in the palm of the left hand, the left thumb rests in the right palm and the right thumb then crosses over the back of the left thumb. Or vice versa.

The hands are at heart-centre level about 2 inches in front of the chest without the hands touching the chest. Your elbows are resting against your ribs.

Eyes:

Your eyes are open but focused on the tip of the nose (which you cannot actually see).

Breathing:

There are four parts to the breathing cycle.

1. Inhale through the nose and exhale through the nose.
2. Inhale through the mouth with the lips puckered, as if to kiss or make a whistle, and exhale through a relaxed mouth.
3. Inhale through the nose and exhale through the mouth.
4. Inhale through puckered lips and exhale through the nose.

Continue the 4-part cycle for 11-31 minutes.

Note: You will likely lose track of where you are in the breathing cycle many times. This is perfect. It means you are becoming empty. Your mind is not active enough to "keep track" of where you are. When it happens, just start at the top.

CHAPTER 21

LIVING IN REALITY

The movie, *A Beautiful Mind*, tells a true story about John Nash, a brilliant mathematician who lives a life that seems to be made just for him. He has an intelligence job with the government where he can use his genius mind. He has a best friend who understands him. He has a lovely wife. His life is truly perfect.

But soon, something goes wrong. Things aren't adding up, and then we realize most of what we see in his life isn't true at all. It is all a fantasy in his mind. The only part of his life that was real was his wife. He had created everything else and he not only fully believed it, he was actually living within it. He was eventually diagnosed with schizophrenia.

This movie absolutely blew my mind. I realized how much we all did this in our lives, every day. I wondered whether John Nash's increased intelligence contributed to the level of elaborate detail in his fantasy. Did his genius "colour in the picture" so vividly that it was impossible for him to tell the difference between fact and fantasy?

I looked at everyone around me carefully. Had I created an image of them that was a combination of who they really are mixed with what I wanted them to be? Was this mixture of fact and fantasy part of my struggles? Was I pretending they were something they weren't and then being disappointed when they didn't live up to my fantasy? Everyone was only being themselves. It was me who had created a vision in my mind of the "ideal" for us all.

I realized how often we do this. We get upset because our in-laws act a certain way or our parents didn't do "this" when we were young, or our neighbour does "that," or our kids aren't good at... but they are all just being authentically themselves.

It is the fantasy that we create about how they *should* be that makes us so crazy.

LIVING A LIFE IN REALITY

I've lived through some terrible things in my life,
Some of which actually happened.
MARK TWAIN

All magic happens in the present moment. It is our only reality.

Yet how many of our thoughts are about this current moment? And how many are focused on fantasy?

Fantasy is anything that isn't real in this moment. It might *seem* fine to lie in bed and replay the day's events, but they are no longer real. What *is* real is that you are lying in your bed, breathing, eyes closed, resting, preparing for sleep. *This* is where you are actually alive.

Do you have conversations with people in your head? It is very common for us to imagine scenarios where "this person" showed up and then we said "this" and then they said "that." It is all fantasy.

Do you worry about events that haven't happened? There's an old saying that worry is like sitting in a rocking chair on the porch. As you rock, you feel like you're doing something, but you're actually not going anywhere. Worry is creating imaginary possibilities in our minds, going into the scenario, and then getting upset about it. Pure fantasy.

This being said, there are times when we are practising healthy mental exercises as opposed to playing out distracting fantasy.

If we have a speech or talk to give, it is normal to rehearse your speech. This is preparing for a future event that is going to happen. Similarly, some athletes and musicians will practise mentally before a race or performance. This mental practising creates neural pathways in our minds of perfect performance. We can do important work mentally to "improve our game" this way. The effect of our mind on our body is so strong, this is an excellent technique for perfecting our craft. Similarly, people with social anxiety will practise what they want to say. This is a healthy way to rehearse to overcome fears.

Also, we might go over something in the past to try to understand what happened. When we consciously do this to grow and unearth a pattern within that we don't want to repeat, this can be good work. We just have to be aware of the effects of this practice on us. Are we learning? Or are we just replaying it over and over again, as if it is happening right now?

THE HABIT OF FANTASY

With fantasy, we create an all-day-long habit of not being present to what is happening in the moment.

Children often play pretend. They play house. They play with trucks and cars. All of this is play. The difference is they *know* it was play. When it's time to come for lunch, playtime is over. It's that simple.

Our tendency to live in fantasy might have begun the first time we got bored in elementary school. We *had* to sit there. We weren't *allowed* to move. We had to *look* like we were paying attention, but our mind was elsewhere. It was a self-preservation mechanism because we weren't allowed to fall asleep, either. Maybe this is the beginning of our fantasy world. Maybe this was the beginning of getting used to having two realities side by side in our brains – what is *actually* happening and what we are *imagining* could be true.

This idea of fantasy is epidemic in our world. We think things like, "I wish it wasn't raining", "I wish it was warmer", "I wish I had more money", "I wish I had a girlfriend", "I wish I could have children", "I wish my dad hadn't died", "I wish I was thinner", "I wish I was taller", "I wish I was more attractive", "I wish I had more friends", "I wish I was younger",... the list is endless.

This habit of fantasizing about a "better" life is also fed to us daily through advertising. A friend told me a story once about a woman who struggled with self-worth and feeling attractive. My friend had an uplifting chat with her and by the end, the woman felt awesome about herself. Then the woman reached into her bag and pulled out a fashion magazine. As she thumbed through the pages, her face slowly fell. Her smile disappeared. By the time she was finished, she wasn't good enough any longer.

She wanted to look like the pictures she saw. Her reality was somehow not OK.

This is the root of so much of our suffering and our inability to be fully present in the moment. This is why we miss most of the magic all around us.

Reality is all there is.

We need to repeat this a thousand times until we undo the idea that if we pretend it isn't true, then another reality will appear.

If I am 5'7, then this is my reality. If it is raining, then this is reality. If I am poor, this is my reality. If I am in a wheelchair, then this is my reality.

We can have all kinds of judgements about our situation and preferences, but they are all irrelevant. They serve no purpose other than distracting us from what is.

Let's imagine that someone wants to paint a beautiful landscape. They head outside, only to find it is raining. They don't want it to be raining. They want sunshine today. They need to be able to paint. They decide they don't accept the reality of the rain. They head out with their easel, canvas, and paint, and they spend the entire day frustrated that their paint is getting water in it and the rain is ruining their painting.

It might seem harsh to compare our struggles we wish weren't real with the desire to paint a pretty picture, but our habit of fantasy is more dangerous to our well-being for many reasons.

If we don't admit, accept, and embrace the truth of our lives, we will waste all of our moments wishing they were different. We will spend our lives dieting instead of enjoying life. We will miss out on a hundred fun opportunities because we wished we had a partner to take with us. We will miss great free opportunities in the city because we wish we had money.

We also won't make the changes that are needed in our lives. Let's say we are in an abusive relationship. The only way we can stay with this person is to tell ourselves it isn't so bad. Our partner actually loves us. It won't always be this way. One day they will stop. They won't hurt us. Or, they won't hurt us again.

Our habit of living in fantasy will keep us in relationships, jobs, and situations long after it is healthy for us.

The minute we stop living in fantasy and we look at what is real, right in front of us, we will be faced with the emotions we don't want to feel. The fear of being alone. The fear of not having enough money. The fear of not being loved. The fear of not being successful. The fear of the unknown.

However, when we face these fears, we find the courage to make real change in our lives. We might need to allow ourselves to get really angry. This anger will give us strength to make a different choice. We might need to feel exactly how disappointed we are and how much we long for something different. Only when we admit to ourselves just how deeply we feel these things will we find the will to make the changes needed to live our own lives.

HEALING OUR PSYCHOLOGICAL WOUNDING

As one falls on the ground,
one must lift oneself by aid of the ground.
KULARNAVA TANTRA

Our personal journey starts with being real about exactly *how* we are.

When we are asked "How are you?" we are taught to say, "I am fine." We might be sad, grieving, lonely, disappointed, afraid, or struggling with a hundred things from our past. Instead of saying that, we say we are fine, to others and to ourselves.

This habit made sense to me after I became a farmer. If we were planting crops or it was haying season, there was no time to think about anything that was bothering us. We had to "make hay while the sun shone." There was no place for complainers, pain, or illness. You had to tough it out until all the hay was safely in the barn. *Then* you could pass out.

All societies have histories (or present-day issues) of great depressions, poverty, war, famine, and struggle, where there was no point complaining about what was bothering you. There was no point focusing on what was wrong with life because there was so much suffering all around you. Previous generations learned to become tough and ignore what was wrong so they could keep moving forward and stay alive.

Those previous generations didn't pretend life was different than it was. They didn't have that luxury. They were in the middle of a war. They were starving. They couldn't keep their children safe. There was no time for fantasy about "how life could be." They were in survival mode.

I believe this is where some of our deeply-ingrained fears of change come from. Maybe all of those generations of people who made the best out of horrible situations still live within us somewhere, and they are whispering their fears to us.

Maybe we have watched too many movies and TV shows, and read too many books about realities other than our own. Maybe we have become used to "leaving our current reality" and entering these other realities. The result is that we often live in two worlds – reality and fantasy – and we struggle to know which is the real one.

How Our Feelings Guide Us

Our feelings will help us come back to our actual reality at any moment.

Let's say there are only two feelings that tell us something about this present moment – happy and sad. Everything else we experience are emotions that take those initial feelings, mix them with thoughts, and create frustration, grief, anger, elation, etc.

In any given moment when you think of something, does your heart lift (happy) or drop (sad)? This tells us how we feel in any moment. We can't change this feeling. Feelings are our truth. They connect us with our reality in that moment.

Yet we often ignore these feelings. We are taught to. We are taught we should feel a certain way, even though feelings are actually our direct experience of what is happening. When we pretend we feel differently than we do, we are creating a fantasy, like children playing a game of pretend.

We even try to change how others feel. We want someone else to love us, or we wish we felt a certain way towards someone, but we don't. It isn't personal. It just isn't reality.

I can walk down the street and see 100 people. Only one person might catch my eye. Why? I don't know. Why do I have a connection with *that* person, but not the person behind them? I have no idea. It's a feeling.

I love to dance. Some nights I think of going to class and my heart lifts and I can hardly wait to get there. Other nights, the thought of going feels like a burden. Why? I don't know. My brain will make up all kinds of stories about possible reasons. But really, I have no idea. It's just the reality of this moment.

These feelings of "yes" or "no" are a direct link to our intuitive guidance. It's like an amoebic response. If it is life-giving, an amoeba moves towards it. If it is dangerous, it moves away. All we have to do is follow it and see what happens in our lives.

This is especially important in relationships. We must be honest about our true feelings about each other. Feelings are not thoughts. You cannot create them or destroy them. You cannot feel something if you don't feel it, any more than you can make someone feel hungry.

Tantra is about truth. It is about what is real. There are no fantasies, not in the bedroom and not in life.

SEXUAL FANTASY

Do you fantasize sexually? This is a particularly fun fantasy because it is exciting. It gets our hearts pumping and can create pleasurable results. Whereas a lot of our mental fantasy is negative and stressful – worry, replaying events, imagining new scenarios with various people in our lives – sexual fantasy is stimulating and exciting. It seems harmless.

In general, it is. Sitting by yourself having fantasies about the most erotic scene you can imagine doesn't hurt anyone. This is true.

But does it help you become more tantric? Does it allow you to connect with the present moment? Does it help you to be more connected with others? Does it help you to be more deeply intimate with a lover?

All fantasy creates specific wiring in the brain, and every sexual fantasy creates scenarios that create pleasure. It is easy for these pleasure pathways to become strong. The stronger these pathways, the harder it is to be present in an intimate encounter.

We forget the point of true intimacy - to connect with *this other human*. To find out what happens when our two unique chemistries interact. It has nothing to do with specific scenes, sexual preferences, or ideas that turn us on.

It is about being fully present, having new experiences. All of the time.

The greater problem with fantasy is we think our personal fantasy is better and far beyond anything possible in real life. For many of us, this might be true so far. The thrill of your favourite fantasy might have far exceeded anything you have experienced in the real world.

This is why we are studying tantra (in terms of lovemaking *and* life).

When we are tantric, what we can experience here in the real world is actually *far beyond* anything you can imagine in your mind. This may seem hard to believe. Yet what is possible between two humans is so far beyond what our minds can grasp that when it happens, all we can do is flow with it. It is absolutely euphoric, blissful, and ecstatic beyond our wildest dreams.

I am not exaggerating.

However, we will miss all of it if our minds are filled with other pictures. Our fantasies tell us stories about "what we like" and "what turns us on." This is true. Yet it is only when we drop all of these ideas that we have the chance to tune in with another person. We have a chance to *feel* their presence. We have a chance to merge with them and experience true bliss.

WE ARE ONLY IN REALITY
WHEN WE ARE WHOLE

Tantra is about being whole. If you have unresolved issues with yourself or others, these must be resolved. There are many techniques in all the spiritual traditions that can help us get to the bottom of what is hurting us so we can heal.

Within tantra, the path is one of listening inside. It is about looking at your family, constructs, and beliefs, and understanding how these form your current life. It is looking at our current life – physically, emotionally, mentally and spiritually – and being very honest with ourselves about where we are. It is about learning to quiet the mind and ask for inner guidance, and then have the courage to follow it.

Perhaps you have always struggled with one of your parents, and your relationship is toxic. Nothing you do is good enough; they make negative comments or you don't see eye to eye. At this point in your life, you might feel like nothing will ever change. You've tried. You accept this fact.

Then you start studying tantra. You meditate, you slow down your thoughts, and soon emotions from your relationship with your parent start to surface. You might even recognize you are playing that relationship out with your current partner.

You might have "accepted" it, but you haven't resolved it.

Tantra adds a new dimension to our healing journey because we truly integrate spirit into the experience. We can actually use our spiritual aspect; it isn't just a concept.

So, we ask for guidance. We listen. We wait for the words to come. We trust in the guidance. We allow ourselves to let go of what we don't want in our lives any more. We choose the present over the past.

When we are comfortable living fully in the present, this is where possibilities appear. We no longer live in the fantasy of the past or future. We don't imagine reality is anything other than it is. We fully accept and embrace our life exactly as it is. This is where the magic is. This is where infinite solutions exist.

This is where we feel fully alive.

PERSONAL EXPLORATION:
STAYING IN REALITY

The practice is to watch your thoughts and see when you are in this current reality or when you are lost in fantasy, and to keep coming back to the moment.

If your thoughts are in the past, future, or an alternate present, then come back to this present moment.

Take a deep breath. Look around you. What is here right now?

Is your current reality actually lovely, but you are distracted? Become really present. Notice smells, textures that you're touching. What do you see around you?

Or is there something about your current state you want to escape from? Is your current relationship a challenge? Do you wish it was different?

If this is the case, then come back to the moment and look at your situation, close your eyes and ask, "What can I do here to take a step in a new direction?"

If you are unhappy about some aspect of who you are, come back to the moment and ask, "Is this something I can change? Or is it my makeup? If so, what if I am made this way for a very specific and perfect purpose?"

If you *can* change your current state, then close your eyes and ask what the first step is. That's all you need.

What about sexual fantasy? Is this a part of your life? Why? If you have a partner, can you be more present with them? Can you explore making love in a more connected way? Can you bring the passion that you get from fantasy into your relationship?

If you don't have a partner right now, where else can you funnel all that passion? Is there a project you would love to accomplish? Sexual energy is creative life force. What have you always wanted to do that you can pour all that energy into?

Where can you apply this energy into your current reality?

CHAPTER 22

INTUITIVE WISDOM

I was a brain-child in school. I even continued on to get a Bachelor's Degree in Mathematics. This, combined with society's heightened respect for intelligence, allowed me to believe my brain knew how to make all the right decisions in my life.

I was wrong.

Years ago, when I got sick and my teacher, Jim, appeared in my life, the number one lesson for me was to learn how to shut my brain off. I had to learn how to trust something I could not explain, see, or justify to anyone. I had to make decisions based on something other than what I'd been told was right, what others would approve of or what I understood.

I had to learn to listen inside. I had to listen for divine guidance. I had to listen to a still place inside of me. I had to have faith in something more than my brain.

It was an incredibly dark time. Not only did I have to give up the one thing I had any pride in, it was also what I believed was my greatest strength. It brought me safety and stability (I thought). I was giving up everything I thought I understood about the world.

This is one of the gifts of being in crisis, of being afraid that you could die. You'll try anything. You have nothing to lose.

I started listening inside for guidance. I asked for help and answers came. I followed inner promptings and felt no need to explain them to anyone. I asked, I listened, and I followed.

And my whole life changed.

Ever since then, my life has been filled with miracles. It's been so incredible that my kids, friends, and family used to call it "Katrina's World."

While renovating my train station turned yoga school, my contractor and I realized we needed a new window above the door. It was an odd size of window, being in such an old building. I closed my eyes and innocently wondered, "Where would we get an old window for this?" Then the thought of a particular used furniture store popped into my head. I asked the contractor for the exact measurements. I got in my car, headed for the little store, and there was a perfect window in the *exact* measurements. It even had a sunrise pattern in the window (that matched all of the sunrise patterns throughout the old station).

It was the little, tiny, invisible decisions that made the biggest differences. It was listening in the quiet moments and making very subtle choices that created miraculous experiences, everywhere I went.

Today, I can't rely on my brain to make decisions. I trust something much greater. In fact, if I can't hear the guidance within, I struggle to make any decision at all. My brain is still great for creating businesses and working a plan. But which way I go and what I choose in my life? This is all based on divine guidance. It is based in something I cannot explain nor justify. And yet, it gives me comforting peace knowing that it's leading me.

The greatest gift I have received is never knowing where the road is going. My brain always had a plan I had to stick to. Now, I listen, trust, and follow.

Life is truly an adventure, never knowing what's coming tomorrow.

(The full story of this journey is the topic of my first book, *What If You Could Skip the Cancer?*)

Being a Modern Mystic

Once the journey to God is finished,
the Infinite journey in God begins.
ANNEMARIE SCHIMMEL

Tantra is a mystical path.

The word "mystical" can bring all kinds of meanings up for us. Sometimes we think of the occult, witches, magick, and psychics. It often seems strange and not part of our normal day-to-day lives, but this isn't mysticism.

To be a mystic is to seek direct experience of the divine in your life. No one stands between you and this experience – no religion, no prophet, no book, and no spiritual teacher. It's just you and God (whatever you consider that to be).

When we live a mystic life, we trust something beyond our intellect. We listen for guidance and believe it. When we have this trust, we have a sense of peace and confidence that the logic and rules of our minds cannot give us. The trust is so complete that we simply make the choice and walk forward in all aspects of our lives.

WHAT IS GOD?

When we say we are connecting to the "divine" and listening to intuition, what are we actually connecting to?

What do *you* believe in?

Maybe you love the classic version of God that your religion describes. Perhaps you prefer the "nothingness" of Zen, or the feeling you have in nature. Maybe you have a sense of being connected to a greater consciousness.

If none of these sit right with you, do you believe you are more than your body? This is good enough. All we need to know is there is a mystery of which we are a part. After all, that is the truth. All religions tell us not to name it because to name it, we must make it smaller. We must humanize it in a way that our minds can grasp. This will limit it and remove all its power and mystery.

LEFTOVER RELIGIOUS BLOCKS

If you were raised in a particular faith and have negative ideas about God or the divine, then it will be important to resolve these on your tantric journey.

Tantra is about integrating the divine into our lives. If you were taught to believe in a jealous or vengeful God or if you have deep issues with a masculine God stereotype, then how will you be able to surrender to and integrate it?

Often, it is healing our relationship with our religion of birth that we need the most. Although we may relate more to another religion or idea today, if we have issues with our original religion, this may create roadblocks on our journey.

In Joan Borysenko's book, "*A Woman's Journey to God,*" she shared her journey from being raised Jewish and being completely turned off religion based on Judaism's treatment of women. She travelled all over the world studying the world's religions, describing herself as a "dyed-in-the-wool-seeker." However, it was returning to her roots and healing her relationship with Judaism that brought her complete peace.

INTUITION: LISTENING FOR GUIDANCE

Seek and you shall find.
Knock and the door will be opened for you.
JESUS

This was my first real teaching in tantra many years ago when I was faced with serious illness. My teacher, Jim, told me that if I wanted to live, I had to learn how to pray.

He said I needed to practise three things:

- Ask for what I wanted

- Listen for an answer

- Act on the guidance

I found this incredibly difficult. It was hard to figure out what I really wanted to know. I knew I was unhappy and afraid of dying, but what was the question I was really asking? If there was divine guidance out there, did I even want to hear it? Did I already know what was wrong in my life and I didn't want to look at it?

My mind was a flurry of fears, "shoulds," pride, emotions, and the voices of everyone around me. I barely knew where to start. Of course, as I shared my confusion, Jim would look at me, smile, let me rant and cry and be frustrated, and then slowly I would come to centre and I would know the question I wanted to ask.

So, how do we do it?

QUIET THE MIND

First, we practise quieting the mind. We want to be clear that the guidance we get is from our expansive, timeless self, not our fears, programming, or the opinions of others. To do this, we practise some form of meditation. Simply stopping what we're doing and breathing deeply will relax our nervous system and change our state of mind. Over time, we will learn how to quiet the chatter, the fears, and the other voices so we can hear our guidance.

We can also find places where our minds naturally become quiet. Some find quiet by the ocean or lake or walking in the woods. Others go for long walks or sit in old churches. Others sit in a café, watching the world go by.

One of my sisters finds her peace sitting in bookstores. My other sister hikes up the hill behind her house and sits under her favourite tree. Another friend finds it during her morning yoga practice. Another goes on long runs to "clear his head."

Where do *you* feel peaceful? Where can you go that your body naturally takes a deep breath and the world stops spinning?

ASK THE QUESTION

The next step is knowing what you would like guidance about. This is often the most challenging step. We know that we don't like what is going on in our life, but what do we *really* want? What are we willing to change?

It's like imagining you are lost in the forest. A guide appears. What would you ask him? What is your burning question?

Don't worry. It doesn't have to be the best question ever. You will have this opportunity to ask anything you want every second of the rest of your life. You only have to know the question in *this* moment.

LISTEN FOR THE ANSWER

There was a time when a spiritual journey meant finding a guru and surrendering to their wisdom. We would release our attachments to being right. We would give up believing we knew anything. We simply trusted the guru. We would listen and follow.

In reality, the true guru exists within us. These "human" teachers showed us what our inner process would look like in physical form. We all have the same divine connection they do. We only have to learn to listen.

What does this inner guidance sound like?

It is the stillest voice in your mind. Our mind is often filled with many "voices" discussing the issues back and forth. Some may sound like our parents, partners, or other authority figures in our life. Maybe the voices are our own hopes, aspirations, expectations, and judgements of ourselves.

None of these have the guidance we are listening for.

Divine guidance is the one still voice that simply repeats the truth. It doesn't discuss or argue. It simply states "what is."

We previously talked about bringing together "oneness" and "duality" in life. Our intuition connects us with the oneness. All of the voices in our minds represent all the possibilities of this multi-faceted world.

Intuition is from the source. It is a singular voice. It isn't just guidance; it shows us the current reality. There is no path. It is our personal window into the reality of this moment.

When we hear it, we simply know it's true, and a peace comes over us.

BECOMING RECEPTIVE

To surrender and listen like this requires us to develop our feminine ability to receive. In our modern day, we understand how to have a strong masculine side that *does* things and argues and stands its ground.

To listen within requires our feminine side. It requires us to be humble before wisdom. To set aside what we previously believed to be true and to open ourselves to new opportunities and new possibilities.

JUST ENOUGH LIGHT FOR THE STEP WE'RE ON

Intuition generally gives us only the next step. We don't tend to see the whole picture or what the end-game looks like. This is quite annoying since it's much easier to trust that this step is "right" when we know what the outcome will be.

But, this is the definition of faith – to trust because you simply know it is true.

For me, my health-crisis-miracle in 1999 tipped the scales towards faith and away from the strength of my mind. Since I started trusting inside, incredible things have appeared in my life that I couldn't have imagined before. Today, it is much easier to trust in faith. I now know my brain can only base its decisions on a limited amount of information, whereas intuition and faith are connected to the whole.

I trust that.

WHAT IF WE DON'T HEAR AN ANSWER?

If we don't hear an answer, it may mean no action is needed right now. Maybe you are meant to breathe and sit still for a while. Maybe other events have to occur in your life before you can take the next step. This can be very frustrating, but it works out in the end.

More often than not, when we can't hear an answer it's because we already know it. We just don't like it. So we wait for another, easier answer. There isn't another answer; our intuition simply states "what is." There is only one answer to receive.

Sometimes this happens when we feel stuck in life. We know what the reality is. We know what the next step is, but we don't want to take it. Perhaps part of us wants to take the next step, but a greater part of us is afraid.

This is a time to look inside at our spiritual connection. Do we *really* trust this guidance? Do we believe it is in our highest good? Do we believe we will be happier once we follow through with this? Because if we *do*, then what are we afraid of?

This is *our* personal journey. Each of us has all kinds of fears and reasons why we don't trust this inner guidance. We need to be kind and compassionate as we navigate these parts of ourselves that are terrified to take this leap of faith.

Perhaps this isn't your time to make this choice. This is good too. All that matters is that we are honest with the guidance we've heard. Maybe we take the step now. Maybe we take the step later. It's all part of the process.

TAKE A LEAP OF FAITH

The final step is to act on the guidance.

In the beginning, we might feel the need to explain our actions to others. When we trust and act on this inner guidance, we can't honestly answer "But why would you do *that?*" We really don't know why. We just know that it's right.

In time, this gets easier. Your friends and family soon understand that you trust something else to guide you in life. When my children were small, they knew there was no arguing with me once I had an answer. This wasn't because I was stubborn. It was because when I was faced with a question or challenge,

I would sit quietly with it. I would remove my own fears and opinions and I would listen inside, and an answer would come.

My kids didn't agree because they were easy-going; they knew I was right, that this was the truth. We can feel when someone says the truth, and we know when someone doesn't.

Yes, there were (and are) times when the guidance isn't clear. In those cases, I would admit that I didn't know the answer. Maybe we needed to discuss it more. Maybe we needed more information. Maybe it wasn't my decision to make.

I must say it was easiest to be intuitive with my children. My protectiveness and fear of doing or saying the wrong thing honed my "mother's intuition" to be incredibly sharp. Whereas in other family relationships and marriage, it was a little murkier and not so clear.

DIVINE COURAGE

Are you looking for the Holy One?
I am in the next seat.
My shoulder is against yours.
KABIR

Developing this connection makes the tantric journey possible. Tantra is about expanding *into* who we are. We need to heal and bring back all of the parts of us that we have "sent away." As we become whole, we can expand into our true potential.

We all know that change can be hard and the process of healing can be painful and scary. There was a reason we blocked certain memories and carry the baggage that we do. We have emotions and pain from the past that we really don't want to revisit... even with the promise of amazing happiness in the end.

And yet, we know we must take the journey. We know it's time.

This is what makes the tantric journey so different. We first strengthen our inner connection. We focus on trusting this divine wisdom in every moment of our lives. When we feel called to heal something that we previously couldn't, we now trust something different. We trust our intuition more than our fears. Deep down, we know our wisdom holds the answers to our lives being whole and happy again.

This is Divine Courage.

This means we aren't making a decision because we "should." There's something "greater" inside of us, pushing us forward. We are aware of a greater wisdom within that will bring our life closer to truth.

Sometimes the pieces of ourselves that require growth and healing are difficult. There was a reason we buried our painful memories a long time ago, and they tend to be emotionally loaded with angst and fears.

Without tantra, we are left on our own. We prefer to avoid them, to try to get through life even though they are brewing under the surface. We've gotten along OK for this long. What's a little more time?

Without divine courage, we must confront these scary places through our willpower alone. All we have are the tools in our minds. However, our minds also hold our accumulated fears, rules, and habits that want to pull us back to our old ways, especially on the low days. Being strong on the "up" days is easy. It's the "low" days where we struggle.

As we integrate the spiritual, infinite, and divine aspects of ourselves, we realize we are so much more than our fears. We are connected to an unending source of hope, strength, and wisdom.

When we look at our challenges through these eyes, they don't look so daunting. They might still be difficult and painful, but we don't get lost in the pain. We experience it. We understand it in a greater context, the context of our whole life and path. Even if we don't understand it, there is now something inside that knows we're heading in the right direction. This divine courage gives us the strength to move forward through the challenge instead of retreating to safer and familiar ground.

We have integrated the wisdom of spirit into our lives. Now we can use it.

COURAGE STRENGTHENS WITH EXPERIENCE

We are the ones who must strengthen the muscle that trusts our intuition, that feels the connection to source. This isn't an intellectual idea. It must be felt. It's like going for a run. We can't understand what a run would feel like for our body. We must do it for our cardiovascular and muscular systems to feel it and adapt to the new experience.

This courage grows every time we listen and follow the inner guidance. Each time, we trust it a little bit more. This muscle gets stronger.

This isn't blind faith. It is a constant testing and expansion of this experience. It is like the Buddhist teaching that we are not to believe anything on faith. If something resonates with us, then we take the leap to follow it further. We see what happens. We test everything in our day-to-day life out in the world.

Then, we won't be "believing it on faith." We will *know* it. We will have experienced it.

This is the journey of tantra.

PERSONAL EXPLORATION: HEARING YOUR INTUITION

On the Mat

Find a place to sit where your mind is easily quiet. It could be in your house in a special place where you can sit cross-legged yogi-style with a candle, or your favourite easy-chair in the backyard. You could sit by a lake, on a quiet park bench, or in a church.

Close your eyes and breathe deeply.

Ask: "What is my question?"

Listen for an answer. This may take a while, but there will be one that keeps repeating itself.

Ask: "What is the answer? What can I do?"

Listen for an answer. Find your centre. Breathe deeply. If you have many thoughts swirling around, that's OK. Keep breathing and let the thoughts flow around you, as if the wind is blowing around you and you are in the centre of it. See what answer comes.

Ask: "What can I do to make this happen?"

Listen for an answer. Perhaps you get a glimpse of something. I once wanted to buy a train station (to turn it into a wellness centre). When I asked this question, I suddenly saw myself inside the station turning off the lights after a class. It was then that I knew it was actually going to happen.

It might not be time to take action. You might only need to know right now that this is the truth and your answer. It might have to sit with you and grow until the timing is right.

In Our Lives

We do this on the mat so we can practise for life. We want to be fully connected to our inner wisdom in every moment of our day.

As you begin your day, observe yourself when you make choices. When you're getting dressed, do you *feel* like wearing something in particular? Do you have a sense that you'd like to take a different route to work? Are there thoughts in your mind that won't go away, that might be interesting to pursue?

Maybe you're planning a conference. Where should it be? What are the options? Which one does your mind continually go back to, regardless of how often the others are discussed? What if you picked it based on this intuition?

Maybe you're walking down the road and feel the compulsion to turn right, then left... This isn't about finding miracles because you made these choices. It is about connecting with this inner mechanism.

It can be any choice from "What do I feed the kids?" to "Where should we hold the conference this year?" There are logical answers to these questions, but what if you sit quietly with the question, stop and *listen*. An answer you've never previously considered might pop in. Play with considering it. Trust this strange thought.

Use this as you communicate with others. Instead of quickly responding or reacting to them (especially with difficult people), take a breath, ask how to have a different experience with them, and wait for the words to come.

All day long, play with listening inside. Go for a walk. Should I turn left or right? Trust. It's fun.

This is how we integrate our divinity into every moment of our lives.

CHAPTER 23

INSPIRED COMMUNICATION

My kids will tell you that I never punished them. Instead, they had to "come sit on the couch" and talk with me. Then, they would roll their eyes and act like they were tortured there.

I never pretended I had all of the answers for my kids. When they were fighting or having trouble in school or they were frustrated or simply angrier than normal, I never got angry. I got concerned. I always wondered what was *really* going on here. What was causing them to act out?

I always honoured that they had to go through whatever was happening in their lives. They were allowed to have "bad days," but once their behaviour disrupted the peace in the home, then those immortal words would be spoken.

"Do you want to come sit on the couch for a while?"

We would sit. I would ask what was wrong. If they didn't know and they just felt angry/frustrated/tired/sick, then we would sit there and look at each other. If the problem was obvious, then the conversation would start there.

I would listen to them intently. Even more so, I was listening inside for guidance as to what to say or do. How could I help here?

Sometimes, I would feel called to tell a story from my own teenage years. Or I would start rambling about something that seemed unrelated. Eventually, they would start talking or crying and the truth of what was going on would surface. It was like magic. I would have no idea why this random story would bring up what was going on in them, but it always worked. Well, except for this one time when my daughter came over to the couch. I started saying something and she looked at me and said, "Oh my god, MOM! Sometimes I'm just an emotional 16-year-old!" And then we laughed, which brought about its own resolution.

As a parent, especially during their teenage years, this brought me a comforting peace inside. Not only did it deeply bond us together, but I always knew that no matter what was going on or how challenging it was, all I had to do was listen inside and wait for the right words to come.

And they always came.

MYSTICS WAIT FOR THE WORDS TO COME

I used to rehearse everything I wanted to say to everyone. I would have conversations over and over again so that I could cover all the options. It was exhausting.

My teacher, Jim, told me the story from the bible where Jesus was going to be killed and his disciples were worried about what they would do if they were captured too. Jesus told them not to worry; He would be there with them and would speak through them.

Jim told me to trust that God is always with me and all I had to do was ask for the right words.

He was right.

When I took the time to stop and ask inside for help, words would come into my mind that I had never thought before. And they weren't mine.

I used this in teaching yoga, meditation, and tantra. I used this raising my children and talking with my husband. I used it speaking to groups and to town councils.

I used this as a counsellor and was always amazed by the experience. When people came to see me, I would look at this incredibly intricate and multifaceted person with thousands of experiences. They could tell me the obvious things, but in between the big things were small, subtle experiences that had also formed them. As their counsellor, how could I ever know enough to give good advice without listening for guidance?

So I would listen. Then words would come. It might be a story, or something off the wall. I would say what came to me, and most of the time they would cry. Later, they would say, "You know when you said *that*? It was *just* what I needed to hear. How did you know to say it?"

The truth is that I often didn't remember saying it. It didn't come from me. It was only for them.

When I spoke to large groups, complete strangers would come up after and say "It's like you were talking right to *me*! How did you know?"

I didn't know. The words that came simply followed the intention I had for speaking that day.

WHAT IS MY INTENTION?

With each communication, we have to be clear about our intention.

Professionally, when I speak, my only goal is to answer the questions that the members of this specific group have in their hearts. I will always have an agenda of the topics I want to cover, but *how* I cover the topics is always completely unique and dependent on who is in the group. It's amazing to me how one topic can be discussed and covered from so many different angles.

In our personal lives, do I want to build a bridge between myself and this person in front of me? Or do I want to prove that I am right? Do I want to help them find the best solution for them? Or do I want to convince them that *my* solution is best for them? These are important distinctions.

When we are clear about our intention, it is easier to trust what comes, even if we have no idea what to say. If we are clear about our intentions, it's easier to take the leap of faith.

It is only when we are unsure or when we aren't being honest with ourselves that we get into trouble.

INSPIRED COMMUNICATION IN CONFLICT

Relationships don't always go the way we plan.

We are all separate people and we have different perspectives. There will be times where we do not agree on topics or hopes or plans. Sometimes there will be misunderstandings. Sometimes we will do the wrong thing. Sometimes we will make mistakes.

Sometimes we have been hurt in the past. Maybe we had been open and vulnerable, and the other person was not careful with us. This can easily create a deep desire to turn around and hurt them back. But of course, this only makes things worse, creating a vicious cycle that you will repeat over and over again.

The key is to be honest with yourself and aware of the end result you want for the conversation. You need to be clear about your intention. If your intention is only to make the other person wrong or to hurt them, then there is not going to be happy resolution. The distance between you will become greater.

If your intention is to be close again, then you must pause, take a deep breath, and listen inside for another solution.

WHEN ARGUING BRINGS YOU CLOSER

I had a lover who had a jealous streak. He used to get upset when I was with other men for any reason. Because of this, there were times I would hide where I was going or what I was doing because I didn't want him to be upset. Although we had a beautiful love between us, this part of our relationship wasn't good at all. (I don't recommend lying or living with jealousy, but sometimes we do strange things in love that we swore we would never do.)

One time, he got upset that I went out with friends. This time I called him on it. I said that I wasn't happy and it wasn't fair for him to be like this. He knew this and he agreed with me. He hated that he was like that - that sometimes his emotions took his mind to crazy places and the demons got bigger and bigger until he couldn't think about anything else. It was just the way it was.

After I got home, we tried to resolve the problem. We repeated everything that had been said earlier and soon came to a stalemate. We sat there, holding hands, looking at each other. There was nothing to say. Neither of us wanted to say anything mean to the other. Neither of us needed to be right. We only wanted to get back to where we were before it happened. It killed us to be mad at each other.

As we sat in silence, he eventually begged me to say something. He couldn't stand that I was angry with him and the silence made it even worse!

I told him I had so many thoughts going through my head. I wasn't sure if they were true or if they were just angry, frustrated thoughts, and I didn't want to say them out loud in case they were hurtful. The last thing I wanted to do was hurt him. He asked me to say them anyway. I agreed to do so, as long as he didn't take what I was saying to heart, or ever repeat anything I said, as if it was true or it was what I thought.

Within this context, within this bubble, I said what came to my mind. They were half-truths and frustrations and emotional words, but saying them moved the energy of the conversation. It created flow. With this movement of energy, the words came. And soon, we were able to have a deeper conversation about the fears that were being triggered inside of us.

In the end, because we had healed deeper wounds within both of us, we ended up even closer than we were before the whole thing started.

I learned so much from this experience. I learned that difficulties, misunderstandings and hurtful experiences can bring us closer if we maintain intimacy and love throughout the experience. If we honour how much we love this other person and do not want to hurt them, there is a beautiful chance of not only resolving the issue at hand, but healing each other in the process.

We recognize that the only reason the difficulty arose is because a wound in our psyche was triggered. Since we love each other, even in conflict, we want to be there to help each other heal.

COMMUNICATION IN INTIMACY

Inspired communication is beautiful in sexual intimacy as well.

In a lovemaking session, our words can add or detract from the connection very quickly. We want to be careful to communicate within the truth of the moment, not from a fantasy in our mind, or we risk creating distance with our partner.

When we are completely open to each other, we are very vulnerable. In every way, our most sensitive parts are exposed. This can be unnerving for both people. It can be scary to be that open and vulnerable, and we also don't want to do or say the wrong thing to our partner.

This is why we practise guided communication in life first. We learn to listen inside and say what we hear. We observe the effects on others around us and then we start to trust this guidance. We understand that it is wise. We can trust it.

When we choose to join together intimately, we are playing in a whole new world. We are using sexual intimacy to merge together to experience bliss. When we choose to speak, the words will come from deep within us, and they will deepen the connection. We will communicate with our bodies, but the inspiration to move will not come from our brains. It will be intuitive. You won't know why you desire to touch here or move there or kiss them this way. You will trust it and simply follow.

In this way, we all completely surrender in the experience. Although one may be playing a masculine role and the other a feminine role, or perhaps you are completely merged into one, everyone is connected to source. Everyone is moving and communicating in an inspired way.

This is what takes us on an incredible journey – never knowing what is coming next and fully trusting the guidance to get there.

PERSONAL EXPLORATION: PRACTICE INSPIRED COMMUNICATION

We want to practise speaking from this inspired place.

Be centred first

When you sit down to chat with someone, whether it is a casual conversation with someone you barely know or a serious conversation with a loved one, first take a deep breath and actually arrive in this present moment.

What is your intention here?

Do you want to have a friendly chat? Then listen inside for topics to chat about. Listen and respond openly with them. See where it goes.

Is there a problem with a partner, child, or friend? Do you want to find a loving solution?

Be aware if your true desire is to hurt them. If this is your truth, then say it. Tell them you really want to talk to them, but right now, you honestly want to hurt them. You need time to look at that, because the truth is that you love them. You want to chat later to find a solution.

Listen for guidance

As you sit with them, say what comes into your mind. Don't be afraid to say things like, "OK. I don't know why I feel called to share this but it keeps rolling around in my mind..." In the beginning, it's often easier to start speaking from inside when we can preface it with, "I don't know why I'm saying this but..."

The point here isn't to sound wise, intelligent, and all-knowing. It's to have an experience with someone or to deepen your connection.

Enjoy the Adventure

When we speak from this inspired place, we let go of controlling where the conversation is going to go. We are open to what the other person is going to say. We are open to whatever we are going to say. Conversations become exciting explorations instead of repeating the same conversation as when you discussed this topic with the last ten people.

If you are using this to resolve conflict, then stay open to the resolution happening. There are many relationships in our lives where we can't imagine there ever being any solution, but have hope. The strangest things happen when we listen inside.

True miracles can happen.

CHAPTER 24

GOING FORWARD FROM HERE

WHAT DOES BEING TANTRIC LOOK LIKE FOR YOU?

There is no specific, "correct" way to *be tantric*. Being tantric doesn't mean we are always calm like the Buddha. It also doesn't mean we are wild, sexual, and unpredictable.

Tantra simply releases the limitations on what we are allowed or supposed to be. We are free to explore ideas that feel true to us. We understand the societal norms we were raised in and consciously work within them or choose to discard them. Either way is perfect.

I've had students who discovered that when they let their guards down and allowed *anything* to be possible, they could speak to animals. Others found their true voice. Some discovered they no longer wanted to be a rebel and exchanged partying for libraries and reading books. Others discovered their sensuality and now feel free to explore their deepest desires in ways they were afraid to before.

Your path going forward is a perfect combination of you, God, and this life you have been given. Where do you feel called to go? What do you feel called to explore? What are you no longer afraid to admit to yourself and the world at large?

This is the perpetual unfolding of your life – exactly as it was designed to be.

TANTRA IN OUR DAY-TO-DAY LIVES

When we become tantric, it doesn't mean we no longer have issues. We are still alive, interacting with others and continuously growing. This means we are always leaving who we once were in order to expand and grow into what's possible. Deep change is always challenging. This can feel painful, sometimes bringing us anxiety, angst, stress and real grief.

This is all part of being human. There is nothing wrong with it. Low energy or sad days are just as valuable as happy, euphoric days. In the same ways that the masculine and feminine we studied in this book play *with* each other, neither is better or worse. They feed and build upon each other. The low days give us the depth we need to truly embrace the happy days. And the happy days give us the lightness, hope and courage to truly face our fears on the low days.

As I was writing this particular chapter, I was actually filled with angst. Maybe it was stressful to write "the last chapter," maybe the stars were in a funny alignment, or maybe I was simply tired. Regardless, I wasn't in my "happy writing place." When I saw my 19-year-old daughter, she asked me how I was doing today. I looked at her, took a deep breath and said, "I am filled with writer's angst." She said, "Ya. I can imagine." We chatted a bit and then went on with our days.

There is a great teaching for people who struggle with anger and fury that you should just imagine your fury like a swimming pool. Dive in and own it. Otherwise, if you sit on the side, it might keep splashing on you, annoying you, making you feel like it controls you. But if you have the courage to dive in and experience it, you retain control. You choose how it plays out.

It is the same with being tantric. Regardless of how we are feeling, we want to dive in. If we are sad or grieving, go all in. Feel it completely. Learn what there is to learn. And then allow it to pass. Similarly, on the "happy" days, dive into them too. Enjoy the sunshine, the ease, and the optimism flowing through you. Be fully present. Receive the gift. Breathe deeply and feel happy to be alive.

In the end, being tantric is simply being who we are in each moment. It is embracing the mystery we are within the limited time and space we have been given. It is knowing there are unlimited solutions in every moment and there is always guidance to help us see the next step. It is knowing that although we look separate, we are all connected. We are never alone.

It is knowing that at any time, we can close our eyes, breathe deeply, and connect with the deepest calm. We can't explain it. That even within the chaos, there is a peace inside... and the excitement in knowing that anything could happen next.

Epilogue

Meister Eckhart once said: "All that exists rejoices in its existence."

This is the quote that will always pull me out of a low day. No matter what is going on, no matter how tired I am or lost I'm feeling, when I remember this quote, I bring my head up out of my sadness, look around me and realize, "Well, I *am* still here. Hmmm."

I'm always thankful for that simple fact.

We can spend our lives trying to understand the world around us, but we are missing the point.

Tantra shows us we are absolutely magnificent, infinite creations walking around this amazing and complex world. At any moment, we have endless possibilities and solutions at our fingertips. All we have to do is ask.

We are capable of unexpected miracles within our own lives and absolute magic when we combine our lives with others.

No matter where we are or what we are doing, there is subtle beauty and magic all around us. All we have to do is take a deep breath, tune in, and be thankful we are here.

Thank you for joining me on this exciting journey together. I wish you all the joy and courage in your adventure going forward!

All the best,
Katrina Bos

MOST COMMONLY ASKED QUESTIONS ABOUT STUDYING TANTRA

CAN I STUDY TANTRA WITHOUT A PARTNER?

This is probably the most common question I am asked. Tantra is often connected with sexuality and relationships because this is one of the main applications where we need the most healing and help.

However, many of us feel drawn to study tantra, when we are on our own. This is perfect; our tantric journey must begin with ourselves. In fact, when we try to apply tantra to our relationships without doing our own work first, it will be quite challenging since we often have hard feelings and issues swept under the rug within the relationship.

If we don't address our own issues and brokenness, how can we create something whole with another? So, even within a relationship, it's important to do your own work first.

The real goal of tantra is to experience our true essence, our true divinity, right here in our lives.

This asks us to learn different philosophies about what life is all about, apply them to our lives, and then experience what happens. This is a very personal experience.

When we become tantric, we are effortlessly this way in all aspects of our lives – in all of our relationships, at work, with our children and friends, and definitely in our sexual intimacy.

MY PARTNER ISN'T INTERESTED. CAN I STILL STUDY TANTRA?

The answer depends on why you want to study tantra.

If your goal is personal growth and the desire to become tantric in all aspects of your life, then the answer is definitely "yes," because tantra is always a personal journey to begin with. The goal is to *become tantric*. It isn't something we *do* or require anyone else for. Our personal journey is our richest journey. This is where we find ourselves, expand, and experience life in whole, new, and wonderful ways.

However, if you want to study tantra because you want to experience something different with your partner, then we have to look at some other questions.

Does your partner know what tantra is?

What is your partner not interested in? Most people have no idea what tantra is, and the very fact that it sounds foreign means it must be weird, strange and not "normal." Of course, tantra is the most natural thing for all of us regardless of culture, but this needs to be explained because it isn't obvious.

There is also a lot of misinformation out there about tantra. There are many services, teachings, and events that are called tantric but have nothing to do with tantra. For some, tantra means kinky sex, orgies, naked retreats, polyamory, etc. These things are not tantra. Kink is kink. Polyamory is polyamory. Nudity is nudity. These are personal choices that have nothing to do with tantra.

Tantric Intimacy is about the quality of the connectedness between you. It's about journeying together to drop the walls, release the expectations and explore what is possible between two people.

Are you looking for different things in your relationship?

If your partner understands all of this and they are still not interested, it might be a sign of something you already know – it's not that they aren't interested in tantra. They aren't interested in connecting in a deeper way with you.

Tantric intimacy asks us to drop our guards and become very close. This is not everyone's path. Your partner might genuinely like your relationship exactly as it is right now and not want to go any deeper.

Your partner might not want to try anything different sexually, either. They might be satisfied with your sex life and don't want to change a thing, or they might be intimidated by trying something new.

The challenge is that sex is more than something you do together in the bedroom. You are the same people with the same relationship, regardless of which room you are in. If they are satisfied sexually but you are not, this might be telling you even more about your relationship.

CAN TANTRA FIX MY RELATIONSHIP?

Tantra looks at our relationships through a different lens than many types of counselling. It gets to the core of who we are and teaches us how to connect in deep and nourishing ways. Whether this will work for you depends on where you are in your relationship.

And so, the answer is "maybe yes" and "maybe no."

If both of you want to grow personally and heal, and you both want to explore a deeper connection, then tantra is a beautiful structure to help you on this journey together.

Tantra gives us a new understanding of love and connection. We can learn how to be safe and trusting with each other. We can learn how to love each other in ways that perhaps we've never even seen before.

Introducing the discipline of 100% kindness into your communications and actions will draw you closer in every moment.

When each of you do your personal work, your relationship will change. This will give you a lot of insight as to where each of you have contributed to the distance that you now feel. The intimacy exercises will allow you to connect in a deep and meaningful way that will create an entirely new foundation for your relationship.

When you are able to let go of all expectations and reactions, you can embrace the infinite possibilities that tantra has to offer.

Yes, tantra can definitely help.

However, you might already know that the answer is "no." If you are the only one who wants to fix your relationship, then no, tantra cannot help. We must work within what is real.

However, tantra might help you see your relationship for what it truly is. Maybe you won't ever have intense passion, but maybe you can have a friendlier and kinder companionship. Tantra redefines love in a way that we can apply it to all depths and kinds of connection. If you are both happy with a friendly, loving companionship, then tantra can help you happily live together.

Moving On When Love Isn't There

When love is disappearing, when happiness has gone, then it might be time to say thank you and move on.

For many of us, this is a radical thought. Historically, we were committed to the institution of marriage. We made a promise and we have to keep it. Within that promise there is no requirement that you are happy or fulfilled or passionate, or that love is even there. Sometimes marriage is a business agreement, and love has little to do with it.

The idea of "till death do you part" is a man-made creation. Staying together for life is not a sign of success. It says nothing about happiness or the fullness of your life. Sometimes it works, and there is great love the whole time. But when it's not like that, there is no reason to be together.

If this is your situation, you will have to look at what is really happening. Has your relationship simply run its course? Perhaps you can look at each other with love, honour your relationship, and take different roads.

Sometimes, there is love in the beginning, but we don't know how to love each other. We know how to lust after each other. We know how to live together. We can have children and pay the bills together, but keeping true love alive takes a different set of skills. This is where we tend to harm the relationship and the love dies.

Instead, we often treat our loved ones – partners and children – worse than friends, colleagues, and even strangers on the street. We "let our hair down" and are "just ourselves" at home because we know that no matter how we act, they won't go anywhere. We act more like fighting siblings than lovers.

True love is not unkind. It isn't moody. It doesn't take out a bad day on another person. It never wants the other person to feel badly. It protects the other person from anything that might upset them.

If you find yourself in a place where you have not been loving toward each other and there are all kinds of hurt feelings and trust issues, but **you both** want to heal the relationship, then tantra can help. You will have to take it very slow and focus on being kind 100% of the time with each other.

If you are treating your partner with anything except kindness and love, it is likely because you are used to this pattern from your childhood and most relationships in your life. Being impeccable with others will be a new skill to develop. It will take thoughtful discipline in the beginning. But it's definitely worth it.

DOES TANTRA APPLY TO GAY COUPLES?

Yes. Definitely. We often imagine it only applies to the heterosexual world, since that has been the dominant culture for a long time.

Regardless of orientation, tantra is first a way of being. It is about integrating our spiritual and physical lives. This is true for all genders and orientations.

Our tantric journey shifts our philosophy so we can heal all of the parts of us we have hidden away. Most people in the LGBTQ community have been forced to hide a lot of who they are and still have to in many cultures. This process of healing is fundamentally important.

How we create loving connection is about how souls connect. Our souls have no gender. We just love. We can have full body orgasms through complete presence and touch. We can be fully clothed, doing nothing sexual at all.

What matters is that when we are complete, infinite possibilities can happen. Truthfully, all couples need this foundation within each person, regardless of orientation.

There is a lot of discussion about the interaction of the masculine and feminine in tantra, which can seem heterosexist. This refers to the masculine and feminine balance within each of us. We all interact in masculine and feminine ways with each other, regardless of orientation. This isn't about sex. It's about the natural magnetism between the two aspects of each of us and how we interact with each other.

It is true that there is much more information and focus on heterosexuality in tantra mostly because historically, we have not been able to discuss same-sex couples, let alone the people who make up the LGBTQ community today.

We live in a time where we can not only talk openly about how everyone loves and connects with each other, but we can study the wisdom of tantra and learn (perhaps for the first time) how this ancient wisdom applies to everyone of all genders and orientations.

The world is ready for it now.

HOW CAN I FEEL SEXUAL AGAIN?

This is a common question for anyone who feels like they aren't feeling everything they could be, lacks libido, or aren't as excited to be sexual and intimate as they once were.

Feeling sexual and sensitive again is part of our healing process. We are naturally sensitive to touch, we feel pleasure, and we have life energy to share with others. When we don't feel this, we have some clues as to what we need to heal on our tantric journey.

Emotional Scarring During Sex

We are incredibly vulnerable when we are sexually intimate. Physically and energetically, our most vulnerable parts are exposed and mingling with another. If we are intimate with someone and they say or do something careless, this can do real damage and stay with us for a long time.

Some men who struggle with erectile dysfunction can trace it back to a partner who made a derogatory comment about them during a sexual encounter. One woman told me she remembers a certain lover making fun of something she did and after that, she was always a little shy about lovemaking. She held back more. She became afraid to let go and enjoy.

Tantra helps us heal these inner wounds through self-love, acknowledging what happened, knowing it wasn't true, or reframing the experience. We never know exactly how these wounds get healed, but somehow in the process of becoming whole and re-integrating all of our lost parts, we gain a new confidence. Those experiences are still part of our memories, but we are now stronger and more sensual because of them.

Mental Stress

When we are stressed out, we are fully engaged in our brains. We are locked into our churning and twisting thoughts about some topic. When we are like this, we cannot be sensual.

To be sensual is to be in our bodies, to feel touch and emotion. It is to connect with another person. None of this is possible if we are lost in our minds.

Taking the time to meditate and get to the bottom of our mental stress is helpful if we are ever to become sexual, sensual, and tantric.

De-Sensitization to Touch and Pleasure:

There is a connection between our emotional walls in life and our ability to experience touch with another. Our ability to feel touch can also be diminished through painful past experiences, whether they were sexual experiences, medical procedures, accidents, etc.

Both of these topics are covered in depth in chapter 5 and chapter 12: "Letting Down Our Walls" and "Tantric Touch."

Medication & Recreational Drugs & Alcohol

Modern society has turned to medicating all unpleasant emotions. There are instances where medication truly saves someone's life and makes it possible for them to live in society, but many medications are prescribed to simply "take the edge off."

We might feel stuck in situations we can't change, or we are still hurting from past pain and trauma we haven't been able to heal. We take medications from the doctors to feel better, or we take recreational drugs or drink alcohol. We self-medicate because we don't want to feel bad any longer.

However, when we "take the edge off" of life, we decrease our virility. We are "taking the edge off" of the life force running through us. We are *choosing* not to feel everything we are feeling. This is going to have a direct effect on our sex drives.

Our sexual desires are directly linked to our excitement to be alive. They are connected to our emotions and how we feel about everything. It is our happiness, sadness, grief, low times, high times, anger and everything in between that makes us feel alive, dynamic, and real. This is what stokes our inner fire – living in each moment.

The anger or sadness inside may be just what you need to make necessary changes. But if you're afraid or feel unable to make those changes, then you might turn to other options to repress what you are feeling. This will affect your ability to feel all over.

If you are on medication, ask your doctor whether it may affect your sex drive and see what other options you have. If you self-medicate with natural or recreational drugs and alcohol, be compassionate with yourself and look at what's really going on.

Once we find a way to self-medicate when we are feeling low, we will never go into those painful feelings. The path of tantra asks us to find our way *through* these challenges. It gives us the divine courage to dig deep and step into the fire, knowing we will come out the other side.

When we can go into those dark parts of our psyches and heal them, we will start to feel alive again. When we can feel the life force flowing through us, we will feel sexual again.

For Women

For many women, sex is quite unsatisfying. Because the primal goal of "regular sex" is for the man to ejaculate, a woman's satisfaction tends to be secondary. (This does not apply to everyone. The goal of many men is to make sure their partner is satisfied.)

It wasn't until the late twentieth century that it was widely accepted women were able to have orgasms at all. Prior to this, you simply had sex until the man ejaculated. Period.

Of course, women *did* have sexual desires. They had intimate needs. They desired connection, but this wasn't necessarily happening. They would become emotional and frustrated. The medical system even created a diagnosis for this called "hysteria." This condition had nearly every possible symptom, including depression, anxiety, nervousness, excessive vaginal lubrication, and sexual thoughts... Hmmm.

When this happened, the most common treatment was a "hysterectomy," the removal of the female organs. The other common treatment was much more enjoyable. She would go to the doctor to have a "vulva massage," which would result in a "paroxysm." In other words, she would be masturbated until orgasm and then she would feel wonderful. Her symptoms would vanish. And so, she would simply go for weekly "treatments."

We think this sounds crazy today, but the diagnosis of "hysteria" existed in diagnostic manuals until the 1980s. It isn't ancient history. Historically, the idea of women enjoying sex is relatively new.

If you are older, you may have had many years of mechanical sex. Sex was an expectation and duty within marriage, whether we felt loving connection or not. Being entered sexually when we didn't want it set up emotional walls within us. This will drastically affect our desire for more of the same. Of course, the other common diagnosis for women was "frigidity." It's not really a surprise.

If you are a younger woman, we have to look at the effects of porn on today's generation. Many boys start watching porn as early as 12 years old. Many girls watch it so they know what to do. This heavily influences what we think is "normal" sexually and therefore what we expect from each other.

One of my students chose to be celibate in his late 20s for a time because he didn't know which sexual desires were *his* and which ones were from all the videos he had watched for so long. Because so much porn is focused on what pleases men (despite the fact that the women act like they are having great pleasure), the men learn nothing about what pleases a woman. There is often no kissing or intimacy at all. Yet these are the acts that create the loving experiences that make women happy.

Both of these situations can cause sexuality to be mechanical and painful for women. I've spoken to women of all ages who believe intercourse is painful, sometimes or at least most of the time. We have to realize that our vaginas hold memories. When we have been hurt, our bodies react with armour. Our bodies learn "when *this* happens," I need to protect myself. We become less sensitive. But when we become less sensitive to pain, we also feel less pleasure.

When we come into our divine feminine and understand the incredible pleasure our bodies are capable of, we can release all of this armour and explore the infinite wonder of the feminine body.

HEALING FROM SEXUAL ABUSE

Sexual abuse affects our ability to physically respond; our bodies are trauma-tized and on high-alert, waiting for the next event.

Sexual abuse has been so common that we sweep it under the rug. In many societies, it historically wasn't even considered abuse. It was normal. Even if it was considered wrong, there was so much shame around it on the parts of both the abuser and the abused that no one talked about it. We have been expected to continue being sexually active, regardless of being abused in the past.

It's like asking a soldier who has been traumatized by war to go back into the field over and over again, without healing. They would either become hardened (out of necessity), or they would break down.

This is how we must treat the effects of sexual abuse. We must recognize there is trauma stored in the body. This must be healed. It is natural to lack desire for more sexual experiences in the same way that a soldier won't want to go back to war. This is the natural response to trauma and fear.

Tantra can help us here, but it is also important to get more help from people experienced in releasing trauma. This must be given the proper attention it needs. It's no small thing. We deserve to heal and desire sexual attention in a healthy and pleasurable way again.

Here are some ways that tantra can help.

Enjoying Touch Again

We want to be able to experience "Original Touch" again. This is the kind of touch that stirs us deep inside and gives us a complete, human, divine experience.

Our mind, emotions and body are all one, so when we experience physical or emotional trauma, it is stored in the tissues. When we are touched, old, painful emotions can rise, which block us from being present to what is happening now. The wounds are like a sinkhole and we disappear into them when the trigger is touched.

Plus, when there has been sexual abuse, the emotions experienced are often around shame, fear, and survival. It is especially important not to ignore the depth of the pain. We don't want to stay here. We want to heal, and it is possible. We are incredible beings.

One of the most powerful aspects of tantra is that we integrate the spiritual with the physical. We integrate the divine into our lives.

When we imagine trying to recover from sexual abuse all on our own, we are only working through the body and mind. But when we integrate spirit into our being and we learn to trust that part of ourselves, we find we have strength and courage to face what we couldn't before.

Trusting Another

This is often a deeper wound to heal than the physical wound.

As a baby, we learn to trust those around us. We are completely dependent, and if those around us are not trustworthy, we will learn to put up walls to protect ourselves. As we continue to grow in that environment, our walls will get higher and higher.

When there is sexual abuse, we put up even higher walls. Sexual abuse affects our feelings around personal safety, survival, and relating to others. We build these walls out of protection and self-preservation. These walls have been important. They are what have kept you alive and sane up until this point.

However, if you are reading this book, then perhaps you want to take these walls down now. They have done their job and now you are finished with them. You would like to deeply connect with someone. You don't want to feel so alone.

This is why tantra is such a personal journey. We must heal ourselves. We must integrate the divine parts of ourselves into our lives. Because when we are centred and happy and we feel guided by our highest self/God/Spirit, we feel much safer opening up.

When we are already complete and whole, opening up won't be so scary because our emotional state, self-worth, or happiness is not dependent on the other person's thoughts or actions. We are tantric ourselves. We are whole. We are open to deeply connecting with another.

CAN TANTRA HEAL MY ADDICTION TO PORN?

This is the most common question I am asked by men around the world.

The messages are all nearly the same. If the man is between 18 and 25, he has been watching porn since he was 12 years old and is now struggling to have a relationship with a real person. If they are older, they started watching porn later in life and it is harming their relationships, they are having trouble getting an erection with a real woman, or they are ejaculating too quickly.

Studying tantra can definitely help.

First of all, I don't think watching porn is bad. There is something exciting and titillating about watching people have sex. We just have to be clear about what porn is.

Porn is entertainment. It isn't about love-making or even having sex. It focuses on the most titillating aspects of various situations. They play out our fantasies – things that we couldn't do ourselves, and maybe wouldn't even want to do in real life. But our minds will hold fantasies like they are real, so it can be difficult to be clear about what is real and what is fantasy.

The people in porn are actors. Even if they are amateurs filming at home on their cameras, they are still playing to a screen and their possible viewers. Whether they are enjoying themselves or not, they are going to act like they are. They are going to make sounds like they are, but it is no more real than a TV show. Real intimacy can seem like a lot of work, and can get quite messy. Porn is so much easier.

If you are addicted to porn right now, you have choices.

The first step is to expand our ideas about what is possible in a sexual encounter. When we believe all that there is is the "procreative sex" model, which is basically "get in, get off, get out." No matter how we dress it up, we will inevitably get bored at some point. The porn industry is also based on this model. This is why they have to make it so edgy. This model is boring, so we bring in bigger boobs, bigger penises, different colours, toys, locations, multiple partners, bondage, rape, animals, you name it. We have to dress it up because at its very core, there's not much going on.

Tantra is a different experience altogether. When we experience this tantric touch, closeness, and intercourse, the multi-faceted pleasure that is possible doesn't even compare to porn. It is the difference between flying a spacecraft to Mars and driving a souped-up bicycle to the corner store.

When we truly understand this, it can create a new desire inside of us. From this desire, we start to crave something else. Something more fulfilling and pleasurable than watching porn. When the desire for something else comes from inside, the pull of addictions disappear.

TANTRA IS THE OPPOSITE OF PORN

(I wrote this article in February 2015. Collective Evolution posted it on their website, and as of the writing of this book, it was shared over 350,000 times from their site. There is definitely something important that we are all looking for here.)

What if studying tantra could heal our addiction to porn? What if tapping into our natural abilities to experience ecstasy changes everything?

I was really nervous when I first realized that I wanted to teach tantra. What would people think? Would they be offended? Talking about sex is such a no-no. I live in a very small conservative community. How was this going to work?

Then a good friend said to me. "Do you realize what you're offering people? Tantra is essentially the OPPOSITE of porn." Once I realized this, I never looked back!!

Porn is a funny thing. It isn't inherently evil. Lots of people truly enjoy watching porn. even couples use it together to have a new experience. Yet there are some real dark sides to porn.

Besides the obvious violence and anything involving children, there are much more insidious issues.

1) What we Look Like Is Everything:

Porn focuses on being stimulated through the bodies. And so we are subconsciously told that sexuality depends on what your body looks like. You must be young, fit, have perky breasts and a large penis otherwise you can't be a good lover. And ironically this sets up a huge self-worth issue in everyone – for the ones who aren't young, fit and perky, and for the ones that are, because they aren't perky enough or big enough. No one leaves happy with themselves.

2) It's All About Successfully Pleasuring the Other:

Porn focuses on pleasing the other. Now obviously there is some part of us deep down that knows that the desire to please our partner is actually a wonderful thing. But that isn't usually how it comes across in porn. It comes across as the only thing that is important. That bringing the other person to orgasm is the only goal. And what's wrong with that you ask? Well it is the message that our unconscious receives, that this is the only goal of lovemaking. That if you can't bring your partner to orgasm, then there is no point making love. Also we end up with performance anxiety on the giver and the receiver's sides – the incredible pressure to please and the pressure to "get it up," "have an orgasm," etc.

3) Connection and Intimacy aren't Important:

Porn has nothing to do with connection. It is simply a series of physical events that two people do together. There is no connection or intimacy. And this isn't always evil. Sometimes a round of rockin' porn sex can be fun. But again it sends programming to our subconscious that this is what sex is about. That the connection doesn't matter. It's just about getting off.

4) This is All We are Capable of:

The worst part of it is that porn makes us believe that this is all that there is. We think that we know what sex is all about and that porn just plays the edge of it, which is what is so titillating. But it isn't true.

THE TRUTH IS that we as humans are using maybe 5% of our sexual abilities. It's like having a piano where we think that there are only 10 keys. So we get really good at playing chopsticks. But the truth is that there are 88 keys and we can actually play phenomenal mind-blowing music. We just didn't know.

Porn deepens the belief that chopsticks is all that there is. So we just play it edgier and edgier so that hearing it still interests us. But we are missing the boat.

So how does Tantra change all this?

It shows us the other 78 keys on the piano... and then teaches us how to play.

1) We are so much more than our physical bodies:

And the sexiest part of us isn't our physicality. A truly sensual person has a presence about them that is absolutely captivating and enthralling. They can look at you and gently touch you in a way that will leave you spellbound. They will bring you into their inner quiet where you will breathe and touch each other sending chills and orgasms throughout your bodies. What their body looks like is quite irrelevant.

2) Pleasuring is greater when it is mutual:

We are energetic beings as well as physical. When we are touching our partner, if we are really present and enjoying the feel of our partner's skin, they will sense this. Your touch will be different than if you are just doing it in order to please them. When you are truly in the moment, there is electricity that comes out your fingers (or other sexy parts) that permeates your partner's entire body. As your partner's body responds to this, this pleasure cycles back to you and who is the giver and who is the receiver starts to become blurred. There is just simply pleasure being shared regardless of who is doing what.

3) Connection is Everything:

We are DESIGNED to connect with each other on a very deep level. Human beings do not do well without feeling deep connection. We call it "neediness" and "being desperate" when someone is feeling disconnected. But it's really just because deep down we know that we are capable of phenomenal connection. And when we feel this amazing connection, things in our lives just get better. Depression lifts. We don't feel as anxious. We notice the joys in life. We appreciate each other. We feel a level of content and happiness that we just don't experience when we are all alone.

In tantra, this connection comes first. This is the foundation of all the sexual play. It's like you first have to "plug into" each other before the energy can flow. And so there is real intention to drop our guards and allow each other inside – to truly connect and experience each other and then the sexiness will ensue which makes it oh so much greater and amazing.

4) Sex is Meant to Be a Multi-Dimensional Experience:

When we actually bring in everything that we truly are into our intimate experiences, we go from having simply physical sex to having an experience involving our minds, emotions, feelings, intuition, passion, presence, plus a pile of dimensions that you can't even explain. They just happen, and they blow your mind.

And the most amazing thing is that it doesn't take any tricks. It doesn't take a pile of methods or fancy sexual abilities. It is actually totally natural and programmed into us. We just haven't accessed it.

Will Tantra Rid the World of Porn?

I don't think so. We love sex. Our sexual desire makes us feel alive. And truthfully, watching other people have sex can be very titillating.

Tantra heals our REAL relationships with REAL people. Learning how to be intimate with others allows us to have incredibly satisfying relationships with the people around us. We feel deeper connections and our intimate experiences heal us and make us feel wonderful about ourselves!

So porn won't go away. But for many, the addiction can fade, because once you start experiencing the opposite side, your true potential, true intimacy, and the sexual experiences that we are designed to have, the porn can't own you. It just doesn't come close to comparing to the experiences you've had.

I mean, Once you've driven a Maserati, driving a child's push car just doesn't compare.

HOW DO I INTRODUCE TANTRA
TO NEW PARTNERS?

The important point here is to understand that tantra is a way of being. Between partners, it is a way of connecting, a depth and quality of relationship.

Your Presence

Your tantra studies and practice must bring you to a place where you simply *are* tantric. You are present. You are open. You are loving. You are kind. You are connected to spirit in every moment. When you bring this to the relationship, the other person will reflect this. If they are closed down, your openness will make them feel safe. If they are distracted, your presence will bring them to the moment. If things are challenging and you listen inwards for guidance instead of reacting, this will take the relationship in a new direction.

The Quality of Your Connection

We often feel the need to explain tantric sex if we are going to jump to sex right away, but it won't work this way. Tantric intimacy isn't a set of practices that you just add to sex. You could *know* all about tantric intimacy, but if there is no love and true connection with the other person, the magic will always elude you anyway.

In order to create this connection, it is often good to refrain from being sexual for a while. If we begin a relationship having sex without deep connection, this can easily create a precedent which is harder to change later. You will naturally default to "regular, procreative" sex. Whereas if you take the time to cultivate and deepen the connection between you, you will become accustomed to having an incredible magnetic charge between you. By the time you are sexually intimate with each other, you will be used to it always being incredible and exciting.

If this is a challenge, it is important to look at why that is. Are you really looking for a tantric, intimate connection? It's OK if you aren't. It's just important to be clear with yourself and your partner what your hopes are.

Talk about what tantra REALLY is

When we study and practise tantra, it's natural to want to share this with a new, potential partner. Share with them what tantra is at its core.

How has it changed your life? How does it bring you peace? Do you act differently in life now? How have your relationships changed? The proof is always in your day-to-day life. Sharing how it has transformed you is the most interesting and important aspect of tantra to share with anyone.

If these ideas scare them off, this is a good sign that perhaps they aren't a great match on a very foundational level.

If they desire truth, emotional connection, love, passion, playfulness, and a sense of adventure, once you have a wonderful foundation, introducing them to the more intimate side of tantra will be natural.

Can tantra help with premature ejaculation?

Many men email me asking if tantra will help them with premature ejaculation. The answer is yes!

Learn How To Relax in Life

It is important that we relax all day long. Becoming tantric brings us to a place where we have a peaceful, still centre within us that we can tap into anytime when we need to slow down, relax, and come to centre.

The more we can be relaxed and centred in life, the easier it will become when we are being sexual.

Personal Control

Many men struggle with the idea that ideally, they don't ejaculate at all during tantric intimacy. This is a challenge for most men, regardless of whether they struggle with being premature or not.

You can if you want, but there are huge benefits when you choose not to.

Men can develop a different connection with their vajra (penis). Instead of being at the whim of what it wants to do, they develop control over when or whether or not they ejaculate at all. It is totally within your control. You could have intercourse for hours. You could choose to come whenever you want. This is actually part of your design.

Whether a man is accustomed to ejaculating after 10 minutes, 1 minute, or 20 minutes, there is a certain training required to be in control.

When I was first experimenting with tantra with my husband, he couldn't wrap his mind around not ejaculating or having that kind of control. Then one day, we were making love and I noticed something was different about him. There was this confidence emanating from him. I realized that he was no longer afraid of coming. I asked him what happened, and he said, "I don't know. I decided that I was in control. And now it's up to me. It's that simple."

Releasing Guilt and Shame

It's important to release any guilt or shame around it because you will never be able to be present and focused if there is fear and shame. I remember one man telling me that lots of guys suffer with this. They spent their teenage years masturbating in the shower. They had to do it quickly and in private so no one knew. Speed and shame combined! Those two things need to be released.

Sets of Nine

This is an exercise that is in the sexuality chapter and is super fun to practise with a partner. Through counted slow and then deep penetration, you can practise breathing and being present, and you get to see which number you get to each time. When you get all the way to nine deep penetrations, you will want to keep on going.

CAN TANTRA HELP WITH ERECTILE DYSFUNCTION?

Much of modern "regular sex" is based in the procreative model, where the fundamental goal is ejaculation and creating children. In this scenario, erections, speed, and physical vigour are important.

When the goal is intimate, sexual union, the penis is an energetic instrument, not a "ramming rod." Within tantric sexuality, we learn how to have beautiful, pleasurable intercourse whether the penis is hard or soft.

We can fully connect with another through connective intimacy, love, attention, touch, and other creative physical ways. We can be orgasmic and still lose ourselves in each other. It's all about the quality of our connection.

If we can be orgasmic fully dressed, simply touching hands, imagine what can happen if we are naked.

Developing the other 95% of you

Many men lose the ability to have an erection due to prostate problems and surgery. One of the first tasks is to see yourself as more than your penis. What you can offer a partner is closer to 5% hard penis and 95% the rest of you.

Society tells us the erection is the sign of your manhood and virility. This creates an over-focus on the erection. In many relationships, this is the majority of what is offered. However, their partner desires more than "just sex." They want love and affection all day long. They want extended foreplay. They want all the pleasures that the rest of you offers. Essentially, they want the rest of you, too.

Tantric intimacy brings us very close. It is the connection, the touch, the breathing that brings us to absolute ecstasy. Ejaculation happens in the penis, but orgasm happens in the brain.

So when faced with the inability to have an erection, we need to find all of those other ways we can enjoy loving and being intimate, without our ego telling us we aren't enough.

Resolving Past Experiences

Unkind words spoken at a particularly vulnerable moment can have long-time effects on our emotions and psyche. This is true for both men and women. We are so vulnerable during intimacy, and our partners (and ourselves) aren't trained in the kindness needed with such openness. Without kindness and wisdom, great psychological damage can happen.

If you remember a moment immediately as you read this, then look at that moment. Pray about it. Yell about it. Talk to a trusted counsellor. Do whatever you feel called to do to heal it.

If you're not sure, but it feels possible, then explore the possibility. This can be explored through tantra on your personal journey and with a trusted partner. Tantra has incredible healing potential.

Medication

There are many medications that can dull our senses (on purpose) and therefore also affect our "get-up-and-go," which can be experienced through erectile dysfunction. Check with your doctor about options if this is a possible side-effect.

Masculine Energy

Regardless of whether your inability to have an erection is due to surgery, psychological trauma, or unknown causes, it is important to ask yourself, "Do You Feel Masculine in Your Life?"

If the answer is "no" or "not really," the best thing to do is to go out and do masculine things.

"Masculine" does not mean "macho" or "tough." It simply means "doing," "giving," or "creating" (please refer to the Masculine & Feminine chapter for more information). Work out. Run. Take a dance class. Volunteer. Give to others. Create structure in your life. Get out in the world and DO.

In relationships, give more. Do more. Sexually, take the initiative. Truly "take charge." This isn't forcing yourself on someone. It is observing your partner and reading what they would like, then doing it.

All of these actions strengthen our masculine energy and pump us up to use the confidence and strength we have inside.

CAN TANTRA HELP WITH LOW SEX DRIVE AFTER MENOPAUSE?

As women, there are many aspects of our sexual lives to look at after we have been through menopause.

The body changes in menopause. Our hormone levels are different. Our bodies don't respond in the same ways they did when our bodies were being prepared to have children. That doesn't mean we can't be sensual, intimate, feminine beings.

In fact, tantra brings us into our deepest feminine experience. If you are going through or have passed menopause at the time of this book's writing (2017), then the feminine has not been honoured much in your life. Tantra awakens what is within us.

There are other factors we need to look at, too.

Women's Non-Orgasmic History

Up until the 1960s, it was widely believed that women couldn't have orgasms. A woman's pleasure in bed was not only unimportant, it was a non-issue. Yet it has always mattered that the man ejaculated. In fact, the sex act typically wasn't complete until this happened. Obviously, there are situations where this isn't true, but it is a persistent pattern even today in our younger generation.

By the time we go through menopause, we likely have over 30 years of sexual experiences under our belt. There might have been a few great moments, lots of so-so sex, and perhaps lots of obligatory, "marital" sex.

None of this leads to a continuing desire for more.

Many men of this age were brought up in the same era and ideas about sex. My widowed aunt once told me she didn't want to ever date again because she didn't want to have to bother washing a man's socks and having to make him feel good about himself.

I'm not saying that everyone feels like that, but it's definitely common.

Past Sexual Trauma

Not only did many women have so-so or bad sex, a lot of women have had a lot of sex they didn't want. Every time a man enters us when we didn't want it or we weren't ready, it leaves a physical and psychic effect on us.

The effects are obvious and intuitive when it is rape. If someone obviously forces themselves onto us and we are entered against our will, it's easy to understand the long-term damage and the healing required for this.

However, it is within long-term relationships that we tend to have the most sex that we don't want. We have sex because our partner wants it and we don't want to upset them or "make" them moody. Or maybe we want to fix their mood. Plus, we promised that we would only be sexual with each other, so we easily felt "If I don't have sex with him, he will go elsewhere."

This training runs deep. Only a few decades ago, women couldn't work, vote, or support themselves and care for their children without a man. The importance of "keeping the man happy" was well-bred into us for good reason.

Lubrication

After menopause, ample lubrication can be more challenging than it was before due to hormonal changes, medications, or surgeries.

It's important to know that women often do not have enough foreplay and pleasure to become lubricated enough - postmenopausal or not!

Tantric intimacy teaches us what excites our whole beings and helps us become naturally lubricated. The feminine is fed through her heart. Most of our sexual stimulus isn't even physical. Do we feel loved? Do we feel seen and respected? Do we feel honoured and adored? Is our partner taking initiative (being masculine)? Are we being swept off our feet?

This puts us into the deep feminine. When our heart is stimulated, our yoni (vagina, etc) naturally opens to connect more deeply.

However, this is a new concept for most of us.

Medication

Many medications have side-effects that will affect our sex drive and our body's ability to respond sexually. For many medications, it isn't the side effects that are the challenge; it is the primary intention of the drug that will dull our responses.

For example, when we are on antidepressants, think about what these do. They are intentionally dulling our responses to painful emotional states. This isn't a judgement about whether you should be on them, but it is important to connect the right dots.

True intimacy happens when we are wide open and feel everything. If we have deep issues that we can't face and we rely on medication to give us a different set-point, this can interfere with a great sex-drive.

Being Feminine

Are you very feminine? Have you been able to be feminine? What has stifled your femininity? Do you trust to receive? Have you ever experienced this? Will you allow yourself to receive?

We have become independent and strong, which is good. However, in many ways, we have only become more like men. We have increased our masculinity and lost our femininity.

In tantra we learn the beautiful balance of masculine and feminine within us and in relationships. Suddenly, there is great value to feminine wisdom, wildness, introspection, emotions, and intuition. We learn receiving is as much of a gift as giving.

We learn what it is to be truly women – strong in both our feminine and masculine.

References

Radiance Sutras, Lorin Roche, 2014

This is a beautiful modern translation of the Vijnana Bhairava Tantra. One of my early struggles was that my tantra revelation came from an unknown place inside. I traveled searching for the roots of this wisdom without any luck until I met Lorin Roche. He was teaching a workshop in California sharing his Radiance Sutras. As he read from the pages of his book, my entire body started vibrating. When he read the sutras in Sanskrit, my body became practically orgasmic. This is when I realized that the tantra that was inside of me came from the same roots as this beautiful set of tantras. Afterwards, I caught up with Lorin and told him how thrilled I was to meet him and how hearing these beautiful sutras made everything that I knew make sense. He looked deep into my eyes (with that guru look) and said, "Ahhh yes. It is because you've already lived this. You are a wisdom-keeper." I was so incredibly thankful for his words and the further affirmation that I was on path.

Women's Anatomy of Arousal, Sheri Winston, 2010

This is an incredible book that all women and those who make love to them must read. When I first read it, I was absolutely devastated that I was 44 years old, had been sexually active for decades, and had even had children and I had no idea how a woman's body actually worked! I have recommended this book to everyone I know. Plus, I am very thankful to Sheri for her beautiful endorsement on this book's cover.

All Books by Osho

I discovered Osho over 20 years ago while I was still living on the farm. His books and philosophy were an absolute saving grace while I wrestled with the normal struggles of marriage, motherhood, farming, business and life. I ordered every book I could find that he had written and devoured every word. Later, when I began studying tantra, all of his books on tantra discuss the most beautiful philosophies for living, connecting and understanding what life is all about.

All books by Diana Richardson

In my early years of studying tantra, Diana Richardson was my lifeboat. In a sea of books describing things that didn't feel right to me at all, her book "The Heart of Tantric Sex" was the first book that made my heart say, "Yes. This is what I'm looking for." Her books specifically for men and women were what I introduced my husband to before we went south to try everything out.

ACKNOWLEDGEMENTS

I want to thank my wonderful children who have inspired me so much on my journey. From the moment they were born, I felt so blessed. I was overwhelmed to think that I had been given these little people to take care of and raise. What an incredible responsibility. It was my fear of doing the wrong thing that led me to dig deep, ask for guidance, and trust my intuition. Having them in my life drove me to find the best in me, so I could give that to them. Who knew this would be the foundation of my teachings in tantra?

I would like to thank all the wonderful friends who have created such rich and wonderful years. Some you have met through the stories in this book. Others live only in my heart, but their gifts, guidance, and love flow through all the words in this book.

I want to thank my editor, Sara Stibitz. I can be very philosophical sometimes and it was a wonderful gift to be able to write freely, knowing that her eyes would be on my words, asking me to expand on certain areas, deleting others, and expertly bringing the reader into the creation of this book at each step. Plus, she's super fun to work with.

I would like to thank Lynn Borth, who designed our Tree of Love. We had been seeking a visual of how the three loves support, and thrive within each other. After reading the chapters on love, she saw the tree in her mind and then drew this beautiful picture for us.

I would like to thank all of my students over the years. The relationship between teacher and student is very intertwined. As much as the student may be learning, the teacher is also constantly changing and growing. This book is the culmination of every question I've ever been asked, every time I've been challenged, and all the insights that have been shared with me along the way.

Overall, I am simply thankful. Thankful for my life. Thankful for the ups, downs, good times and bad times. I couldn't ask for a more wonderful, gifted, and blessed life.

About the Author

Because tantra is truly about integrating spirituality into our physical lives, some might say Katrina Bos' life was perfectly designed so that one day, this is exactly what she would be teaching.

Katrina was born in 1969 in Toronto, Canada, the eldest child in a very loving home. She was interested in Eastern thought and natural healing from an early age, giving shiatsu treatments to her family and friends when she was 13. At age 18, she began studying mathematics at the University of Waterloo. Her study of mathematics fed her passion to understand and see patterns in the universe, which fed her deeper desire for spiritual connection. Her other great influences at the time were Carl Jung, Viktor Frankl, and Gandhi.

When Katrina was 22, her mom was diagnosed with breast cancer. This deepened her study into mind-body connection and spirituality in an effort to save her mom and understand why all the women in her family were dying of cancer. Then, at age 23, this philosophical, computer-programming, mathematician fell in love with a farmer, left the city, and moved to the country.

This was the beginning of the "grounded" years. Her mom died when Katrina was 25 and pregnant with her son. Soon, there wasn't much room for philosophical theories and ideals with days filled with diapers, milking cows and "feeding the menfolk." Four years later, she had her own health crisis - lumps growing in her breast, two small children, and the fear that if she didn't figure this out, she would be passing the legacy onto her daughter. Meeting her teacher Jim and her subsequent journey and healing was the incredible turning point in her life where her spirituality became part of her daily life. The full story is in her first book, *What If You Could Skip the Cancer?*

The following years were a mix of happy family times, working on the farm, and teaching dance, kundalini yoga, and meditation in neighbouring towns. In 2009, they sold the farm and moved to town, and Katrina bought an old, vacant train station which she renovated into a centre for all things joyful, healing, and fun. She called it East Street Station. This was the gathering place of all her passions – dance, spirituality, meditation, yoga, kids' homework clubs, music concerts, kids camps, art classes, and eventually tantra.

Katrina now lives in Toronto, teaches online courses through her school, Fusion Tantra, and travels to teach all around the world. Her passion is teaching "grounded spirituality" and understanding and exploring exactly what we as humans are truly capable of.

For more information about Katrina or her school, Fusion Tantra, please check out katrinabos.ca and fusiontantra.com.

Made in United States
North Haven, CT
29 July 2023

39702440R00183